FOREWORD

This textbook is one of eight (8) textbooks written under my hand and supervision:

'Injia on Criminal Offences in Papua New Guinea and the Pacific'

'Injia on Criminal Practice and Procedure in Papua New Guinea and the Pacific'

'Injia on Sentencing in Papua New Guinea and the Pacific'

'Injia on Statutory Interpretation in Papua New Guinea and the Pacific'

'Injia on Coronial Proceedings in Papua New Guinea and the Pacific'

'Injia on Investigatory Practice in Papua New Guinea and the Pacific'

'Injia on Contempt of Court in Papua New Guinea and the Pacific'

'Injia on Evidence in Papua New Guinea and the Pacific'

Each of those textbooks is an effort to offer to Judicial officers, legal practitioners and students of law a comprehensive set of principles and practical guidelines on criminal law and practice in Papua New Guinea and the Pacific. The work undertaken under the auspices of AusAID through the PNG-Australia Law and Justice Partnership Project is an extension of a similar project undertaken previously in writing the textbook *Criminal Law and Practice in Papua New Guinea* co-authored by myself, Professor Don Chalmers, Dr Weisbrot and Justice Andrew.

The textbooks will be of great benefit to the criminal justice system in Papua New Guinea and the Pacific and specifically will assist judges, magistrates, lawyers, law students and police officers in the performance of their duties.

The assistance of AusAID and its development practitioner Mr Errol Gibson who provided research and spent countless hours in the production of these textbooks is acknowledged.

Sir Salamo Injia, Kt

Chief Justice of Papua New Guinea

22nd September 2013

Injia on Evidence in Papua New Guinea and the Pacific

Salamo Injia

University of Papua New Guinea Press and Bookshop, 2013

Injia on Evidence in Papua New Guinea and the Pacific

ISBN: 978-9980-87-918-9

PUBLISHED BY:

The University of Papua New Guinea Press and Bookshop
PO Box 413
University PO, NCD
Papua New Guinea
Email: upngpress@gmail.com

TABLE OF CONTENTS

TABLE OF CONTENTS

TABLE OF CONTENTS

TABLE OF CONTENTS

TABLE OF CONTENTS

TABLE OF CONTENTS

TABLE OF CONTENTS

TABLE OF CONTENTS

TABLE OF CONTENTS

INTRODUCTION TO EVIDENCE

In a criminal trial, it is not safe to rely on suspicion and what the Court thinks. The Court must be guided by the evidence adduced in a case in order to make a finding of guilt.[1]

Courts should have the fullest possible access to all relevant material.[2]

Whereas in a non-legal sense 'evidence' means something which makes a fact or facts apparent or obvious; in a legal sense it means that which the law accepts as providing proof of facts in a trial situation.[3]

The term is also used to describe the law relating to evidence. Evidence in that sense has traditionally included various topics, but the reasons why the law of evidence has included any particular topic are not always clear.[4]

The law of evidence:

- is considered to serve the purpose of the trial process, including the pursuit of truth, party freedom and procedural fairness[5]; and

- in criminal cases is really nothing more than a set of practical rules that experience has shown to be best fitted to elicit the truth about guilt without causing undue prejudice to an accused person.[6]

---

[1] See *The State v Kokara Fova* CR 1494 of 2006.

[2] See *Rex v Hardy* (1794) 24 St Tr 199; *Marks v Beyfus* (1890) 25 QBD 494 and *Conway v Rimmer* [1968] AC 910.

[3] See New Zealand Law Commission, 1991, 'Evidence Law: Principles for Reform -- A Discussion Paper', Preliminary Paper 13, page 3.

[4] See New Zealand Law Commission, 1991, 'Evidence Law: Principles for Reform -- A Discussion Paper', Preliminary Paper 13, page 3.

[5] See New Zealand Law Commission, 1996, 'The Evidence of Children and Other Vulnerable Witnesses – A Discussion Paper', Preliminary Paper 26, page 19.

[6] See *Thompson v R* (1918) 13 Cr App R 61, [1918] AC 221, per Lord Dunedin at 226.

See also: *R v Christie* [1914] AC 545, (1914) 24 Cox CC 249, (1914) 10 Cr App R 141, per Lord Reading at 164.

INTRODUCTION TO EVIDENCE

Evidence is information that can be put before a Court; and not only to police officers, but to the general public.[7]

The central focus of evidence law is a trial at which witnesses are questioned by the parties to the proceeding. Most issues about the admissibility of evidence arise in the context of questioning witnesses.[8]

All evidence that is sought to be admitted must be tendered in compliance with the law.[9]

The trite and often repeated statement that in order to adduce proof of each element of a charge[10] the maxim:

> 'The best evidence must be given of which the nature of the court case permits'

is considered a fundamental principle of the law of evidence, ie., the 'best evidence rule'.[11]

The basic principle is:

> Only the 'best' evidence should be placed before a Court, that is, the evidence that is most likely to be reliable.[12]

In *The State v Warun*[13] the Court stated:

> 'The accused's right to protection of the law means that the State must prove its case in conformity with the rules of evidence. [...]

---

[7] See *R v Osbourne and Virtue* [1973] 2 WLR 209, [1973] 1 All ER 649, [1973] 1 QB 678, [1973] Crim LR 178, (1973) 57 Cr App R 297, per Lawton LJ at 307.

[8] See New Zealand Law Commission, 1999, 'Evidence. Volume 1: Reform of the Law and Evidence. Volume 2: Evidence Code and Commentary', Report 55, page 102.

[9] See for example, *Mary Bomai Michael v The State* (2004) SC737.

[10] Refer also to the section titled 'Proof Of Elements' in the chapter titled 'Proof Of Issues' in the text titled 'Injia on Criminal Practice and Procedure in Papua New Guinea and the Pacific'.

[11] See *The State v John Bill White (No. 1)* (1996) N1441.

[12] See *R v Horncastle and others* [2009] UKSC 14.

[13] [1988-89] PNGLR 327 at 332-333.

INTRODUCTION TO EVIDENCE

When it is said that the State must prove its case, the State must bring witnesses who give testimony[14], generally on oath[15]. The witnesses may identify and prove a document which may be used because of its contents in testimonial manner[16], or as either circumstantial[17] or real evidence[18]: *Cross*, par. 1.26 at 14 – 15. The witness may give testimony to identify things put in evidence, like an axe, or a knife, as real evidence. In all these cases a witness is required to get the evidence properly before the court'.

When defending a client on a criminal charge, a legal representative shall endeavour to protect his or her client from being convicted except by a competent tribunal and upon legally admissible evidence sufficient to support a conviction for the offence with which his or her client is charged.[19]

In conformity with the rules of evidence, neither the prosecution nor the defence are permitted to give evidence from the bar table.

Therefore, all evidence must be given by witnesses on oath or solemn declaration or affirmation[20], with the exception of:

- an accused person who gives an 'unsworn statement'[21];
- the tendering of evidence without the calling of a witness[22];

---

[14] Refer also to the section titled 'Witness Attendance' in the chapter titled 'Witnesses' in the text titled 'Injia on Criminal Practice and Procedure in Papua New Guinea and the Pacific'.

[15] Refer also to the section titled 'Examination-in-Chief' in the chapter titled 'Examination Of Witnesses' in the text titled 'Injia on Criminal Practice and Procedure in Papua New Guinea and the Pacific'.

[16] Refer also to the chapter titled 'Documentary Evidence'.

[17] Refer also to the chapter titled 'Circumstantial Evidence'.

[18] Refer also to the chapter titled 'Forensic Evidence'.

[19] See section 16(2) of the *Professional Conduct Rules 1989* ['Defending a Person Accused of Crime'].

[20] Refer also to the section title 'Competency And Compellability' in the chapter titled 'Witnesses' in the text titled 'Injia on Criminal Practice and Procedure in Papua New Guinea and the Pacific'.

[21] Refer also to the section titled 'The Defence Case' in the chapter titled 'Court Procedure' in the text titled 'Injia on Criminal Practice and Procedure in Papua New Guinea and the Pacific'.

[22] Refer also to the section titled 'Admission Of Evidence Without The Calling Of A Witness' in the chapter titled 'Court Procedure' in the text titled 'Injia on Criminal Practice and Procedure in Papua New Guinea and the Pacific'.

- documentary evidence admitted by virtue of a statutory provision[23];
- the evidence of a 'formal admission'[24]; and
- evidence that it is judicially noticed[25].

Irrespective of whether the prosecution or defence object to the admission of certain evidence, it is the overall duty of the Court to ensure that only legally admissible evidence goes into the record of the trial.[26]

A Court has a discretion to exclude legally admissible evidence if justice so requires.[27]

A Court has the discretion whether to exclude 'relevant' evidence on the question of fairness to an accused person[28] when:

- its prejudicial effect.

---

[23] Refer also to the chapter titled 'Documentary Evidence'.

[24] Refer also to the section titled 'Formal Admission' in the chapter titled 'Court Procedure' in the text titled 'Injia on Criminal Practice and Procedure in Papua New Guinea and the Pacific'.

[25] Refer also to the section titled 'Judicial Notice' in the chapter titled 'Court Procedure' in the text titled 'Injia on Criminal Practice and Procedure in Papua New Guinea and the Pacific'.

[26] See *Epeli Devinga v The State* [1995] PNGLR 263 and *Awoda v The State* [1984] PNGLR 165, [1984] PGSC 1.

See also: *R v Gibson* (1887) 18 QBD 537; *Stirland v DPP* [1944] AC 315 and *R v Slack* (2003) A Crim R 314.

However, section 25(1)(a) of the *Juvenile Courts Act 1991* ['Conduct of Proceedings Generally'] provides that in respect to hearings under that Act a Court 'shall allow proceedings to be conducted so as to receive all matters, facts and opinions into evidence and shall not be bound by strict rules of evidence'.

[27] See *Myers v Director of Public Prosecutions* [1965] AC 1001, per Lord Reid at 1024, (1964) 48 Cr App R 348, [1964] 2 All ER 881, [1964] 3 WLR 145.

[28] See *Harris v DPP* [1952] 1 All ER 1044, (1952) 36 Cr App R 235, [1952] AC 694 per Viscount Simon at 707 and *R v Christie* [1914] AC 545, per Lord Reading at 564, (1914) 24 Cox CC 249 at 257, (1914) 10 Cr App R 141.

See also: *Driscoll v R* (1977) 137 CLR 517 at 541, (1977) 15 ALR 47, [1977] HCA 43.

In this context, prejudice means the danger of improper use of the evidence[29] and therefore, capable of causing damage to the prospects of a fair trial[30].

It does not mean damage to the defence case.[31]

outweighs[32]

- its probative value[33].[34]

---

[29] See *HML v R; SB v R; OAE v R* (2008) 235 CLR 334, (2008) 82 ALJR 723, [2008] HCA 16.

[30] See *R v Morris* [1996] 2 Qd R 68 at 72 and *Festa v R* (2001) 208 CLR 593.

[31] See *R v Morris* [1996] 2 Qd R 68 at 72 and *Festa v R* (2001) 208 CLR 593.

[32] Prejudicial effect and probative value are incommensurables, as stated by McHugh J in *Pfennig v R* (1995) 182 CLR 461 at 528, (1995) 69 ALJR 147, (1995) 127 ALR 99, (1995) 77 A Crim R 149, [1995] HCA 7.

Furthermore, a great deal of judicial and other decision-making involves forming a judgement about where the balance is to be struck between competing considerations that are not amenable to any fixed standard of comparison, see *HML v R; SB v R; OAE v R* (2008) 235 CLR 334, (2008) 82 ALJR 723, [2008] HCA 16, per Gleeson CJ.

[33] See also: *Sutton v R* (1984) 152 CLR 528 at 534 and 565, (1984) 51 ALR 435, [1984] HCA 5 and *R v Sang* [1980] AC 402, per Lord Diplock at 434-435, (1979) 69 Cr App R 282, [1979] 3 WLR 263, [1979] 2 All ER 1222, [1979] Crim LR 282, [1979] UKHL 3.

[34] See *Harris v DPP* [1952] 1 All ER 1044, (1952) 36 Cr App R 235, [1952] AC 694 at 707; *Kuruma v R* [1955] AC 197, [1955] 1 All ER 236 and *Selvey v DPP* [1970] AC 304, [1968] 2 WLR 1494, [1968] 2 All ER 497, (1968) 52 Cr App R 443.

See also: *Driscoll v R* (1977) 137 CLR 517 at 523 and 541, (1977) 15 ALR 47, [1977] HCA 43; *Alexander v R* (1981) 149 CLR 395 at 402-3, 417-18, 428-30 and 435, (1981) 34 ALR 289, [1981] HCA 17; *Sutton v R* (1984) 152 CLR 528 at 534, 558-9 and 565, (1984) 51 ALR 435, [1984] HCA 5; *Doney v R* (1990) 171 CLR 207 at 212, (1990) 50 A Crim R 157 at 159, (1990) 96 ALR 539, [1990] HCA 51; *Harriman v R* (1989) 167 CLR at 594, 608 and 633, [1989] HCA 50; *R v Sang* (1979) 69 Cr App R 282, [1980] AC 402 at 437, [1979] 3 WLR 263, [1979] 2 All ER 1222, [1979] Crim LR 282, [1979] UKHL 3 and *Ridgeway v R* (1995) 184 CLR 19, (1995) 129 ALR 41 at 49, (1995) 69 ALJR 484, [1995] HCA 66.

As Justice Scalia once put it, this is like asking 'whether a particular line is longer than a particular rock is heavy', see *Bendix Autolite Corp v Midwesco Enterprises Inc* (1988) 486 US 888 at 897.

It is always a question of degree in each case, as Lord Mackay stated in *DPP v P* [1991] 2 AC 447, [1991] 3 WLR 161, [1991] 3 All ER 337, (1991) 93 Cr App R 267, [1992] Crim LR 4.

The concept of probative value involves relevance and weight. The probative value of evidence must be considered by reference to the purpose or purposes for which it is used.[35]

In order to determine probative value, the evidence must be:

- taken at its highest[36];
- assumed that the evidence would be accepted[37]; and
- assumed to be true[38].

Furthermore, a Court may also exclude 'relevant' evidence:

- when the strict rules of admissibility would operate unfairly against an accused person[39] and particularly if the evidence has no or little weight[40];
- when the evidence has been ascertained or procured by unlawful or improper conduct on the part of those whose task it is to enforce the law[41], although there is no general rule that a Court will reject evidence that has been illegally obtained[42].

---

35 See *HML v R; SB v R; OAE v R* (2008) 235 CLR 334, (2008) 82 ALJR 723, [2008] HCA 16, per Gleeson CJ.

36 See *R v Singh-Bal* (1997) 92 A Crim R 397 and *R v Yates* [2002] NSWCCA 520.

37 See *Adam v R* (2001) 207 CLR 96, per Gaudron J.

38 See *R v AB* [2001] NSWCCA 496.

39 See *Stephens v R* (1985) 156 CLR 664 at 669, [1985] HCA 30; *Driscoll v R* (1977) 137 CLR 517 at 541, (1977) 15 ALR 47, [1977] HCA 43 and *Harris v DPP* [1952] 1 All ER 1044, (1952) 36 Cr App R 235, [1952] AC 694, per Viscount Simon at 707.

40 See *R v Christie* [1914] AC 545 at 560, (1914) 24 Cox CC 249 at 257, (1914) 10 Cr App R 141; *Noor Mohamed v R* [1949] AC 182 at 192, [1949] 1 All ER 365; *Harris v DPP* [1952] 1 All ER 1044, (1952) 36 Cr App R 235, [1952] AC 694 at 707; *Kuruma v R* [1955] AC 197, per Lord Moulton at 204, [1955] 1 All ER 236 and *Driscoll v R* (1977) 137 CLR 517, per Gibbs J at 541, (1977) 15 ALR 47, [1977] HCA 43.

41 See *R v Ireland* (1970)126 CLR 321 at 334-335, [1970] ALR 727, (1970) 44 ALJR 263, [1970] HCA 21 and *Bunning v Cross* (1978) 141 CLR 54 at 64-65, 72 and 74-75, (1978) 19 ALR 641, [1978] HCA 22.

42 See *Cleland v R* (1982) 151 CLR 1, per Gibbs CJ at 9, (1982) 43 ALR 619, [1982] HCA 67.

However, evidence that has been unlawfully obtained is not necessarily inadmissible[43];

- when the evidence involves an inordinate amount of time which is not commensurate with its value[44];
- when the evidence is misleading in the sense that its effect on the Court is out of proportion to its reliability[45]; or
- when the evidence places the accused person at risk of being improperly convicted[46], such as because its weight and credibility cannot be effectively tested[47].

The power is based on a Court's duty in a criminal trial to ensure that an accused person receives a fair trial.[48]

---

[43] See *R v Ireland* (1970)126 CLR 321 at 334-335, [1970] ALR 727, (1970) 44 ALJR 263, [1970] HCA 21; *Bunning v Cross* (1978) 141 CLR 54 at 66, (1978) 19 ALR 641, [1978] HCA 22 and *Cleland v R* (1982) 151 CLR 1 at 9, (1982) 43 ALR 619, [1982] HCA 67.

[44] See *R v Mohan* [1994] 2 SCR 9 at 21, 1994 SCC 80 and *R v Jabarianha* [2001] 3 SCR 430, 2001 SCC 75.

[45] See *R v Mohan* [1994] 2 SCR 9 at 21, 1994 SCC 80 and *R v Jabarianha* [2001] 3 SCR 430, 2001 SCC 75.

[46] See *McDermott v R* (1948) 76 CLR 501, per Dixon J at 511-515 and *Driscoll v R* (1977) 137 CLR 517, per Gibbs J at 541, (1977) 15 ALR 47, [1977] HCA 43.

[47] See *McDermott v R* (1948) 76 CLR 501, per Dixon J at 511-515 and *R v Lee* (1950) 82 CLR 133 at 144, [1950] HCA 25.

[48] See *R v Noor Mohamed* [1949] AC 182 at 192, [1949] 1 All ER 365; *Harris v DPP* [1952] 1 All ER 1044, (1952) 36 Cr App R 235, [1952] AC 694, per Viscount Simon at 707 and *R v Christie* [1914] AC 545, per Lord Reading at 564, (1914) 24 Cox CC 249, (1914) 10 Cr App R 141.

See also: *C (A Minor) v DPP* [1996] AC 1, per Lord Lowry at 35; *Lobban v R* [1995] 1 WLR 877, [1995] 2 All ER 602, [1995] 2 Cr App R 573 at 583; *Bunning v Cross* (1978) 141 CLR 54 at 66, (1978) 19 ALR 641, [1978] HCA 22; *R v Ireland* (1970) 126 CLR 321 at 335, [1970] ALR 727, (1970) 44 ALJR 263, [1970] HCA 21; *Ridgeway v R* (1995) 129 ALR 41 at 49, (1995) 69 ALJR 484, [1995] HCA 66; *R v Coombs* [1985] 1 NZLR 318 at 321; *R v Dally* [1990] 2 NZLR 184; *R v Grayson and Taylor* [1997] 1 NZLR 399; *R v Convery* [1968] NZLR 426; *R v Sang* (1979) 69 Cr App R 282, [1980] AC 402, [1979] 3 WLR 263, [1979] 2 All ER 1222, [1979] Crim LR 282, [1979] UKHL 3; *R v Hasler* [1987] 1 Qd R 239; *Driscoll v R* (1977) 137 CLR 517 at 541, (1977) 15 ALR 47, [1977] HCA 43; *R v Baker* [1989] 3 NZLR 635 at 639-640; *Murdoch v Murphy* (1987) 33 A Crim R 118 at 126-127; *Dominic v R* (1972) 128 CLR 114, [1972] HCA 71; *Alexander v R* (1981) 149 CLR 395 at 402-3, 417-18, 428-30 and 435, (1981) 34 ALR 289, [1981] HCA 17; *Harriman v R* (1989) 167 CLR 590, [1989] HCA 50 and *Pfennig v R* (1995) 182 CLR 461, (1995) 69 ALJR 147, (1995) 127 ALR 99, (1995) 77 A Crim R 149, [1995] HCA 7.

The onus is on the defence to prove on the 'balance of probabilities' that a Court should exercise its discretion to exclude 'relevant' evidence.[49]

The defence may renew its application to a Court to exclude evidence in light of what transpires during the course of a trial.[50]

It is a complete mistake to think that a document that is otherwise inadmissible can be made admissible simply because it is put to an accused person in cross-examination.[51]

The admissibility of evidence may be the subject of a 'voir dire proceedings'.[52]

---

[49] See *Public Prosecutor v Mohd Farid bin Mohd Sukis and another* (2002) 3 MLJ 401 and *Francis Antonysamy v Public Prosecutor* (2005) 3 MLJ 389.

[50] See *R v Wilson* [1981] 1 NZLR 316 at 323 and *R v Watson* [1980] 2 All ER 293.

[51] See *R v Treacy* (1944) 30 Cr App R 93.

[52] See *Independent Publishing Company Ltd v Attorney General of Trinidad and Tobago and another (Trinidad and Tobago)* [2005] 1 AC 190, [2005] 1 All ER 499, [2004] UKPC 26, [2004] 3 WLR 611, [2005] AC 190.

Refer also to the section titled 'Voir Dire Proceedings' in the chapter titled 'Confessional Evidence'.

RELEVANCE

The basic rule is that evidence is admissible (ie, may be offered as evidence in a proceeding) if it is 'relevant'.[53]

A fundamental prerequisite for admissibility of evidence at common law is:

> Relevance.[54]

'Relevance' means:

- Relevant according to the ordinary common law rules of evidence; and
- Relevant to the case as it is being put.[55]

The basic principle of admissibility of evidence is:

> Unless there is some good reason for not receiving it, evidence that is 'relevant' is admissible.[56]

Evidence that is 'relevant' is admissible, unless excluded by an evidentiary rule.[57]

The common law rules of exclusion arise for consideration only with respect to evidence which is 'relevant'.[58]

---

[53] See *R v Jabarianha* [2001] 3 SCR 430, 2001 SCC 75.

See also:

- New Zealand Law Commission, 1992, 'Criminal Evidence: Police Questioning', Preliminary Paper 21, page 70, and
- *R v Apicella* (1986) 82 Cr App R 295, [1986] Crim LR 238; *Pollitt v R* (1992) 174 CLR 558 at 571, [1992] HCA 35; *Smith v R* (2001) 206 CLR 650; *Goldsmith v Sandilands* (2002) 190 ALR 370 and *R v Wilson* [1991] 2 NZLR 707 at 711.

[54] See *MJH v The State of Western Australia* [2006] WASCA 167 and *Smith v R* (2001) 206 CLR 650.

[55] See *Viola* (1982) 75 Cr App R 125, [1982] 3 All ER 73 and *R v Funderburk* [1990] 2 All ER 482, [1990] 1 WLR 587, [1990] Crim LR 405, (1990) 90 Cr App R 466 at 469.

[56] See *HML v R; SB v R; OAE v R* (2008) 235 CLR 334, (2008) 82 ALJR 723, [2008] HCA 16, per Gleeson CJ.

[57] See *Smith v R* (2001) 206 CLR 650, [2001] HCA 50 and *R v Jabarianha* [2001] 3 SCR 430, 2001 SCC 75.

[58] See *Papakosmas v R* (1999) 196 CLR 297, per Gleeson CJ and Hayne J at 306, [1999] HCA 37.

RELEVANCE

A determination as to whether evidence is 'relevant' may require careful analysis.[59]

In determining 'relevance', it is fundamentally important to identify the issues of the trial.[60]

On a criminal trial the ultimate issues will be expressed in terms of the elements of the offence with which the accused person stands charged. They will, therefore, be issues about the facts which constitute those elements. Behind those ultimate issues there will often be many issues about facts relevant to facts in issue.[61]

Evidence is 'relevant':

> If it could rationally affect, directly or indirectly[62], the assessment of the probability of the evidence of fact in issue, ie., whether the accused person committed the offence, subject to the discretion of the Court.[63]

Evidence may be 'relevant' if it assists in the evaluation of other evidence.[64]

Such an assessment involves consideration of:

- what the evidence discloses; and
- how the evidence relates to what is in issue in the trial.[65]

---

[59] See *Smith v R* (2001) 206 CLR 650, [2001] HCA 50.

[60] See *Smith v R* (2001) 206 CLR 650, [2001] HCA 50.

[61] See *Smith v R* (2001) 206 CLR 650, [2001] HCA 50.

[62] See *Roach v R* [2011] HCA 12.

[63] See *Goldsmith v Sandilands* (2002) 190 ALR 370; *HML v R; SB v R; OAE v R* (2008) 235 CLR 334, (2008) 82 ALJR 723, [2008] HCA 16, per Gleeson CJ and *Smith v R* (2001) 206 CLR 650 at 654, [2001] HCA 50.

See also: Australian Law Reform Commission, 2005, 'Uniform Evidence Law', Report 112, NSWLRC Report 102 and VLRC Final Report, paragraph 16.10.

[64] See *HML v R; SB v R; OAE v R* (2008) 235 CLR 334, per Gleeson CJ at 352, (2008) 82 ALJR 723, [2008] HCA 16.

[65] See Australian Law Reform Commission, 2005, 'Uniform Evidence Law', Report 112, NSWLRC Report 102 and VLRC Final Report, paragraph 10.94.

WEIGHT

Any proposed evidence must be relevant to the issues being determined:

> In other words, it must have what is called 'probative value'[66] or 'weight'.

Upon evidence being ruled admissible, and therefore 'relevant', a Court must then determine what 'weight' or 'probative value' the evidence should be given, ie., the amount of importance.

Even if evidence is of some, albeit slight, 'probative value', it is still admissible subject to some principle of exclusion.[67]

A Court is entitled to put what 'weight' it wishes to the evidence of each witness.[68]

Questions as to the 'weight' of evidence are not determined by arbitrary rules, but by the application of:

- common sense;
- logic; and
- experience.[69]

In relation to the weighing of evidence and drawing inferences from it each case presents its own peculiarities and in each common sense and shrewdness must be brought to bear upon the facts elicited.[70]

---

[66] See Law Reform Commission of Ireland, 2010, 'Hearsay in Civil and Criminal Cases', Introduction.

See also: *DPP v Hester* [1972] 2 WLR 910, [1972] 3 All ER 440, (1973) 57 Cr App R 212, [1973] AC 296 and *R v Wilson* (1991) 2 NZLR 707.

[67] As Gleeson CJ observed in *Festa v R* (2001) 208 CLR 593 at 599.

[68] Section 25(2) of the *Juvenile Courts Act 1991* ['Conduct of Proceedings Generally'] provides that in respect to hearings under that Act where a matter, fact or opinion has been received into evidence the weight to be given to such matter, fact or opinion, as the case may be, shall be as determined by the magistrate.

Refer also to the section titled 'Court Decision' in the chapter titled 'Court Procedure' in the text titled 'Injia on Criminal Practice and Procedure in Papua New Guinea and the Pacific'.

[69] See *Dalu v R* [1993] SBHC 54.

[70] See *R v Madhub Chunder* (1874) 21 W R Cr 13, per Birch J at 19.

WEIGHT

All evidence is to be weighed according to:

- The proof that it was in the power of one side to have it produced; and
- The power of the other side to have it contradicted.[71]

[71] As observed by Lord Mansfield in *Blatch v Archer* [1774] EngR 2, (1774) 1 Cowp 63 at 65, [1774] EngR 2, (1774) 98 ER 969.

See also: *Rosa Angitai v The State* [1983] PNGLR 185, [1983] PGSC 7 and *Fairfield v Glenhaven Funeral Services Ltd* [2003] 1 AC 32, per Lord Bingham at 46.

DISCRETION TO EXCLUDE RELEVANT EVIDENCE

[1.0] STATUTORY PROVISIONS

[1.1] CRIMINAL PRACTICE RULES

Order 2, Division 1, rule 6 of the *Criminal Practice Rules 1987* ['Practice Directions'] states (in part):

> At a hearing under this rule counsel shall inform the Court --
>
> (f) of exhibits which are to be provided and whether they are to be admitted by consent; and
>
> (h) of any point of law which may arise on trial, any question as to the admissibility of evidence which then appears on the face of the papers and of any authority on which either party intends to rely as far as can be possibly envisaged at that stage'.

Rule 3 states (in part):

> 'An application under this order may be made within a reasonable time prior to the hearing --
>
> (a) Where directions are sought under Rule 6, before any Judge of the Court in Chambers'.

[1.2] PROFESSIONAL CONDUCT RULES

Section 16(2) of the *Professional Conduct Rules 1989* ['Defending a Person Accused of Crime'] states:

> 'When defending a client on a criminal charge, a lawyer shall endeavour to protect his client from being convicted except by a competent tribunal and upon legally admissible evidence sufficient to support a conviction for the offence with which his client is charged'.

[2.0] GENERAL PRINCIPLES

If evidence is either 'relevant' or it is not, no discretion arises.[72]

If it is not 'relevant', no further question arises about its admissibility, for irrelevant evidence should not be received.[73]

---

[72] See *Smith v R* (2001) 206 CLR 650 at 653-654.

[73] See *Roach v R* [2011] HCA 12.

DISCRETION TO EXCLUDE RELEVANT EVIDENCE

The application of the rules of evidence is not based on sportsmanship.[74]

There is no authority to suggest that a Court has any power to admit, as a matter of discretion, evidence which is inadmissible under an exclusionary rule of law.[75]

It is the duty of both the prosecution and defence to object to the admissibility of evidence as soon as practicable after reason for the objection emerges.[76]

A Court is expected to ensure that no inadmissible evidence is admitted, irrespective of whether there is an objection to its admission[77], otherwise there may be a miscarriage of justice[78].

However, evidence that has been unlawfully obtained is not necessarily inadmissible.[79]

---

[74] See *The People (Attorney-General) and O'Brien v McGrath* (1965) 99 Irish Law Times 59, per Davitt P.

[75] See Blackstone's Criminal Practice, 2005, page 2143.

[76] See *R v Rogers* (1983) 9 A Crim R 209.

[77] See *Luingi Yandasingi v The State* [1995] PNGLR 268.

[78] See *R v Chai* [2002] NSWCCA 512.

Refer also to the chapter titled 'Appeals' in the text titled 'Injia on Criminal Practice and Procedure in Papua New Guinea and the Pacific'.

[79] See *Kuruma v R* [1955] AC 197, [1955] 1 All ER 236.

See also: *R v Ireland* (1970) 126 CLR 321 at 334, [1970] ALR 727, (1970) 44 ALJR 263, [1970] HCA 21; *Bunning v Cross* (1978) 141 CLR 54 at 66, (1978) 19 ALR 641, [1978] HCA 22; *Marchant v R* (1971) 126 CLR 414, [1971] ALR 736, (1971) 45 ALJR 310; *R v Demicoli* [1971] Qd R 358; *R v Barnsley* [1972] 2 NSWLR 220; *R v Warneminde* [1978] Qd R 371; *R v Shea* (1978) 18 SASR 591; *R v Conley* (1979) 21 SASR 166; *Cleland v R* (1982) 151 CLR 1 at 9, (1982) 43 ALR 619, [1982] HCA 67; *R v Fox* [1986] 1 AC 281 and *R v Khan* [1996] 2 Cr App R 440.

DISCRETION TO EXCLUDE RELEVANT EVIDENCE

In deciding whether to exclude evidence although 'relevant' but which has been unlawfully obtained a Court may:

- exercise its common law discretionary power to reject such evidence; and

- exercise its power as provided for by section 57 of the *Constitution of the Independent State of Papua New Guinea* ['Enforcement of Guaranteed Rights and Freedoms'] to reject the evidence, depending on the circumstances.[80]

The onus of proving the admissibility of the evidence lies with both the prosecution[81] and defence.

A Court has a discretion to exclude legally admissible evidence if justice so requires.[82]

A Court has the discretion whether to exclude 'relevant' evidence on the question of fairness to an accused person[83] when:

- its prejudicial effect.

---

[80] See *Alex v Golu* [1983] PNGLR 117 and *The State v James Bero Popo* [1987] PNGLR 286.

In Canada evidence obtained in breach of the *Canadian Charter of Rights and Freedoms* will be excluded if its admission is likely to bring the administration of justice into disrepute, see *R v Collins* [1987] 1 SCR 265.

In New Zealand evidence obtained in breach of the semi-constitutional provisions of the *New Zealand Bill of Rights Act 1990* is prima facie inadmissible, but subject to exceptions created by the overriding demands of justice, see *Howden v Ministry of Transport* [1987] 2 NZLR 747 and *R v Grayson and Taylor* [1997] 1 NZLR 399.

See also: *HKSAR v Chan Kau Tai* [2006] 1 HKLRD 400.

[81] See *R v Mallinson* [1993] 1 NZLR 528 at 531.

[82] See *Myers v Director of Public Prosecutions* [1965] AC 1001, per Lord Reid at 1024, (1964) 48 Cr App R 348, [1964] 2 All ER 881, [1964] 3 WLR 145.

[83] See *Harris v DPP* [1952] 1 All ER 1044, (1952) 36 Cr App R 235, [1952] AC 694 per Viscount Simon at 707 and *R v Christie* (1914) 10 Cr App R 141, [1914] AC 545, (1914) 24 Cox CC 249, per Lord Reading at 564 and 257 respectively.

See also: *Driscoll v R* (1977) 137 CLR 517 at 541, (1977) 15 ALR 47, [1977] HCA 43.

In this context, prejudice means the danger of improper use of the evidence[84] and therefore, capable of causing damage to the prospects of a fair trial[85].

It does not mean damage to the defence case.[86]

outweighs[87]

- its probative value[88].[89]

---

[84] See *HML v R; SB v R; OAE v R* (2008) 235 CLR 334, (2008) 82 ALJR 723, [2008] HCA 16.

[85] See *R v Morris* [1996] 2 Qd R 68 at 72 and *Festa v R* (2001) 208 CLR 593.

[86] See *R v Morris* [1996] 2 Qd R 68 at 72 and *Festa v R* (2001) 208 CLR 593.

[87] Prejudicial effect and probative value are incommensurables, as stated by McHugh J in *Pfennig v R* (1995) 182 CLR 461 at 528, (1995) 69 ALJR 147, (1995) 127 ALR 99, (1995) 77 A Crim R 149, [1995] HCA 7.

Furthermore, a great deal of judicial and other decision-making involves forming a judgement about where the balance is to be struck between competing considerations that are not amenable to any fixed standard of comparison, see *HML v R; SB v R; OAE v R* (2008) 235 CLR 334, (2008) 82 ALJR 723, [2008] HCA 16, per Gleeson CJ.

[88] See also: *Sutton v R* (1984) 152 CLR 528 at 534 and 565, (1984) 51 ALR 435, [1984] HCA 5 and *R v Sang* [1980] AC 402, per Lord Diplock at 434-435, (1979) 69 Cr App R 282, [1979] 3 WLR 263, [1979] 2 All ER 1222, [1979] Crim LR 282, [1979] UKHL 3.

[89] See *Harris v DPP* [1952] 1 All ER 1044, (1952) 36 Cr App R 235, [1952] AC 694 at 707; *Kuruma v R* [1955] AC 197, [1955] 1 All ER 236 and *Selvey v DPP* [1970] AC 304, [1968] 2 WLR 1494, [1968] 2 All ER 497, (1968) 52 Cr App R 443.

See also: *Driscoll v R* (1977) 137 CLR 517 at 523 and 541, (1977) 15 ALR 47, [1977] HCA 43; *Alexander v R* (1981) 149 CLR 395 at 402-3, 417-18, 428-30 and 435, (1981) 34 ALR 289, [1981] HCA 17; *Sutton v R* (1984) 152 CLR 528 at 534, 558-9 and 565, (1984) 51 ALR 435, [1984] HCA 5; *Doney v R* (1990) 171 CLR 207 at 212, (1990) 50 A Crim R 157 at 159, (1990) 96 ALR 539, [1990] HCA 51; *Harriman v R* (1989) 167 CLR at 594, 608 and 633, [1989] HCA 50; *R v Sang* (1979) 69 Cr App R 282, [1980] AC 402 at 437, [1979] 3 WLR 263, [1979] 2 All ER 1222, [1979] Crim LR 282, [1979] UKHL 3 and *Ridgeway v R* (1995) 184 CLR 19, (1995) 129 ALR 41 at 49, (1995) 69 ALJR 484, [1995] HCA 66.

As Justice Scalia once put it, this is like asking 'whether a particular line is longer than a particular rock is heavy', see *Bendix Autolite Corp v Midwesco Enterprises Inc* (1988) 486 US 888 at 897.

It is always a question of degree in each case, as Lord Mackay stated in *DPP v P* [1991] 2 AC 447, [1991] 3 WLR 161, [1991] 3 All ER 337, (1991) 93 Cr App R 267, [1992] Crim LR 4.

DISCRETION TO EXCLUDE RELEVANT EVIDENCE

The concept of probative value involves relevance and weight. The probative value of evidence must be considered by reference to the purpose or purposes for which it is used.[90]

In order to determine probative value, the evidence must be:

- taken at its highest[91];
- assumed that the evidence would be accepted[92]; and
- assumed to be true[93].

Furthermore, a Court may also exclude 'relevant' evidence:

- when the strict rules of admissibility would operate unfairly against an accused person[94] and particularly if the evidence has no or little weight[95];
- when the evidence has been ascertained or procured by unlawful or improper conduct on the part of those whose task it is to enforce the law[96], although there is no general rule that a Court will reject evidence that has been illegally obtained[97].

---

[90] See *HML v R; SB v R; OAE v R* (2008) 235 CLR 334, (2008) 82 ALJR 723, [2008] HCA 16, per Gleeson CJ.

[91] See *R v Singh-Bal* (1997) 92 A Crim R 397 and *R v Yates* [2002] NSWCCA 520.

[92] See *Adam v R* (2001) 207 CLR 96, per Gaudron J.

[93] See *R v AB* [2001] NSWCCA 496.

[94] See *Stephens v R* (1985) 156 CLR 664 at 669, [1985] HCA 30; *Driscoll v R* (1977) 137 CLR 517 at 541, (1977) 15 ALR 47, [1977] HCA 43 and *Harris v DPP* [1952] 1 All ER 1044, (1952) 36 Cr App R 235, [1952] AC 694, per Viscount Simon at 707.

[95] See *R v Christie* [1914] AC 545 at 560, (1914) 24 Cox CC 249 at 257, (1914) 10 Cr App R 141; *Noor Mohamed v R* [1949] AC 182 at 192, [1949] 1 All ER 365; *Harris v DPP* [1952] 1 All ER 1044, (1952) 36 Cr App R 235, [1952] AC 694 at 707; *Kuruma v R* [1955] AC 197, per Lord Moulton at 204, [1955] 1 All ER 236 and *Driscoll v R* (1977) 137 CLR 517, per Gibbs J at 541, (1977) 15 ALR 47, [1977] HCA 43.

[96] See *R v Ireland* (1970)126 CLR 321 at 334-335, [1970] ALR 727, (1970) 44 ALJR 263, [1970] HCA 21 and *Bunning v Cross* (1978) 141 CLR 54 at 64-65, 72 and 74-75, (1978) 19 ALR 641, [1978] HCA 22.

[97] See *Cleland v R* (1982) 151 CLR 1, per Gibbs CJ at 9, (1982) 43 ALR 619, [1982] HCA 67.

However, evidence that has been unlawfully obtained is not necessarily inadmissible[98];

- when the evidence involves an inordinate amount of time which is not commensurate with its value[99];
- when the evidence is misleading in the sense that its effect on the Court is out of proportion to its reliability[100]; or
- when the evidence places the accused person at risk of being improperly convicted[101], such as because its weight and credibility cannot be effectively tested[102].

The power is based on a Court's duty in a criminal trial to ensure that an accused person receives a fair trial.[103]

---

[98] See *R v Ireland* (1970)126 CLR 321 at 334-335, [1970] ALR 727, (1970) 44 ALJR 263, [1970] HCA 21; *Bunning v Cross* (1978) 141 CLR 54 at 66, (1978) 19 ALR 641, [1978] HCA 22 and *Cleland v R* (1982) 151 CLR 1at 9, (1982) 43 ALR 619, [1982] HCA 67.

[99] See *R v Mohan* [1994] 2 SCR 9 at 21, 1994 SCC 80 and *R v Jabarianha* [2001] 3 SCR 430, 2001 SCC 75.

[100] See *R v Mohan* [1994] 2 SCR 9 at 21, 1994 SCC 80 and *R v Jabarianha* [2001] 3 SCR 430, 2001 SCC 75.

[101] See *McDermott v R* (1948) 76 CLR 501, per Dixon J at 511-515 and *Driscoll v R* (1977) 137 CLR 517, per Gibbs J at 541, (1977) 15 ALR 47, [1977] HCA 43.

[102] See *McDermott v R* (1948) 76 CLR 501, per Dixon J at 511-515 and *R v Lee* (1950) 82 CLR 133 at 144, [1950] HCA 25.

[103] See *R v Noor Mohamed* [1949] AC 182 at 192, [1949] 1 All ER 365; *Harris v DPP* [1952] 1 All ER 1044, (1952) 36 Cr App R 235, [1952] AC 694, per Viscount Simon at 707 and *R v Christie* [1914] AC 545, per Lord Reading at 564, (1914) 24 Cox CC 249, (1914) 10 Cr App R 141.

See also: *C (A Minor) v DPP* [1996] AC 1, per Lord Lowry at 35; *Lobban v R* [1995] 1 WLR 877, [1995] 2 All ER 602, [1995] 2 Cr App R 573 at 583; *Bunning v Cross* (1978) 141 CLR 54 at 66, (1978) 19 ALR 641, [1978] HCA 22; *R v Ireland* (1970) 126 CLR 321 at 335, [1970] ALR 727, (1970) 44 ALJR 263, [1970] HCA 21; *Ridgeway v R* (1995) 129 ALR 41 at 49, (1995) 69 ALJR 484, [1995] HCA 66; *R v Coombs* [1985] 1 NZLR 318 at 321; *R v Dally* [1990] 2 NZLR 184; *R v Grayson and Taylor* [1997] 1 NZLR 399; *R v Convery* [1968] NZLR 426; *R v Sang* (1979) 69 Cr App R 282, [1980] AC 402, [1979] 3 WLR 263, [1979] 2 All ER 1222, [1979] Crim LR 282, [1979] UKHL 3; *R v Hasler* [1987] 1 Qd R 239; *Driscoll v R* (1977) 137 CLR 517 at 541, (1977) 15 ALR 47, [1977] HCA 43; *R v Baker* [1989] 3 NZLR 635 at 639-640; *Murdoch v Murphy* (1987) 33 A Crim R 118 at 126-127; *Dominic v R* (1972) 128 CLR 114, [1972] HCA 71; *Alexander v R* (1981) 149 CLR 395 at 402-3, 417-18, 428-30 and 435, (1981) 34 ALR 289, [1981] HCA 17; *Harriman v R* (1989) 167 CLR 590, [1989] HCA 50 and *Pfennig v R* (1995) 182 CLR 461, (1995) 69 ALJR 147, (1995) 127 ALR 99, (1995) 77 A Crim R 149, [1995] HCA 7.

DISCRETION TO EXCLUDE RELEVANT EVIDENCE

The onus is on the defence to prove on the 'balance of probabilities' that a Court should exercise its discretion to exclude 'relevant' evidence.[104]

The defence may renew its application to a Court to exclude evidence in light of what transpires during the course of a trial.[105]

Despite the possible advantages that may flow from a pre-trial ruling as to the admissibility of evidence[106], there is no principle of law under which an accused person is entitled to request a Court to give a pre-trial ruling on the law in respect to evidence that he or she proposes to give when that evidence is not accepted by the prosecution.[107]

---

[104] See *Public Prosecutor v Mohd Farid bin Mohd Sukis and another* (2002) 3 MLJ 401 and *Francis Antonysamy v Public Prosecutor* (2005) 3 MLJ 389.

[105] See *R v Wilson* [1981] 1 NZLR 316 at 323 and *R v Watson* [1980] 2 All ER 293.

[106] See *R v Vickers* (1975) 61 Cr App R 48.

[107] See *R v Reid* [2002] NZCA 161.

Refer also to the section titled 'Pre-trial' in the chapter titled 'Court Procedure' in the text titled 'Injia on Criminal Practice and Procedure in Papua New Guinea and the Pacific'.

BEST EVIDENCE AND SECONDARY EVIDENCE RULES

The trite and often repeated statement that in order to adduce proof of each element of a charge[108] the maxim:

> 'The best evidence must be given of which the nature of the court case permits'

is considered a fundamental principle of the law of evidence, ie., the 'best evidence rule'.[109]

The basic principle is:

> Only the 'best' evidence should be placed before a Court, that is, the evidence that is most likely to be reliable.[110]

There is the expectation of the Courts that original evidence will be tendered by the prosecution, and defence, whenever possible.[111]

Where the contents of a document are to be proved, the law of evidence requires that the original must be produced or its absence explained. This is usually called 'the secondary evidence rule'.[112]

Primary evidence may be defined as 'the best evidence, or that kind of proof which, under any possible circumstances, affords the greatest certainty of the fact in question', whereas secondary evidence is 'all evidence falling short of this'.[113]

---

[108] Refer also to the section titled 'Proof Of Elements' in the chapter titled 'Proof Of Issues' in the text titled 'Injia on Criminal Practice and Procedure in Pqapua New Guinea and the Pacific'.

[109] See *The State v John Bill White (No. 1)* (1996) N1441.

See also: *R v Nowaz (alias Karim)* (1976) 63 Cr App R 178, [1976] 3 All ER 5, [1976] 1 WLR 830; *R v Governor of Pontville Prison and another; ex parte Osman* [1989] 3 All ER 701, (1990) 90 Cr App R 281, [1990] 1 WLR 277; *R v Uxbridge Justices; ex parte Sofaer and another* (1987) 85 Cr App R 367 and *R v Stipendiary Magistrate at Lambeth and another; ex parte McComb* [1983] 1 All ER 321.

Refer also to the section titled 'Missing Exhibit' in the chapter titled 'Exhibits'.

[110] See *R v Horncastle and others* [2009] UKSC 14.

[111] Refer also to the chapter titled 'Exhibits'.

[112] See New Zealand Law Commission, 1994, 'Evidence Law: Documentary Evidence and Judicial Notice – A Discussion Paper', Preliminary Paper 22.

[113] See New Zealand Law Commission, 1994, 'Evidence Law: Documentary Evidence and Judicial Notice – A Discussion Paper', Preliminary Paper 22.

BEST EVIDENCE AND SECONDARY EVIDENCE RULES

The admissibility of secondary evidence, ie., a copy of an original document, has been considered in the courts. If a copy or a copy of a copy is sought to be tendered there must be evidence so that it is proved to be a true copy of the original.[114]

The 'secondary evidence rule' may be seen as the last vestige of the 'best evidence rule', now largely obsolete.[115]

The only remaining instance of that rule is:

> If an original document is available it must be produced and a witness cannot give secondary evidence by producing a copy, if the original is available[116],

subject to statutory exceptions[117].

---

[114] See *R v Collins* (1960) 44 Cr App R 170 at 174.

[115] See New Zealand Law Commission, 1994, 'Evidence Law: Documentary Evidence and Judicial Notice – A Discussion Paper', Preliminary Paper 22.

[116] See *Garton v Hunter* [1969] 2 QB 37 at 44.

See also: *Kajala v Noble* (1982) 75 Cr App R 149, per Ackner LJ at 152.

Refer also to the chapter titled 'Documentary Evidence'.

[117] See:

- section 55 ['Secondary Evidence of Registered Deed or Document, etc.']; and
- Division 6 of Part IV ['Photographic and Machine Reproductions']

of the *Evidence Act* (Ch. 48).

CHARACTER EVIDENCE

[1.0] INTRODUCTION

The law assumes that a person is of either good or bad character and nothing in between. Although logically there is no compelling reason for distinguishing between good and bad character evidence, the common law has treated evidence of an accused person's good or bad character differently.[118]

An accused person's character is often inferred, therefore, from such matters as the accused person's previous convictions[119], associations, conduct and way of life.[120]

Character evidence is traditionally admitted for the following reasons:

- to attack or support the credibility of a witness; or
- to prove the witness acted in the way alleged.[121]

Evidence of character and evidence of credibility can both be of great assistance to a Court, to the extent of being decisive. But such evidence can also be of little or no relevance with the result that its introduction may be distractful. Moreover, for an accused person evidence of character and credibility can be unfairly prejudicial.[122]

When considering that evidence of 'character' is potentially damaging to an accused person there are specific rules based on statutory law and the common law for their protection.

---

[118] See *Durani v The State of Western Australia* [2012] WASCA 172.

[119] Refer also to the section titled 'Previous Convictions' in the section titled 'Wording Of Charges' in the chapter titled 'Charges' in the text titled 'Injia on Criminal Practice and Procedure in Papua New Guinea and the Pacific.

[120] See New Zealand Law Commission, 1997, 'Evidence Law – Character and Credibility A Discussion Paper', Preliminary Paper 27, page 56.

[121] See New Zealand Law Commission, 1999, 'Evidence. Volume 1: Reform of the Law and Evidence. Volume 2: Evidence Code and Commentary', Report 55, page 44.

[122] See New Zealand Law Commission, 1999, 'Evidence. Volume 1: Reform of the Law and Evidence. Volume 2: Evidence Code and Commentary', Report 55, page 44.

CHARACTER EVIDENCE

Character has the following evidential aspects:

- evidence in relation to 'reputation'; and
- evidence of 'disposition'.[123]

[2.0] REPUTATION

[2.1] ACCUSED PERSON

[2.1.1] GOOD CHARACTER EVIDENCE

Although evidence of 'bad character' can be admitted against an accused person at common law, stringent conditions as to its 'probative value' have to be complied with[124], although no such conditions are applied to evidence of 'good character'.[125]

If evidence constitutes evidence of 'good character' it is admissible even when, as often happens, it throws little, if any, light on whether the accused person committed the offence in question.[126]

The basis for allowing evidence of 'good character' to be used 'is not logic but the "policy and humanity" of the common law'.[127]

Evidence of 'good character' is relevant to issues of an accused person's credibility and guilt.[128]

The assumptions which underpin these accepted areas of relevance are as follows:

- as to credibility, it is thought a person of 'good character' is more likely to be an honest witness, and is thus more believable; and

---

[123] See New Zealand Law Commission, 1997, 'Evidence Law – Character and Credibility A Discussion Paper', Preliminary Paper 27, page 11.

[124] See *Pfennig v R* (1995) 182 CLR 461, (1995) 69 ALJR 147, (1995) 127 ALR 99, (1995) 77 A Crim R 149, [1995] HCA 7.

[125] See *Durani v The State of Western Australia* [2012] WASCA 172.

[126] See *Melbourne v R* (1999) 198 CLR 1, [1999] HCA 32, per McHugh J.

[127] As commented by McHugh J by *Melbourne v R* (1999) 198 CLR 1, [1999] HCA 32.

[128] See *Durani v The State of Western Australia* [2012] WASCA 172.

- as to guilt, a person of 'good character' is thought to be less likely to commit an offence, and therefore less likely to have committed the offence or offences before the Court.[129]

An accused person is always entitled to call evidence of his or her 'good character' or other evidence in disproving his or her own guilt of the offence charged.[130]

The test to be applied is:

Whether the evidence is relevant or not to the question of guilt.[131]

Where credibility is in issue, a 'good character direction' is always relevant.[132]

When an accused person is of 'good character', ie., has no convictions of any relevance or significance, he or she is entitled to the benefit of a 'good character direction', tailored to fit the circumstances of the case.[133]

However, it does not follow that an accused person who has no previous convictions is inevitably of good character.[134]

---

[129] See *Durani v The State of Western Australia* [2012] WASCA 172.

However, both McHugh J and Kirby J commented that such assumptions are dubious, see *Melbourne v R* (1999) 198 CLR 1, [1999] HCA 32.

[130] See *R v Stannard* (1837) 7 Car & P 673 at 674.

See also: *R v Trimboli* (1979) 21 SASR 577.

[131] See *R v Thompson, Sinclair and Maver* [1995] 2 Cr App R 589.

As regards 'character evidence' generally, see also: *Braysich v R* [2011] HCA 14; *Melbourne v R* (1999) 198 CLR 1; *Smith v R* (1980) 144 CLR 319; *Berry v R* [1992] 2 AC 364; *Sealey and Headley v The State* [2002] UKPC 52; *R v Broadhurst, Meanley and Hill* (1918) 13 Cr App R 125; *R v Lloyd* [2000] 2 Cr App R 355; *R v Martin* [2000] 2 Cr App R 42; *R v Jackson and Harim* (1988) 33 A Crim R 413; *R v Noble* (1928) 20 Cr App R 191; *R v Brownhill* (1912) 8 Cr App R 118 at 120; *R v Thompson* [1966] 1 WLR 405, [1966] 1 All ER 505, (1966) 50 Cr App R 91; *R v Bellis* (1966) 50 Cr App R 88 at 89 and *R v Murphy* [1985] 4 NSWLR 42.

[132] See *Berry v R* [1992] 2 AC 364 at 381; *Barrow v The State* [1998] AC 846 at 850; *Sealey and Headley v The State* [2002] UKPC 52 and *Teeluck and another v The State (Trinidad and Tobago)* [2005] 1 WLR 2421, [2005] UKPC 14.

[133] See *Thompson v R* [1998] AC 811; *R v Aziz and other appeals* [1995] 3 All ER 149, [1995] 2 Cr App R 478, [1996] 1 AC 41, [1995] 3 WLR 53; *R v Vye, R v Wise and R v Stephenson* [1993] 1 WLR 471, [1993] 3 All ER 241, (1993) 97 Cr App R 134; *Teeluck and another v The State (Trinidad and Tobago)* [2005] 2 Cr App R 25, [2005] 1 WLR 2421, [2005] UKPC 14 and *R v Gray* [2004] 2 Cr App R 30.

[134] See *Gilbert v R* (Practice Note) [2006] UKPC 15, [2006] 1 WLR 2108.

CHARACTER EVIDENCE

The evidence of 'good character' is primarily a matter that goes to credibility[135] and must be evidence of 'general reputation'[136], and not dependent upon particular acts or actions[137].

In order to raise evidence of 'good character' an accused person must:

- give evidence of his or her 'good character'[138];
- cross-examine a witness called by the prosecution as to his or her 'good character'[139]; or
- call a witness to give evidence of his or her 'good character'.[140]

  The appropriate evidence is from an individual who knows:

  - the accused person; and
  - other people who know the accused person.[141]

---

135 See *R v Bellis* (1966) 50 Cr App R 88.

See also: *R v Marr* (1990) 90 Cr App R 154 and *Berry v R* [1992] 3 WLR 153 at 166.

136 See *R v Rowton* (1865) 10 Cox CC 25, [1865] EngR 53, (1865) 169 ER 1497, Le & Ca 520.

See also: *R v Falealili* (1996) 14 CRNZ 157 and *Donaldson v The State of Western Australia* (2007) 176 A Crim R 488, [2007] WASCA 216, per Buss JA.

137 See *R v Rowton* (1865) 10 Cox CC 25, [1865] EngR 53, (1865) 169 ER 1497, Le & Ca 520 and *R v Butterwasser* [1948] 1 KB 4, per Goddard LCJ at 6.

138 See *Barrow v State* [1998] AC 846 at 852; *Thompson v R* [1998] AC 811 at 844 and *Teeluck and another v The State (Trinidad and Tobago)* [2005] 2 Cr App R 25, [2005] 1 WLR 2421, [2005] UKPC 14.

139 See *R v de Vere* [1981] 3 All ER 473; *Barrow v The State* [1998] AC 846 at 852; *Thompson v R* [1998] AC 811 at 844 and *Teeluck and another v The State (Trinidad and Tobago)* [2005] 2 Cr App R 25, [2005] 1 WLR 2421, [2005] UKPC 14.

140 See *Barrow v The State* [1998] AC 846 at 852; *Thompson v R* [1998] AC 811 at 844; *Teeluck and another v The State (Trinidad and Tobago)* [2005] 2 Cr App R 25, [2005] 1 WLR 2421, [2005] UKPC 14; *Gilbert v R* [2006] UKPC 15 and *R v de Vere* [1981] 3 All ER 473.

141 See *Re T and Director of Youth and Community Services* [1980] 1 NSWLR 392.

CHARACTER EVIDENCE

The purpose of evidence of 'good character' is to:

- bolster the credibility of an accused person, as any person of 'good character' is entitled to claim and establish that because he or she has lived his or her life to the age he or she is and has remained a person of 'good character', he or she is less likely to commit an offence[142]; and

- bolster the credibility of the accused person's version of events[143].

However,

> what inference can properly be drawn about the character of an accused person beyond the bare statement that he or she has no previous convictions?[144]

The reality is that evidence as to 'good character', in the run-of-the mill case, can seldom 'weigh[145]' heavily in the scales in favour of an accused person, though evidence of 'bad character' might be extremely prejudicial.[146]

---

[142] See *R v Richardson and Longman* [1968] 2 All ER 761, (1968) 52 Cr App R 317, [1968] 3 WLR 15, [1967] 1 QB 299.

See also: *Attwood v R* (1960) 102 CLR 353; *Simic v R* (1980) 144 CLR 319; *R v Lawrence* [1984] 3 NSWLR 674; *R v Bryant and Oxley* [1978] 2 All ER 689, (1978) 67 Cr App R 157, [1979] QB 108, [1978] 2 WLR 589, [1978] Crim LR 307; *R v Marr* (1990) 90 Cr App R 154, [1989] Crim LR 743; *R v Cohen* (1990) 91 Cr App R 125; *Barrow v The State* [1998] AC 846; *R v Vye, R v Wise and R v Stephenson* [1993] 3 All ER 241, [1993] 1 WLR 471, (1993) 97 Cr App R 134; *R v Aziz and other appeals* [1995] 3 All ER 149, [1995] 2 Cr App R 478, [1996] 1 AC 41, [1995] 3 WLR 53; *R v Thompson* [1966] QWN 47; *R v Nilon* (1980) 5 A Crim R 385; *R v Lee Kam Yuen* [1995] 1 HKCLR 264 at 266 and *Teeluck and another v The State (Trinidad and Tobago)* [2005] 2 Cr App R 25, [2005] 1 WLR 2421, [2005] UKPC 14.

[143] See *R v Nilon* (1980) 5 A Crim R 385; *Barrow v State* [1998] AC 846; *R v Vye, R v Wise and R v Stephenson* [1993] 1 WLR 471, [1993] 3 All ER 241, (1993) 97 Cr App R 134; *R v Aziz and other appeals* [1995] 3 All ER 149, [1995] 2 Cr App R 478, [1996] 1 AC 41, [1995] 3 WLR 53 and *Teeluck and another v The State (Trinidad and Tobago)* [2005] 2 Cr App R 25, [2005] 1 WLR 2421, [2005] UKPC 14.

[144] See *Tang Siu Man v HKSAR* [1998] HKCFA 45, [1997-98] 1 HKFCAR 107, [1998] 1 HKLRD 350, [1998] HKC 371.

[145] Refer also to the chapter titled 'Weight'.

[146] See *Tang Siu Man v HKSAR* [1998] HKCFA 45, [1997-98] 1 HKFCAR 107, [1998] 1 HKLRD 350, [1998] HKC 371.

CHARACTER EVIDENCE

An accused person's character will in most cases depend on matters unrelated to the offence for which he or she is being tried.[147]

People do commit offences for the first time.[148]

Once any aspect of an accused person's character is put in issue, it is all put in issue.[149]

The failure to ensure that an accused person's 'good character' is brought before the Court may result in a guilty verdict being unsafe[150], depending on whether such evidence would have made a difference as to the result[151].

The omission of a good character direction is not necessarily fatal to:

- the fairness of the trial; or
- the safety of a conviction.[152]

[2.1.2] BAD CHARACTER EVIDENCE

Evidence of an accused person's 'bad character' is ordinarily inadmissible because it may inappropriately be relied upon to establish guilt.[153]

Before evidence of 'bad character' can be admitted against an accused person at common law, stringent conditions as to its 'probative value' have to be complied with.[154]

---

[147] See *Oui v R* [2006] WASCA 76 and *R v Lee Kam Yuen* [1995] 1 HKCLR 264 at 266.

[148] See *Palazoff* (1986) 23 A Crim R 86.

[149] See *R v Winfield* (1939) 27 Cr App R 139.

[150] See *Nigel Brown v State of Trinidad and Tobago* [2012] 1 WLR 1577, [2012] UKPC 2; *Nyron Smith v R* (2008) 74 WIR 379, [2008] UKPC 34; *Sealey and Headley v The State* (2002) 61 WIR 491, [2002] UKPC 52 and *Teeluck and another v The State (Trinidad and Tobago)* [2005] 2 Cr App R 25, [2005] 1 WLR 2421, [2005] UKPC 14.

[151] See *Bhola v The State* (2006) 68 WIR 449, [2006] 4 LRC 268, [2006] UKPC 9.

[152] See *Bhola v The State* (2006) 68 WIR 449, [2006] 4 LRC 268, [2006] UKPC 9.

[153] See New Zealand Law Commission, 1997, 'Evidence Law – Character and Credibility A Discussion Paper', Preliminary Paper 27, page 53.

[154] See *Pfennig v R* (1995) 182 CLR 461, (1995) 69 ALJR 147, (1995) 127 ALR 99, (1995) 77 A Crim R 149, [1995] HCA 7.

CHARACTER EVIDENCE

It is not generally permissible to ask questions of an accused person:

- about his or her previous 'bad character'; or

- which tend to show that he or she has previously committed some criminal offence[155], whether before or after the offence charged[156].

  The reception of inadmissible evidence of a prior conviction offends against one of the most deeply rooted and jealously guarded principles of criminal law.[157]

However, the prosecution may lead evidence of an accused person's 'bad character' as follows:

- as provided for by section 15 of the *Evidence Act* (Ch. 48) ['Accused as Witness as to Previous Convictions, etc'].[158]

  It is impossible and would be unwise to lay down hard and fast rules as to how a Court should exercise its discretion, as provided for by section 15.[159]

  The critical question is whether or not leave to cross-examine should have been given having regard to the prejudice involved[160]; and

---

[155] See *R v Miller and others* (1952) 36 Cr App R 169, per Lord Steyn at 171.

See also: *Lui Mei Lin v R* [1989] AC 288, [1989] 2 WLR 175, [1989] 1 All ER 359, (1989) 88 Cr App R 296, [1989] Crim LR 364 and *R v Randall* [2004] 1 WLR 56

[156] See *R v Wood* [1920] 2 KB 179.

[157] See *Maxwell v DPP* (1934) 24 Cr App R 152, [1935] AC 309 at 317.

[158] Refer also to the subsection titled 'Questioning Credibility Of An Accused Person' in the section titled 'Cross-examination' in the chapter titled 'Examination Of Witnesses' in the text titled 'Injia on Criminal Practice and Procedure in Papua New Guinea and the Pacific'.

[159] See *R v Edwards* [1991] 1 WLR 207, per Lane LCJ at 216.

Refer also to the subsection titled 'Questioning Credibility Of An Accused Person' in the section titled 'Cross-examintion' in the chapter titled 'Examination Of Witnesses' in the text titled 'Injia on Criminal Practice and Procedure in Papua New Guinea and the Pacific'.

[160] See *R v Jenkins* (1945) 31 Cr App R 1, per Singleton J at 15.

See also: *R v Kalo* [1984] 1 CRNZ 413 and *R v Fisher* [1964] NZLR 1063 at 1065.

- when an accused person offers evidence of 'good character' that is not correct then the prosecution may offer evidence of 'bad character' in rebuttal even if the accused person does not testify[161].

  However, the prosecution cannot rebut evidence of an accused person's 'good character' by asking questions about a previous charge on which the accused person had been acquitted[162].

[2.2] WITNESSES GENERALLY

[2.2.1] PREVIOUS CONVICTIONS

STATUTORY PROVISION

Section 25 of the *Evidence Act* (Ch. 48) ['Proof of Previous Conviction of Witness'] states:

> 'A witness may be questioned as to whether he has been convicted of an offence, and if on being so questioned, he denies or does not admit the fact, or refuses to answer, the cross-examining party may prove the conviction'.[163]

GENERAL PRINCIPLES

A witness may be cross-examined about his or her previous convictions, provided:

- the questioning does not become oppressive[164]; and
- the offence is of such a nature as to tend to weaken confidence in the credit of the witness, that is to say, in his or her character or trustworthiness as a witness of truth[165].

---

[161] See New Zealand Law Commission, 1997, 'Evidence Law – Character and Credibility A Discussion Paper', Preliminary Paper 27, page 54.

[162] See *Maxwell v DPP* (1934) 24 Cr App R 152, [1935] AC 309.

[163] Refer also to the subsection titled 'Proof Of A Previous Conviction' in the section titled 'Wording Of Charges' in the chapter titled 'Charges' in the text titled 'Injia on Criminal Practice in Papua New Guinea and the Pacific'.

[164] See *Hally v Starkey; ex parte Hally* [1962] Qd R 474 at 478.

[165] See *Bugg v Day* (1949) 79 CLR 442, per Dixon J at 467.

CHARACTER EVIDENCE

Evidence of a complainant's previous conviction may be relevant when self-defence is an issue.[166]

A witness who has a criminal conviction may be considered to be a 'Suspect Witness'.[167]

[2.2.2] REPUTATION FOR VERACITY

A witness may be called in order to be asked:

- whether he or she has knowledge of the impugned witness's general reputation for veracity;
- whether from such knowledge he or she would believe the impugned witness's sworn testimony; and
- to express his or her individual opinion based upon his or her personal knowledge as to whether another witness is to be believed upon his or her oath, solemn declaration or affirmation and is not to be confined to giving evidence merely of 'general reputation'.[168]

[2.2.3] SEXUAL REPUTATION

Section 37G of the *Evidence Act* (Ch. 48) states:

> 'In a proceeding with respect to a sexual offence, evidence of the sexual reputation, of the Complainant whether general or specific, is not admissible'.[169]

---

[166] See *R v Davis* [1980] 1 NZLR 257 at 262 and *R v Wilson* [1991] 2 NZLR 707.

[167] Refer also to the section titled 'Suspect Witness' in the chapter titled 'Witnesses' in the text titled 'Injia on Criminal Practice and Procedure in Papua New Guinea and the Pacific'.

[168] See *R v Richardson and Longman* [1968] 2 All ER 761, (1968) 52 Cr App R 317, [1968] 3 WLR 15, [1967] 1 QB 299 and *R v Gunewardene* [1951] 2 KB 600, (1951) 35 Cr App R 80.

See also: *R v Moloney* (1988) 14 VLR 934; *R v BDX* [2009] VSCA 28; *Bell v R* (1985) 7 FCR 555 at 563 and *R v Hanrahan* [1967] 2 NSWR 717 at 718-719.

[169] This type of legislation is generally described as 'rape-shield legislation', see New Zealand Law Commission, 1997, 'Evidence Law – Character and Credibility A Discussion Paper', Preliminary Paper 27, page 103.

Refer also to the section titled 'Vulnerable And Intimidated Witness' in the chapter titled 'Witnesses' in the text titled 'Injia on Criminal Practice and Procedure in Papua New Guinea and the Pacific'.

CHARACTER EVIDENCE

[3.0] DISPOSITION

Evidence of 'disposition' relates to an individual's:

- inherent personality; and
- habitual behaviour.[170]

[170] See New Zealand Law Commission, 1997, 'Evidence Law – Character and Credibility A Discussion Paper', Preliminary Paper 27, page 11.

Refer also to:
- the chapter titled 'Similar Fact Evidence'; and
- the section titled 'Cross-examination' in the chapter titled 'Examination Of Witnesses' in the text titled 'Injia on Criminal Practice and Procedure in Papua New Guinea and the Pacific'.

CIRCUMSTANTIAL EVIDENCE

The law allows for a conviction on 'circumstantial evidence' even where there is no direct evidence.[171]

A case is not defective or bound to fail merely because it relies upon 'circumstantial evidence' to the exclusion of 'direct evidence'.[172]

'Circumstantial evidence' is evidence:

- of a basic fact or facts from which the Court is asked to infer a further fact or facts[173]; and
- which, if accepted, tends to prove a fact from which the existence of a fact in issue may be inferred[174].

Direct evidence is evidence which, if accepted, tends to prove a fact in issue.[175]

It has been said that 'circumstantial evidence' is very often the 'best evidence'.[176]

The strength of 'circumstantial evidence' lies in its ability to show that according to the common course of human affairs, the degree of probability that the occurrence of the facts proved would be accompanied by the occurrence of the fact to be proved is so high that the contrary cannot reasonably be supposed.[177]

Where there is 'circumstantial evidence' connecting an accused person to the commission of an offence, a Court is entitled to draw inferences from such evidence to return a guilty verdict.[178]

---

[171] See *Denden Tom and others v The State* (2008) SC967; *Garitau Bonu and Rosanna Bonu v The State* (1997) SC528 and *The State v Koivi Ipai* (2010) N3972.

[172] See *R v Taylor, Weaver and Donovan* (1928) 21 Cr App R 20, per Hewart LCJ at 21.

[173] See *Shepherd v R (No. 5)* (1990) 170 CLR 573, per Dawson J at 579, (1990) 51 A Crim R 181, (1990) 65 ALJR 132, [1990] HCA 56.

[174] See *Festa v R* (2001) 208 CLR 593, [2001] HCA 72.

[175] See *Festa v R* (2001) 208 CLR 593, [2001] HCA 72.

[176] See *R v Taylor, Weaver and Donovan* (1928) 21 Cr App R 20, per Hewart LCJ at 21.

[177] See *Martin v Osborne* (1936) 55 CLR 367, per Dixon J at 375, [1936] HCA 23.

[178] See *Denden Tom and others v The State* (2008) SC967; *Garitau Bonu and Rosanna Bonu v The State* (1997) SC528 and *The State v Koivi Ipai* (2010) N3972.

CIRCUMSTANTIAL EVIDENCE

It is not necessary for every inference leading ultimately to a conclusion of guilt to be:

- the only inference reasonably open[179]; or
- proven 'beyond reasonable doubt[180]'.[181]

A case based on 'circumstantial evidence' can prove the intention of an accused person.[182]

Motive is 'circumstantial evidence' and may be used as a factual basis for an inference of guilt.[183]

---

[179] See *Cooley v The State of Western Australia* [2005] WASCA 160.

[180] Refer also to the chapter titled 'Proof Of Issues' in the text titled 'Injia on Criminal Practice and Procedure in Papua New Guinea and the Pacific'.

[181] See *Shepherd v R (No. 5)* (1990) 170 CLR 573, (1990) 51 A Crim R 181, (1990) 65 ALJR 132, [1990] HCA 56; *Stewart v R* [1977] 2 SCR 748 at 759-61, [1976] 6 WWR 644; *R v Morin* [1988] 2 SCR 345 at 354, 44 CCC (3d) 193, 66 CR (3d) 1, 30 OAC 81 and *Cooley v The State of Western Australia* [2005] WASCA 160.

[182] See *The State v Raphael Kuanande* [1994] PNGLR 512 at 514 and *The State v Titus Aiko and others* (2008) N3324.

[183] See *Chamberlain v R (No. 2)* (1984) 153 CLR 521, (1984) 51 ALR 225, [1984] HCA 7.

See also: *Penney v R* (1998) 155 ALR 605, (1998) 72 ALJR 1316, [1998] HCA 51; *R v Murphy* (1985) 4 NSWLR 42, at 59-60; *R v Pantoja* [1998] NSWSC 565; *R v Plevac* [1999] NSWCCA 351; *R v Fowler* (2003) 151 A Crim R 166, [2003] NSWCCA 321; *R v Kotzmann* [1999] 2 VR 123, (1999) 105 A Crim R 243, [1999] VSCA 27; *R v Koeleman* [2000] 2 VR 20, [2000] VSCA 141; *R v Nguyen* (2001) 118 A Crim R 479, [2001] VSCA 1; *R v Cummins* (2004) 10 VR 15, [2004] VSCA 164 and *Neill-Fraser v Tasmania* [2012] TASCCA 2.

Refer also to the section titled 'Motive' in the chapter titled 'Criminal Responsibility' in the text titled 'Injia on Criminal Offences in Papua New Guinea and the Pacific'.

CIRCUMSTANTIAL EVIDENCE

The offence of 'Wilful murder' is a serious offence as a conviction makes the person liable to be sentenced to death.[184] Therefore, a Court must insist on the highest degree of proof, within the standard of 'beyond reasonable doubt[185]', that is known to the law. That does not, however, entail an obligation that the State prove its case beyond a shadow of a doubt. Nor does it mean that 'eyewitness evidence' is necessary.[186] Therefore, an accused person may be convicted of the offence of 'Wilful Murder' and the other homicidal offences[187] based solely on 'circumstantial evidence'.

[184] See however the section titled 'Sentence Of Death' in the chapter titled 'Sentencing Options' in the text titled 'Injia on Sentencing in Papua New Guinea and the Pacific'.

[185] Refer also to the chapter titled 'Proof Of Issues' in the text titled 'Injia on Criminal Offences in Papua New Guinea and the Pacific'.

[186] See *The State v David Yakuye Daniel* (2005) N2869, [2005] PGNC 89.

[187] See also the section titled 'Homicidal Offences' in the chapter titled 'Offences Against The Person' in the text titled 'Injia on Criminal Offences in Papua New Guinea and the Pacific'.

CIRCUMSTANTIAL EVIDENCE

The underlying principle as regards a case based on 'circumstantial evidence' is:

> An accused person is entitled to be acquitted, unless the circumstances are such as to be inconsistent with any reasonable hypothesis[188], other than his or her guilt.[189]

That statement of principle is uncontroversial. It is really no more than an amplification of the rule that the prosecution must prove its case 'beyond reasonable doubt[190]'.[191]

To enable a Court to be satisfied 'beyond reasonable doubt[192]' of the guilt of an accused person in a case based solely on 'circumstantial evidence' it is necessary that:

- not only that the guilt of the accused person should be a 'rational inference'; but

---

[188] An hypothesis cannot be reasonable if it is contrary to proved facts or if it is obviously fanciful, impossible, incredible or not tenable or too remote or too tenuous, see *East v Repatriation Commission* (1987) 16 FCR 517 at 532, [1987] FCA 242.

The inference of guilt must be the only 'rational inference' open on the evidence, see *Thomas v R* (1960) 102 CLR 584, [1960] HCA 2 and *Plomp v R* (1963) 110 CLR 234 at 243, [1963] HCA 44.

[189] See *Saka v The State* [2003] PGSC 18, (2003) SC719; *The State v Derrick Sakatea Niso (No. 1)* (2005) N2929, [2005] PGNC 25; *The State v Tom Morris* [1981] PNGLR 493; *Paulus Pawa v The State* [1981] PNGLR 498; *Allan Oa Koroka And Mariano Wani Simon v The State* [1988-89] PNGLR 131 at 139, [1988] PGSC 21; *R v Koito* [1967-68] PNGLR 217, [1967] PGSC 26; *Anos Naime Maraga and others v The State* (2009) SC968, [2009] PGSC 5; *Garitau Bonu and Rosanna Bonu v The State* (1997) SC528; *The State v Paul Yepei (No. 1)* (2004) N2570; *The State v Jupui Kapera* (1986) N567; *The State v Iamge Waea* (1990) N915; *The State v Koivi Ipal* (2010) N3972; *The State v Nigel Ongapa* (2008) N3314; *The State v Dakoa* (2009) N3587, [2009] PGNC 13 and *The State v Paul Dimon Asilip* (2011) N4197, [2011] PGNC 3.

See also: *Hodge's Case* (1838) 2 Lewin 227, 168 ER 1136, (1838) 2 Law CC 227; *Barca v R* (1975) 133 CLR 82 at 104, [1975] HCA 42; *Plomp v R* (1963) 110 CLR 234 at 243, [1963] HCA 44; *Peacock v R* (1911) 13 CLR 619 at 634, [1911] HCA 66; *Cutter v R* (1997) 71 ALJR 638; *Shepherd v R (No. 5)* (1990) 170 CLR 573, per Dawson J at 578, (1990) 51 A Crim R 181, (1990) 65 ALJR 132, [1990] HCA 56; *Hoch v R* (1988) 165 CLR 292; *Phillips v R* (2006) 80 ALJR 531, (2006) 224 ALR 216, [2006] HCA 4; *Chamberlain v R (No. 2)* (1984) 153 CLR 521, (1984) 51 ALR 225, [1984] HCA 7; *Abbott v The State of Western Australia* [2005] WASCA 42; *R v Ramage* [1985] 1 NZLR 392 at 393; *Police v Pio* [1999] WSSC 50; *Edwards v R* (1993) 178 CLR 193 at 203; *McGreevy v DPP* (1973) 57 Cr App R 424 and *Wood v R* [2012] NSWCCA 21, per McClellan CJ at CL.

[190] Refer also to the chapter titled 'Proof Of Issues' in the text titled 'Injia on Criminal Practice and Procedure in Papua New Guinea and the Pacific'.

[191] See *Knight v R* (1992) 175 CLR 495 at 502, [1992] HCA 56 and *Shepherd v R (No. 5)* (1990) 170 CLR 573, per Dawson J at 578, (1990) 51 A Crim R 181, (1990) 65 ALJR 132, [1990] HCA 56.

[192] Refer also to the chapter titled 'Proof Of Issues' in the text titled 'Injia on Criminal Practice and Procedure in Papua New Guinea and the Pacific'.

- that it should be the 'only rational inference' that the circumstances would enable the Court to draw.[193]

However, for an inference to be 'reasonable' it must rest upon something more than mere conjecture.[194]

In any case substantially dependent on 'circumstantial evidence' the question to be asked is:

> Do the proven facts lead reasonably to only one conclusion – that the accused person did all the things constituting the elements of the offence?
>
> If yes, the accused person is guilty.

---

[193] See *The State v Tom Morris* [1981] PNGLR 493; *Paulus Pawa v The State* [1981] PNGLR 498; *Allan Oa Koroka And Mariano Wani Simon v The State* [1988-89] PNGLR 131 at 139; *Garitau Bonu and Rosanna Bonu v The State* (1997) SC528; *The State v Derrick Sakatea Niso (No. 1)* (2005) N2929, [2005] PGNC 25; *The State v Nelson Tuli* (1997) N1534; *The State v Jupui Kapera* (1986) N567; *The State v Iamge Waea* (1990) N915; *The State v Koivi Ipai* (2010) N3972; *The State v Paul Yepei (No. 1)* (2004) N2570; *The State v Nigel Ongapa* (2008) N3314; *The State v Dakoa* (2009) N3587, [2009] PGNC 13 and *The State v Paul Dimon Asilip* (2011) N4197, [2011] PGNC 3.

See also: *Hodge's Case* (1838) 2 Lewin 227, 168 ER 1136, (1838) 2 Law CC 227; *Chamberlain v R (No. 2)* (1984) 153 CLR 521, (1984) 51 ALR 225, [1984] HCA 7; *Abbott v The State of Western Australia* [2005] WASCA 42; *R v Ramage* [1985] 1 NZLR 392 at 393; *Police v Pio* [1999] WSSC 50; *Edwards v R* (1993) 178 CLR 193 at 203; *McGreevy v DPP* (1973) 57 Cr App R 424; *Knight v R* (1992) 175 CLR 495 at 509-510; *Plomp v R* (1963) 110 CLR 234, per Dixon CJ at 243; *Shepherd v R (No. 5)* (1990) 170 CLR 573, per Dawson J at 578, (1990) 51 A Crim R 181, (1990) 65 ALJR 132, [1990] HCA 56; *R v Griffin* [2009] 2 SCR 42, 2009 SCC 28 and *R v Comba* [1938] SCR 396 at 397.

[194] See *The State v Tom Morris* [1981] PNGLR 493; *Paulus Pawa v The State* [1981] PNGLR 498; *Allan Oa Koroka And Mariano Wani Simon v The State* [1988-89] PNGLR 131 at 139; *Garitau Bonu and Rosanna Bonu v The State* (1997) SC528; *The State v Derrick Sakatea Niso (No. 1)* (2005) N2929, [2005] PGNC 25; *The State v Nelson Tuli* (1997) N1534; *The State v Jupui Kapera* (1986) N567; *The State v Iamge Waea* (1990) N915; *The State v Koivi Ipai* (2010) N3972; *The State v Paul Yepei (No. 1)* (2004) N2570; *The State v Nigel Ongapa* (2008) N3314; *The State v Dakoa* (2009) N3587, [2009] PGNC 13 and *The State v Paul Dimon Asilip* (2011) N4197, [2011] PGNC 3.

See also: *Hodge's Case* (1838) 2 Lewin 227, 168 ER 1136, (1838) 2 Law CC 227; *Chamberlain v R (No. 2)* (1984) 153 CLR 521, (1984) 51 ALR 225, [1984] HCA 7; *Abbott v The State of Western Australia* [2005] WASCA 42; *R v Ramage* [1985] 1 NZLR 392 at 393; *Police v Pio* [1999] WSSC 50; *Edwards v R* (1993) 178 CLR 193 at 203; *McGreevy v DPP* (1973) 57 Cr App R 424; *Knight v R* (1992) 175 CLR 495 at 509-510; *Plomp v R* (1963) 110 CLR 234, per Dixon CJ at 243; *Shepherd v R (No. 5)* (1990) 170 CLR 573, per Dawson J at 578, (1990) 51 A Crim R 181, (1990) 65 ALJR 132, [1990] HCA 56; *R v Griffin* [2009] 2 SCR 42, 2009 SCC 28 and *R v Comba* [1938] SCR 396 at 397.

As to the distinction between an 'inference' and 'conjecture', see *Allan Oa Koroka v The State* [1988-89] PNGLR 131, per Kapi DepCJ at 136.

If no, the accused person is entitled to an acquittal.[195]

A circumstantial case may be compared to a rope. Unlike a chain which is only as strong as its weakest link, a rope takes its strength from all of its strands woven together.[196]

Similarly, Lord Cairns[197] likened 'circumstantial evidence' to a ray of light. Even though no single ray can clear away the darkness to be expelled a number of converging rays may produce the necessary body of illumination.

A Court should not reject one circumstance because, considered alone, no inference of guilt can be drawn from it. Instead a Court must consider the 'weight[198]' or 'probative value' which is to be given to all of the circumstances put together.[199]

As it is often the case that one piece of evidence resolves doubts as to another.[200]

'Circumstantial evidence' must not be considered on a piecemeal basis. It must be evaluated:

- in its entirety[201]; and therefore,
- holistically[202].

---

[195] See *Paulus Pawa v The State* [1981] PNGLR 498; *Devlyn David v The State* (2005) SC881; *The State v Dakoa* (2009) N3587, [2009] PGNC 13 and *The State v Paul Dimon Asilip* (2011) N4197, [2011] PGNC 3.

[196] See *R v Exall* (1866) 4 F & F 922, per Chief Baron Pollock at 929.

[197] See *The Belhaven and Stenton Peerage Case* (1875) 1 App Cas 278 at 279.

[198] Refer also to the chapter titled 'Weight'.

[199] See *The Belhaven and Stenton Peerage Case* (1875) 1 App Cas 278 at 279.

See also: *R v Van Beelen* (1973) 4 SASR 353 at 373; *Thomas v R* [1972] NZLR 34 at 37-38 and 40; *Plomp v R* (1963) 110 CLR 234, per Dixon CJ at 242 and *Chamberlain v R (No. 2)* (1984) 153 CLR 521 at 535, (1984) 51 ALR 225, [1984] HCA 7.

[200] See *Chamberlain v R (No. 2)* (1984) 153 CLR 521 at 535, (1984) 51 ALR 225, [1984] HCA 7.

[201] See *Belhaven and Stenton Peerage* (1875) 1 App Cas 278, per Lord Cairns at 279.

See also: *R v Hillier* (2007) 228 CLR 618, per Gummow, Hayne and Crennan JJ at 637-638, [2007] HCA 13; *Chamberlain v R (No. 2)* (1984) 153 CLR 521, per Gibbs CJ and Mason J at 535, (1984) 51 ALR 225, [1984] HCA 7; *R v Duke* (1979) 22 SASR 46, per King CJ at 52; *R v Fuhner* [1961] VR 500 at 509; *R v Kalajzich* (1989) 39 A Crim R 415 at 427-429; *R v Laugalis* (1993) 10 CRNZ 350, per Hardie Boys J at 359 and *R v Eade* (1924) 34 CLR 154 at 158.

[202] See *R v Hillier* (2007) 228 CLR 618, [2007] HCA 13.

CIRCUMSTANTIAL EVIDENCE

A Court must weigh and consider the totality of the admissible evidence before reaching a conclusion on the whole of the evidence, that:

- it was open to it to be persuaded 'beyond reasonable doubt[203]' of guilt; or
- a doubt persists such that it would be dangerous to allow the verdict of guilty to stand.[204]

The necessary inference must be drawn from the overall view of all the evidence.[205]

In doing so, the Court ought not:

- stretch credulity; or
- engage in tortuous reasoning

in order to explain away each and every individual circumstance as being consistent with innocence.[206]

The evaluation of 'circumstantial evidence' involves the application of common sense.[207]

Inferences drawn by a Court must be logical and from proven facts, and not mere speculation or conjecture.[208]

An inference must be logically based, that is, it must bear some logical relationship to the evidence from which it proceeds.[209]

---

[203] Refer also to the chapter titled 'Proof Of Issues' in the text titled 'Injia on Criminal Practice and Procedure in Papua New Guinea and the Pacific'.

[204] See *R v Hillier* (2007) 228 CLR 618, [2007] HCA 13.

[205] See *The State v Tom Morris* [1981] PNGLR 493, *Paulus Pawa v The State* [1981] PNGLR 498 and *The State v Dire* (2001) N2178, [2001] PGNC 32.

See also: *Camilleri* (2001) 119 A Crim R 106.

[206] See *R v Micallef* (2002) 136 A Crim R 127, [2002] NSWCCA 480, per Dunford J and *Burrell v R* [2009] NSWCCA 193, per Giles JA.

[207] See *Vaii Rocky Maury v The State* (2001) SC668, [2001] PGSC 16; *Gari Tau Bonu and Rossana Bonu v The State* (1997) SC528; *The State v Nigel Ongapa* (2008) N3314 and *The State v Paul Yepei (No. 1)* (2004) N2570.

[208] See *R v Puttick* (1985) 1 CRNZ 644.

[209] See *Holloway v McFeeters* (1956) 94 CLR 470, [1956] HCA 25 and *Peacock v R* (1911) 13 CLR 619 at 661, [1911] HCA 66.

CIRCUMSTANTIAL EVIDENCE

Where there are a number of competing inferences it is a 'question of fact' for the Court to decide which:

- inferences should be drawn;
- inferences should be rejected;
- inferences are reasonable; and
- inferences are mere conjecture,

and which party, if any, those inferences favour.[210]

When drawing the inferences of the guilt of an accused person a Court must be sure that there are no other co-existing circumstances that:

- weaken; or
- destroy

the inferences.[211]

But if there are two or more possible inferences and one is consistent with the innocence of an accused person then he or she should be found not guilty.[212]

However, hypotheses consistent with innocence may cease to be rational or reasonable in the absence of evidence to support them when that evidence, if it exists at all, must be within the knowledge of the accused person.[213]

---

210 See *The State v Tom Morris* [1981] PNGLR 493.

211 See *Teper v R* [1952] AC 480 at 489.

212 See *R v Oates* (1997) 15 CRNZ 95 at 102.

213 See *Weissensteiner v R* (1993) 178 CLR 217 at 227-228, (1993) 68 ALJR 23.

See also: *Dyers v R* (2002) 210 CLR 285, [2002] HCA 45.

CIRCUMSTANTIAL EVIDENCE

In *Onama Andrew v The State*[214] the Supreme Court stated:

> 'The Supreme Court in *Paulus Pawa's case*[215] adopted the conclusions of Professor O'Regan in his article *Adverse Inferences from Failure of an Accused Person to Testify* 1965 Crim LR 711. These conclusions are useful to test the particular circumstances of a case against the criteria for whether or not the court should draw an adverse inference:
>
> The failure of an accused person to testify is not an admission of guilt and no inference of guilt may be drawn from such failure to testify.
>
> Failure to testify may, however, tell against an accused person in that it may strengthen the State case by leaving it uncontradicted or unexplained on vital matters;
>
> Failure to testify only becomes a relevant consideration when the Crown has established a prima facie case;
>
> The weight to be attached to failure to testify depends on the circumstances of the case. Significant circumstances include:
>
> (a) whether the truth is not easily ascertainable by the Crown but probably well known to the accused;
>
> (b) whether the evidence implicating the accused is direct or circumstantial;
>
> (c) whether the accused is legally represented;
>
> (d) whether the accused has before trial given an explanation which the Crown has adduced in evidence'.

However, an accused person is not obliged to give evidence.[216]

---

[214] (2009) SC997.

Refer also to the section titled 'The Defence Case' in the chapter titled 'Court Procedure' in the text titled 'Injia on Criminal Practice and Procedure in Papua New Guinea and the Pacific'.

[215] See *Paulus Pawa v The State* [1981] PNGLR 498.

[216] Refer also to:

- the section titled 'The Defence Case' in the chapter titled 'Court Procedure' in the text titled 'Injia on Criminal Practice and Procedure in Papua New Guinea and the Pacific'; and
- the chapter titled 'Interviewing Suspects' in the text titled 'Injia on Investigatory Practice in Papua New Guinea and the Pacific'.

CONFESSIONAL EVIDENCE

[1.0] INTRODUCTION[217]

There is nothing in the law that prevents a person from making a voluntary, informed decision to admit having committed an offence. However, there are limits as to how police officers may investigate offences and take statements from suspects. The law of confessions is aimed at ensuring the reliability of incriminating admissions, as well as controlling the methods used to obtain such admissions. When the standards imposed by the law are breached, the resulting confession may be ruled to be inadmissible.[218]

When an accused person makes a confession to:

- a police officer; or
- another person

then that person may give evidence of that confession and it may be accepted by a Court as being truthful[219], referred to as an 'admission against interest'.[220]

---

[217] As regards:

- eliciting confessional evidence from a police officer, refer to the subsection titled 'Eliciting Evidence' in the section titled 'Examination-in-Chief' in the chapter titled 'Examination of Witnesses in the text titled 'Injia on Criminal Practice and Procedure in Papua New Guinea and the Pacific'; and
- a confession of an accused person with a mental illness, see *R v Miller* (1986) 83 Cr App R 192 and *Sinclair v R* (1946) 73 CLR 316, [1946] HCA 55.

See also: Procedure Governing The Admissibility Of Confessional Statements in Criminal Proceedings [2000] HKLRC 2.

[218] See New Zealand Law Commission, 1999, 'Evidence. Volume 1: Reform of the Law and Evidence. Volume 2: Evidence Code and Commentary', Report 55, page 28.

[219] See *Slatterie v Pooley* (1840) 151 ER 579, per Parke V at 581.

See also: *Osifelo v R* [1995] SBCA 3; *Mule v R* (2005) 199 CLR 620, (2005) 221 ALR 85, (2005) 79 ALJR 1573, [2005] HCA 49; *R v Duncan* (1981) 73 Cr App R 359 and *R v Hamand* (1986) 82 Cr App R 65.

Refer also to the chapter titled 'Hearsay Evidence'.

[220] See *R v Bathurst* (1968) 52 Cr App R 251, [1968] 2 WLR 1092, [1968] 2 QB 99, [1968] 1 All ER 1175.

See also: *Straker v R* (1977) 15 ALR 103 and *Willis v R* (2001) 25 WAR 217.

CONFESSIONAL EVIDENCE

Historically, confessions were treated by the law as a special category of evidence, governed by particular rules of admissibility. This reflected concerns about:

- the reliability of confessions; and
- the need to protect people from coerced self-incrimination.[221]

Notwithstanding that a confession is a direct admission of guilt or of some fact or facts which may tend to prove an accused person's guilt[222], it must be:

- closely scrutinised and tested and only after examining the considerations, if any, supplying hypotheses by which the making of the confession may be explained more or less reasonably consistent with innocence[223]; and
- proved to be unequivocal and true[224].

A confession is 'primie facie' evidence of the incriminatory matters unequivocally admitted to therein.[225]

Confessional material in a record of interview is *prima facie* evidence of the facts as against the maker of the statement and can be given full weight.[226]

A confession well proved is the best evidence that can be adduced.[227]

---

[221] See New Zealand Law Commission, 2013, 'The 2013 Review of the Evidence Act 2006', Report 127, page 47.

[222] See *McKay v R* (1935) 54 CLR 1, per Dixon J at 8; *R v Doyle; ex parte Attorney-General* [1987] 2 Qd R 732; *Attorney-General for New South Wales v Martin* (1909) 9 CLR 713 and *Jayalal Anandagola v R* [1962] 1 WLR 817.

[223] See *R v Namiropa Koinbondi* [1969-70] PNGLR 94, [1969] PGSC 20.

[224] See *Burns v R* (1975) 132 CLR 258 at 261; *Timoteo v Police* [1970-1979] WSLR 208, [1978] WSCA 1; *R v Chan Yun Hung* [1987] 2 HKC 228 at 231 and *R v Kelsey* [1953] 1 SCR 220.

[225] See *The State v Steven Torila and Benedict Okole* (1980) N216.

[226] See *The State v John Warkaul Ingilin* [2007] PGNC 127; *The State v Steven Tolira and Benedict Okole* (1980) N216 and *The State v Famundi Badi Moibamo (No. 2)* (2011) N4344, [2011] PGNC 74.

This principle applies equally to a 'Voluntary Statement'.

[227] See *R v Baldry* (1852) 2 Den 430, (1852) 169 ER 568, per Erle J at 446 and 574.

CONFESSIONAL EVIDENCE

A free[228] and voluntary confession is deserving of the highest credit because it is presumed to flow from the strongest sense of guilt.[229]

An accused person may only confess to his or her own:

- acts;
- omissions;
- knowledge; or
- intentions,

but he or she cannot confess as to the acts or omissions of other persons whom he or she did not see and of which he or she can only have knowledge based on 'hearsay[230]'.[231]

A failure by the prosecution to prove an essential element in the offence cannot be cured by an 'admission' of this nature.[232]

---

[228] See sections 32(2)(c) ['Right to Freedom'] and 49 ['Right to Privacy'] of the *Constitution of the Independent State of Papua New Guinea*.

[229] See *R v Warickshall* (1783) 1 Leach 263 at 263, 168 ER 234 at 234.

[230] Refer also to the chapter titled 'Hearsay Evidence'.

[231] See *Eiserman v Nanatsi* [1978] PNGLR 457 and *The State v Robin Erick and Emil Basilio* (2006) N3023, [2006] PGNC 41.

See also: *Suriypaul v R* [1958] 3 All ER 300, [1958] 1 WLR 1050, (1958) 42 Cr App R 266.

Refer also to the chapter titled 'Hearsay Evidence'.

[232] See *Eiserman v Nanatsi* [1978] PNGLR 457 and *The State v Robin Erick and Emil Basilio* (2006) N3023, [2006] PGNC 41.

See also: *Suriypaul v R* [1958] 3 All ER 300, [1958] 1 WLR 1050, (1958) 42 Cr App R 266.

Refer also to the chapter titled 'Hearsay Evidence'.

Furthermore, a confession based on:

- a faulty inference;
- mere assumption, or
- a 'wavering preference for one of two or more possible hypotheses'

will weaken or destroy the 'weight[233]' or 'probative value' of the confession.[234]

An accused person who admits something of which he or she knows nothing about is of no real evidential or 'probative value'.[235]

When the evidence that an accused person has made a confession is not the only evidence a Court is entitled to consider all of the evidence in determining whether the prosecution has proven its case 'beyond reasonable doubt[236]'.[237]

Therefore, clearly the prosecution is expected to present the strongest possible case that requires statements to be taken from all possible witnesses who are able to give 'material evidence'. Evidence is material if it is relevant to an issue in the case.[238] An investigating officer should not rely solely on confessional evidence, rather than conducting a comprehensive investigation.[239]

Whilst an accused person has an obvious motive to claim that he or she did not confess, a Court must be forever mindful that the police must always act according to the law.[240]

---

233 Refer also to the chapter titled 'Weight'.

234 See *The State v Steven Tolira and Benedict Okole* (1980) N216.

235 See *Comptroller of Customs v Western Lectric Co Ltd* [1966] AC 367 at 371.

236 Refer also to the chapter titled 'Proof Of Issues' in the text titled 'Injia on Criminal Practice and Procedure in Papua New Guinea and the Pacific'.

237 See *Burns v R* (1975) 132 CLR 258 at 263.

238 See *R v Reading JJ; ex parte Berkshire County Council* [1996] 1 Cr App R 239.

239 See *The State v Man Turi* [1986] PNGLR 221 at 226.

240 See *Driscoll v R* (1977) 137 CLR 517 at 539, (1977) 15 ALR 47, [1977] HCA 43.

CONFESSIONAL EVIDENCE

Considering that confessional evidence[241] is the best evidence available there must not be any unfair means used in order to obtain the confession.[242]

A police officer is required to act fairly when investigating offences and that requires compliance with:

- sections 37 ['Protection of the Law'] and 42 ['Liberty of the Person'] of the *Constitution of the Independent State of Papua New Guinea*[243];
- section 28 of the *Evidence Act* (Ch. 48) ['Confessions Induced by Threats'];
- the Judges' Rules; and
- the relevant common law.

An accused person should not be:

- arrested; or
- detained

without consent merely for the purpose of asking questions.[244]

---

[241] ie., a 'Record of Interview' or a 'Voluntary Statement'.

[242] See *The State v Lakio Tambai and two others* (1980) N235 and *The State v Steven Tolira and Benedict Okole* (1980) N216.

[243] See *The State v Mana Turi* [1986] PNGLR 221.

[244] See *Mackenzie v R* [2004] WASCA 146; *Williams v R* (1986) 161 CLR 278 at 284-285; *Salihos v R* (1987) 78 ALR 509, per Burt CJ at 513 and Kennedy J at 521 and *Norton v R* (2001) 24 WAR 488.

Refer also to the section titled 'Arrest And Detain' in the chapter titled 'Police Powers' in the text titled 'Injia on Investigatory Practice in Papua New Guinea and the Pacific'.

CONFESSIONAL EVIDENCE

Prior to conducting a record of interview an investigating officer should have prepared his or her interview. The officer should have determined:

- what offence/s had been committed;
- what elements need to be proven; and
- what possible defence/s may be raised.[245]

There is nothing wrong with an officer preparing his or her questions before an interview. Having prepared them, he or she is wise to write them down. However, a record of interview in which those questions are put to an accused person must be prepared in such a way that all the relevant conversation is recorded[246].[247]

If an accused person makes an answer and the investigating officer shortens or paraphrases that answer and in doing so twists the meaning, then that answer could be excluded.[248]

No investigating officer is bound by an accused person's answers. In many cases, the officer is wise, despite a denial, to:

- rephrase the question; or
- try a different approach to the same topic.[249]

Sometimes it is worth returning to it after other matters have been explored. This may all take time and that, in itself, is not necessarily wrong. However, if the protection of the caution is to have any reality, there must be some limit. That limit will vary according to:

- the circumstances of the case;
- the characteristics of the accused person; and

---

[245] Refer also to the chapter titled 'Interviewing Suspects' in the text titled 'Injia on Investigatory Practice in Papua New Guinea and the Pacific'.

[246] See *The State v Goi Mubin* [1990] PNGLR 99 at 102.

[247] See *R v Lokumana and Ihonoda* (Solomon Islands Criminal Case No. 32 of 1987).

[248] See *The State v Goi Mubin* [1990] PNGLR 99 at 102.

[249] See *R v Lokumana and Ihonoda* (Solomon Islands Criminal Case No. 32 of 1987).

- the conditions of the interview.[250]

Therefore, confessional evidence may be held to be inadmissible when obtained as a consequence of persistent questioning.[251]

In whatever language confessional evidence is taken or conducted then that is the language in which it should be recorded, otherwise it would be unfair to the accused person. If it is not conducted in English then an English translation of the confessional evidence should also be prepared.[252]

Interviewing officers and witnessing officers should in the presence of the accused person sign below where the caution had been recorded to certify that:

- the caution had been duly given as recorded; and

- the accused person did understand what the caution meant[253] after the confessional evidence had been read to the accused person in accordance with Rule 9 of the Judges' Rules ['Statements to be Read Over and Signed'][254].

In order to assist in preventing any denial that confessional evidence was true and correct:

- an accused person should be given the opportunity to make changes to it[255] and sign it; and

- an accused person should be served with a copy immediately upon its completion[256].

---

[250] See *R v Lokumana and Ihonoda* (Solomon Islands Criminal Case No. 32 of 1987).

[251] See *R v Bai-Uneme* (1959) No. 145.

[252] See *Balo v R* [1975] PNGLR 378 at 386 and *The State v Konts Kot* (1987) N623.

See however: *R v Ieme* [1973] PNGLR 1, [1973] PGSC 21.

[253] See *R v Motui* [1998] SBHC 95.

See also: *R v Todd* (1981) 72 Cr App R 299, [1981] Crim LR 621.

[254] See Rule 9 of the Judges' Rules ['Statements to be Read Over and Signed'].

[255] See Rule 9 of the Judges' Rules ['Statements to be Read Over and Signed'].

See also: *The State v Thomas Some* (1982) N366.

[256] See *R v William Taupa Tovarula and others* [1973] PNGLR 140 at 183.

See also: *R v Ragen* (1964) 81 WN (NSW) Pt 1 572.

CONFESSIONAL EVIDENCE

Whilst it is not intrinsically unconstitutional or unfair to:

- conduct a record of interview; and
- take a voluntary statement[257]

each case must be assessed on its merits[258], including whether the initial confessional evidence was obtained unlawfully[259]. An accused person must be advised of his or her rights under the *Constitution of the Independent State of Papua New Guinea* prior to the taking of a record of interview and voluntary statement. Furthermore, an accused person must again be cautioned in compliance with the Judges Rules.

An accused person is entitled to have a 'voir dire proceedings' conducted if there is a real question as to:

- voluntariness;
- unfairness; or
- impropriety

and therefore, the admissibility of confessional evidence.[260]

The actual truth of the admission is however not part of such a proceedings.[261]

---

[257] See Rule 4 of the Judges' Rules ['Statement Volunteered'].

[258] See *The State v Dakoa* (2009) N3586, [2009] PGNC 8 and *The State v David Yakuye Daniel* (2005) N2869, [2005] PGNC 89.

See however: *The State v Anton Turik and Wickie Jack Peltam* [1986] PNGLR 138, *The State v Simon Tanuma* [1999] PNGLR 475; *The State v Michael Balana* [2007] PGNC 12; *The State v Mana Turi* [1986] PNGLR 221; *The State v Allan Honiem* (1983) N421(M) and *The State v John Julio and others* (1996) N1446.

[259] See *The State v William Nanua Kapris and others* (2010) N4139, [2010] PGNC 146.

[260] See *MacPherson v R* (1981) 147 CLR 512, per Mason J at 534 and 536 and Aitkin J at 537, (1981) 37 ALR 81, [1981] HCA 46 and *Thongiai v R* [1997] 3 WLR 667 at 682.

[261] See *R v Fatu* [1989] 3 NZLR 419 at 429.

CONFESSIONAL EVIDENCE

An accused person is not entitled to tender his or her record of interview or voluntary statement if it contains his or her self-serving or exculpatory statements[262] and the prosecution cannot be compelled to tender a record of interview or voluntary statement that only contains self-serving statements.[263]

However, if the prosecution seeks to tender a record of interview that contains self-serving statements and admissions then the entire record of interview becomes evidence upon which the Court may consider.[264]

But full weight need not be given to exculpatory statements.[265]

That is simply a rule of fair play. The fact that self-serving statements are admitted does not change their character as 'hearsay'.[266]

---

[262] See *Kochnieff v R* (1987) 33 A Crim R 1, per Connolly J at 4.

[263] See *Prosecutor's Request No. 1 of 1974* (1974) FC 67.

See also: *R v Newsome* (1980) 71 Cr App R 325; *R v Wogandt* (1988) 33 A Crim R 31; *Kochnieff v R* (1987) 33 A Crim R 1 and *R v Callaghan* [1994] 2 Qd R 300 at 304, [1993] QCA 419.

[264] See *R v Joseph Haiai Sarufa* [1974] PNGLR 173; *The State v Gaius Helex Malaia of Kapakada* (1978) N158, [1978] PGNC 8 and *The State v John Michael Awa; The State v Eric Steven Gituthe; The State v Degemba Michael; The State v John Michael Awathe; The State v Eric Steven Gituthe; The State v Degemba Michael; The State v Harry Ewag* (2000) N2012.

See also: *R v Higgins* (1829) 172 ER 565, 3 C & P 603, per Parke J at 604; *R v Williamson* [1972] 2 NSWLR 281 at 294-296; *Herbert, Sampson and Wurrawilya v R* (1982) 42 ALR 631; *Small v R* (1994) 33 NSWLR 575; *R v Smith; R v Tonkins* [1981] 2 NZLR 170; *Button v R* [2001] WASCA 7; *Mule v R* (2005) 199 CLR 620, (2005) 221 ALR 85, (2005) 79 ALJR 1573, [2005] HCA 49; *McCarrol v R* [2004] WASCA 131; *Slater v R* [2004] WASCA 151; *R v Callaghan* [1994] 2 Qd R 300 at 304, [1993] QCA 419; *Gardner v Duve* (1978) 19 ALR 695 at 703-704; *R v Herbert* (1982) 6 A Crim R 1 at 29-32; *Spence v Demasi* (1988) 48 SASR 536, per Cox J at 540-546; *R v Sharp (Colin)* [1988] 1 WLR 7, (1988) 86 Cr App R 274, [1988] 1 All ER 65, [1988] Crim LR 303 and *R v Aziz and other appeals* [1995] 3 All ER 149, [1995] 2 Cr App R 478, [1996] 1 AC 41, [1995] 3 WLR 53.

[265] See *The State v John Warkaul Ingilin* [2007] PGNC 127 and *The State v Steven Tolira and Benedict Okole* (1980) N216.

See also: *R v Duncan* (1981) 73 Cr App R 359 and *R v Hamand* (1986) 82 Cr App R 65.

[266] See *Jack v Smail* (1905) 2 CLR 684, per Griffiths CJ at 695.

Refer also to the chapter titled 'Hearsay Evidence'.

However, a Court may give different 'weight' to different parts of a record of interview.[267] The incriminating parts are likely to be true (otherwise why say them?), whereas the self-serving statements do not have the same weight.[268]

But there is a general discretion to reject the truth in an admission if its truth is called into serious question by the self-serving statement accompanying the admission.[269]

It is not a rule of law that if an accused person gives sworn evidence rebutting what he or she said to the police the Court must by necessity give more 'weight' to the sworn evidence. The 'weight' to be attached to the sworn testimony of an accused person will depend on the normal factors that decide whether any witness's evidence is believed such as the witness's demeanour and the credibility of his or her evidence in light of the other evidence[270].[271]

Once confessional evidence is admitted into evidence it becomes evidence in the trial, the value of which is to be assessed when weighed alongside and against other pieces of evidence that are admitted.[272] Therefore, such evidence may be used in assessing whether there are inconsistencies in the other evidence.[273]

---

[267] See *R v Higgins* (1829) 3 C & P 603, 172 ER 565.

[268] See *R v Duncan* (1981) 73 Cr App R 359 at 365; *R v Sharp (Colin)* [1988] 1 WLR 7, (1988) 86 Cr App R 274, [1988] 1 All ER 65, [1988] Crim LR 303 and *Mule v R* (2005) 199 CLR 620, (2005) 221 ALR 85, (2005) 79 ALJR 1573, [2005] HCA 49.

[269] See *The State v John Michael Awa; The State v Eric Steven Gituthe; The State v Degemba Michael; The State v John Michael Awathe; The State v Eric Steven Gituthe; The State v Degemba Michael; The State v Harry Ewag* (2000) N2012.

[270] Refer also to the section titled 'Court Decision' in the chapter titled 'Court Procedure' in the text titled 'Injia on Criminal Practice and Procedure in Papua New Guinea and the Pacific'.

[271] See *The State v John Baimo Kaole and others* (2009) N4013 and *The State v Stafford Hambo* (2010) N4036.

See also: *The State v Ali Kei Paiya* (2005) CR No. 478 of 2004 and *The State v Martin Maso Naipo* (2005) CR No. 92 of 2004.

Refer also to the section titled 'Court Decision' in the chapter titled 'Court Procedure' in the text titled 'Injia on Criminal Practice and Procedure in Papua New Guinea and the Pacific'.

[272] See *The State v Stafford Hambo* (2010) N4036.

[273] See *The State v Peter Malihombu* (2003) N2365 and *The State v Tolly Amindi* (2004) N2683.

CONFESSIONAL EVIDENCE

The 'weight' to be attached to confessional evidence will need to be assessed having regard to:

- the circumstances in which any incriminating statements were made to the police; and
- whether any objection was made to their admission into evidence.[274]

If the police want a comment by an accused person in relation to a sketch plan of a crime scene, it is the responsibility of the investigating officer to prepare a sketch plan and to give the accused person the opportunity of commenting on it. There is no obligation on an accused person to assist police with their enquiries by preparation of a sketch plan and there should be no unfavourable comment or inference drawn by reason of their alleged failure to do so.[275]

As a matter of practice, when a record of interview is admitted as an exhibit the prosecution should also identify any documents or items that are sufficiently identified in it and those things should be admitted also.[276]

What 'weight' may be given to such a document or item is a different matter, and it is not relevant to the question of admissibility.[277]

Generally a claim of innocence made to:

- a police officer; or
- any other person

is entirely inadmissible[278] because no person can bolster[279] the evidence of an accused person by telling a Court that the accused person told him or her that he or she was innocent.

---

[274] See *The State v John Baimo Kaole and others* (2009) N4013.

[275] See *Fred Bukoya v The State* (2007) SC887.

[276] See *Joshua Yaip Avini and Plaridel Nony Acosta v The State* [1997] PNGLR 212, (1997) SC523, [1997] PGSC 21.

[277] See *Joshua Yaip Avini and Plaridel Nony Acosta v The State* [1997] PNGLR 212, (1997) SC523, [1997] PGSC 21.

[278] See *R v Beck* [1990] 1 Qd R 30.

[279] Refer also to the subsection titled 'Bolster Or Credibility Rule' in the section titled 'Examination-in-Chief' in the chapter titled 'Examination Of Witnesses' in the text titled 'Injia on Criminal Practice and Procedure in Papua New Guinea and the Pacific'.

Furthermore, according to the 'inevitable discovery doctrine', real evidence obtained as a consequence of confessional evidence that was ruled to be inadmissible in itself may still be admissible if it can be proven that it would have been undoubtedly discovered by the police during the course of their investigation in any event.[280] However, its relevance must be established without resorting to any part of the confessional evidence.[281]

[2.0] UNCORROBORATED CONFESSION

The possibility that an accused person may confess to offences he or she did not commit is now accepted and there would be obvious risks in convicting on the basis of such evidence alone.[282]

Whilst an uncorroborated confession may be the basis of a conviction[283]:

- such a confession must be subjected to scrutiny[284] and tested, and any supplying hypotheses must be explained more or less reasonably consistent with innocence[285];

---

[280] See *R v Loe* [1969-70] PNGLR 17.

See also: *R v Warickshall* (1783) 1 Leach 263, 168 ER 234; *R v Lockhart* (1785) 1 Leach 386; *Black v R* [1989] SCR 138; *R v Butcher* [1992] 2 NZLR 257; *R v Shaheed* [2002] 2 NZLR 377; *Bunning v Cross* (1978) 141 CLR 54, (1978) 19 ALR 641, [1978] HCA 22 and *R v Scott; ex parte Attorney-General* [1993] 1 Qd R 537.

[281] See *R v Beere* [1965] Qd R 370.

[282] See New Zealand Law Commission, 1999, 'Evidence. Volume 1: Reform of the Law and Evidence. Volume 2: Evidence Code and Commentary', Report 55, page 124.

[283] See *R v Namiropa Koinbondi* [1969-1970] PNGLR 94, [1969] PGSC 20; *Eddie Sam v The State* (2007) SCRA No. 11 of 2004 and *The State v Jeffery Harold Malepo (No. 2)* (1996) N1449.

See also: *R v McKay* (1935) 54 CLR 1; *Republic v Karl* [1986] LRC (Crim) 158, [1985] NRSC 1; *Timoteo v The Police* [1970-1979] WSLR 208, [1978] WSCA 1; *Chan Wai-keung v R* [1987] 2 AC 160 and *R v Sykes* [1913] Cr App R 233.

See however: *R v Hame Manga* (1970) No. 596.

[284] See *R v Mon and Debong* [1965-66] PNGLR 42 at 51, [1965] PGSC 28.

[285] See *R v Namiropa Koinbondi* [1969-70] PNGLR 94, [1969] PGSC 20; *The State v Joe Foe Leslie Leslie* (1996) N1552; *R v Mon and Debon* [1965-1966] PNGLR 42 at 51, [1965] PGSC 28 and *The State v Terrence Yabok Hiafrie (No. 1)* (2008) N3365, [2008] PGNC 57.

- such a confession must be convincingly proved, and in itself must be cogent and satisfactory evidence[286];

- the Court must carefully examine:

    - the nature and extent of the confession; and

    - the circumstances in which it was made

  to exclude any reasonable doubt that it is a false or unreliable confession[287];

- the Court should examine the surrounding circumstances to ascertain if the confession is consistent with other facts which have been proved[288];

- the Court must apply the principles applying to 'circumstantial evidence' in order to determine the guilt of the accused person[289]:

  > 'Do the proven facts lead reasonably to only one conclusion – that the accused person did all the things constituting the elements of the offence?'
  >
  > If yes, the accused person is guilty.
  >
  > If no, the accused person is entitled to an acquittal[290]; and

- the Court should, as a matter of practice, warn itself of the danger of convicting on the basis of such evidence alone[291].

---

[286] See *R v Fa'aoso* [1996] Tonga LR 36.

[287] See *Onama Andrew v The State* (2009) SC997; *Billy Nara v The State* (2007) SCRA No. 27 of 2005; *R v Mon and Debong* [1965-66] PNGLR 42, [1965] PGSC 15; *The State v Ungum Ovohe* (1980) N245; *The State v Thomas Some* (1982) N366(M); *The State v Malepo (No. 2)* [1996] PNGLR 252; *R v Namiropa Koinbondi* [1969-70] PNGLR 94, [1969] PGSC 20; *The State v Ungum Ovohe* (1980) N245; *The State v Malepo (No. 2)* [1996] PNGLR 252 and *The State v Stafford Hambo* (2010) N4036.

[288] See *Sykes v R* (1912) 8 Cr App 233, per Ridley J at 236.

[289] See *Onama Andrew v The State* (2009) SC997.

Refer also to the chapter titled 'Circumstantial Evidence'.

[290] See *Devlyn David v The State* (2005) SC881.

[291] See *McKinney and Judge v R* (1991) 171 CLR 468 at 476, [1991] HCA 6 and *R v Black* (1993) 68 ALJR 91 at 96.

CONFESSIONAL EVIDENCE

[3.0] VOIR DIRE PROCEEDINGS

[3.1] INTRODUCTION

A 'voir dire', also referred to as a 'trial within a trial', is a hearing within a trial and is pronounced as 'vwah deer'.[292]

Whilst this section deals specifically with the conduct of a 'voir dire' in order to determine the admissibility of confessional evidence[293], such proceedings may also be held in order to determine:

- the admissibility of previous convictions[294];
- the admissibility of similar fact evidence[295];
- the admissibility of any prejudicial matter[296];
- the competency of a witness[297];
- the competency of a witness called to give opinion evidence of an expert[298]; and

[292] See *The State v William Nanua Kapris and others* (2011) N4232, [2011] PGNC 24.

[293] See *Independent Publishing Company Ltd v Attorney General of Trinidad and Tobago and another (Trinidad and Tobago)* [2005] 1 AC 190, [2005] 1 All ER 499, [2004] UKPC 26, [2004] 3 WLR 611, [2005] AC 190.

[294] See *Independent Publishing Company Ltd v Attorney General of Trinidad and Tobago and another (Trinidad and Tobago)* [2005] 1 AC 190, [2005] 1 All ER 499, [2004] UKPC 26, [2004] 3 WLR 611, [2005] AC 190.

[295] See *Independent Publishing Company Ltd v Attorney General of Trinidad and Tobago and another (Trinidad and Tobago)* [2005] 1 AC 190, [2005] 1 All ER 499, [2004] UKPC 26, [2004] 3 WLR 611, [2005] AC 190.

[296] See *Independent Publishing Company Ltd v Attorney General of Trinidad and Tobago and another (Trinidad and Tobago)* [2005] 1 AC 190, [2005] 1 All ER 499, [2004] UKPC 26, [2004] 3 WLR 611, [2005] AC 190.

[297] Refer also to the section titled 'Competency And Compellability' in the chapter titled 'Witnesses' in the text titled 'Injia on Criminal Practice and Procedure in Papua New Guinea and the Pacific'.

[298] Refer also to the chapter titled 'Opinion Evidence'.

- the validity of a search warrant[299].

The wording of the oath of a witness in a 'voir dire proceedings' is as follows:

> 'The evidence that you give will be the truth, the whole truth and nothing but the truth. So help you God!'.[300]

The wording of the oath of an interpreter in a 'voir dire proceedings' is as follows:

> 'You swear that you understand (*describe the language*) which is understood by the witness (*or* accused person *or* accused), and are able to interpret between him and the court and all persons who understand the English language. So help you God!
>
> You will well and truly interpret and give true explanations between the witness (*or* accused person *or* accused) and the court and all persons who understand the English language to the best of your knowledge, skill and ability, and the evidence that you give will be the truth, the whole truth and nothing but the truth. So help you God!'[301]

However, instead of taking an oath:

- a witness may make of a solemn declaration or affirmation[302]; and

---

[299] Refer also to the section titled 'Search And Seize' in the chapter titled 'Police Powers' in the text titled 'Injia on Investigatory Practice in Papua New Guinea and the Pacific'.

[300] See section 3 ['Voir Dire'] and Form 3 of the *Oaths, Affirmations and Statutory Declarations Act* (Ch. 317).

[301] See section 4(1)(b) ['Interpreter's Oath'] and Form 5 of the *Oaths, Affirmations and Statutory Declarations Act* (Ch. 317).

[302] Section 45 of the *Constitution of the Independent State of Papua New Guinea* ['Freedom of Conscience, Thought and Religion'] states (in part):

> '(4) No person may be compelled to take an oath that is contrary to his religion or belief, or to take an oath in a manner or form that is contrary to his religion or belief.
> (5) A reference in this section to religion includes a reference to the traditional religious beliefs and customs of the peoples of Papua New Guinea'.

See also: section 5(2)(a) ['Declaration or Affirmation Instead of Oath'] and Form 9 of the *Oaths, Affirmations and Statutory Declarations Act* (Ch. 317).

- an interpreter may make of a solemn declaration or affirmation[303].[304]

In *The State v Mana Turi*[305] McDermott J outlined the following questions which should be used to determine whether confessional evidence should be admissible:

'1. Was the person then arrested or detained[306]?

2. Was the person then a suspect or a likely witness?

3. Was the person spoken to in a language which he properly understands?

4. Was the person treated with dignity?

5. Was the person informed of the provisions of the *Constitution*, s. 42(2)?

6. Was the person given reasonable and adequate opportunity to exercise those rights?

7. Did the person make a statement or answer questions in an interview?

8. Was the person in any way disabled by injury, illness, fatigue, alcohol or drugs at the time of making the statement or when questioned?[307]

9. Was the person cautioned before such statement was made or interview took place in these terms?[308]

"You are not obliged to say anything unless you wish to do so. Anything you say will be taken down in writing and may later be given to the court?"

10. Did the person understand this caution?

---

[303] See section 5(2)(b) ['Declaration or Affirmation Instead of Oath'] and Form 10 of the *Oaths, Affirmations and Statutory Declarations Act* (Ch. 317).

[304] See also: section 8 of the *Oaths, Affirmations and Statutory Declarations Act* (Ch. 317) ['Modes of Binding Interpreters in Certain Cases'].

Refer also to the section titled 'Examination-in-Chief' in the chapter titled 'Examination Of Witnesses' in the text titled 'Injia on Criminal Practice and Procedure in Papua New Guinea and the Pacific'.

[305] [1986] PNGLR 221 at 226.

[306] Refer also to the chapter titled 'Police Powers' in the text titled 'Injia on Investigatory Practice in Papua New Guinea and the Pacific'.

[307] Refer also to the section titled 'Voluntariness' in this chapter.

[308] Refer also to the section titled 'Judges Rules' in this chapter.

11. Was a written record taken of the person's statement or interview?[309]

12. If the person made a statement was he asked if he wished to write it personally?[310]

13. Was the record taken in the language spoken by the person or in the language of an interpreter?

14. At the conclusion of the statement or interview:

(a) Did the person:

(i) read the record of it; or

(ii) was it read back to him?

(b) Was the person asked to make any corrections or alterations?

(c) Did the person then agree as to the correctness of the record?[311]

15. Does the following appear on the record:

(a) The time, date and place where it was made; and

(b) The caution; and

(c) The signatures of:

(i) the person;

(ii) the witnesses present;

---

[309] This is referred to as a 'Voluntary Statement'.

Refer also to the chapter titled 'Interviewing Suspects' in the text titled 'Injia on Investigatory Practice in Papua New Guinea and the Pacific'.

[310] This is referred to as a 'Confessional Statement'.

Refer also to the chapter titled 'Interviewing Suspects' in the text titled 'Injia on Investigatory Practice in Papua New Guinea and the Pacific'.

[311] Refer also to the section titled 'Adoption' in this chapter.

Refer also to the chapter titled 'Interviewing Suspects' in the text titled 'Injia on Investigatory Practice in Papua New Guinea and the Pacific'.

(iii) an interpreter?[312]

16. After the statement was given or the record of interview taken, was the person further questioned otherwise than for the purpose of:

(a) preventing or minimising harm or loss to any person or property or the public at large; or

(b) to clarify any ambiguity or uncertainty, in the previous statement or record of interview?

17. If the person was further questioned for this purpose was he further [questioned] before being so cautioned?

18. If the person was shown a statement or answer made by another:

(a) Was the person asked to reply or comment upon it?

(b) If the person did so voluntarily was he cautioned before he replied or commented?'

A Court may on its own volition conduct a 'voir dire proceedings'.[313]

As a rule of law and of procedure:

> where the prosecution seeks to rely on confessional evidence that is objected to by the defence, a 'voir dire proceedings' should be conducted.[314]

---

[312] This is referred to as a 'Voluntary Statement'.

Refer also to the chapter titled 'Interviewing Suspects' in the text titled 'Injia on Investigatory Practice in Papua New Guinea and the Pacific'.

[313] See *The State v Dakoa* (2009) N3586, [2009] PGNC 8; *John Alex v Martin Golu* [1983] PNGLR 117 and *The State v Silih Sawi* [1983] PNGLR 234 at 237.

[314] See *Mecklina Kar Poning v The State* (2005) SC814.

CONFESSIONAL EVIDENCE

An accused person is entitled to have a 'voir dire proceedings' conducted if there is a real question as to the admissibility of the confessional evidence based on:

- the issue of voluntariness[315];
- the issue of unfairness or impropriety[316]; or
- the exercise of the public policy discretion[317].

Irrespective, there is no general rule that a Court will reject confessional evidence that was obtained voluntarily but had been illegally obtained. On the contrary, the rejection of confessional evidence for that reason alone is most exceptional.[318]

---

[315] See *Uda Liki Gasika v The State* [1983] PNGLR 58 at 60.

See also: *McPherson v R* (1981) 147 CLR 512, per Mason J at 534-536 and Aitken J at 537, (1981) 37 ALR 81 and *Thongiai v R* [1997] 3 WLR 667 at 682.

[316] See *Uda Liki Gasika v The State* [1983] PNGLR 58 at 60.

See also: *McPherson v R* (1981) 147 CLR 512, per Mason J at 534-536 and Aitken J at 537, (1981) 37 ALR 81 and *Thongiai v R* [1997] 3 WLR 667 at 682.

[317] See *R v Ireland* (1970) 126 CLR 321 at 334, [1970] ALR 727, (1970) 44 ALJR 263, [1970] HCA 21; *Bunning v Cross* (1978) 141 CLR 54 at 72, (1978) 19 ALR 641, [1978] HCA 22; *R v Foster* (1993) 67 ALJR 550 at 554, (1993) 113 ALR 1 at 7, (1993) 66 A Crim R 112, [1993] HCA 80; *R v Pollard* (1992) 176 CLR 177 at 196, (1992) 110 ALR 385, (1992) 67 ALJR 173, (1992) 64 A Crim R 393; *Cleland v R* (1982) 151 CLR 1, (1982) 43 ALR 619, [1982] HCA 67; *R v Swaffield; Pavic v R* (1998) 192 CLR 159 at 175-181, 190-191 and 211-14, (1998) 72 ALJR 339, (1998) 151 ALR 98, [1998] HCA 1; *McDermott v R* (1948) 76 CLR 501; *Van der Meer v R* (1988) 62 ALJR 656 at 660, (1988) 82 ALR 10, [1988] HCA 56; *R v Stead* (1992) 62 A Crim R 40 at 48-49 and *R v O'Neill* [1996] 2 Qd R 326, (1995) 81 A Crim R 458.

[318] See *Cleland v R* (1982) 151 CLR 1, (1982) 43 ALR 619, per Gibbs CJ at 9 and 624, [1982] HCA 67; *Collins v R* (1980) 31 ALR 257, per Brennan J at 317, [1980] FCA 72; *R v D'Arrigo* [1994] 1 Qd R 603, (1991) 58 A Crim R 71; *Foster v R* (1993) 113 ALR 1, (1993) 67 ALJR 550, (1993) 66 A Crim R 112; *Polland v R* (1992) 176 CLR 177, (1992) 110 ALR 385, (1992) 67 ALJR 173, (1992) 64 A Crim R 393 and *Ridgeway v R* (1995) 129 ALR 41, (1995) 69 ALJR 484, [1995] HCA 66.

CONFESSIONAL EVIDENCE

A Court does not have to hold a 'voir dire proceedings' when:

- it is merely being used as a fishing expedition[319];
- it is merely being used as a means of testing in advance the evidence of the prosecution witnesses[320]; or
- the sole basis for holding it is that an accused person claims that the confessional evidence was not accurately recorded[321].

A Court should proceed to hold a 'voir dire proceedings' if an accused person denies making a confession.[322]

The prosecution cannot re-open the issue of admissibility of confessional evidence upon a 'voir dire proceedings' being completed.[323]

[319] See *R v Williams* (1976) 14 SASR 1, per Wells J at 3.

[320] See *MacPherson v R* (1981) 147 CLR 512, (1981) 37 ALR 81, [1981] HCA 46.

[321] See *The State v Joseph Maino* [1977] PNGLR 216.

[322] See *The State v John Yambra Pai* (1986) N535.

See also: *MacPherson v R* (1981) 147 CLR 512, per Gibbs CJ and Wilson J at 522-523, (1981) 37 ALR 81, [1981] HCA 46 and *Ajodha and others v The State* [1981] 3 WLR 1, (1981) 73 Cr App R 129, [1982] AC 204, per Lord Bridge at 220.

[323] See *The State v Paro Wampa (No. 2)* [1987] PNGLR 281.

[3.2] APPLICATION

[3.2.1] NATIONAL COURT OF JUSTICE

At a pre-trial review the defence should advise the Court as to whether it will be challenging the admissibility of confessional evidence and the legal basis thereof.[324]

There is no hard-and-fast rule that only grounds raised in a Notice of Objection can be considered by the National Court.[325]

The filing of a Notice of Objection to the admission of a voluntary statement or a record of interview is not required by the Rules of the National Court. It is a practice, and it is a good practice, that has developed over the years. But it should not be elevated to the status of pleadings in civil proceedings or even to the status of an alibi notice in criminal proceedings (which must be filed under the *Criminal Practice Rules 1987*).[326]

Allowing an accused person to depart from the grounds of objection in a Notice of Objection is a matter for the discretion of the trial judge whilst having regard to:

- the circumstances of the particular case;
- the seriousness of the alleged unfairness, particularly where breaches of human rights are alleged;

---

[324] Order 2, Division 1, rule 6(h) of the *Criminal Practice Rules 1987* ['Practice Directions'] states:

> 'At a hearing under this rule counsel shall inform the Court of any point of law which may arise on trial, any question as to the admissibility of evidence which then appears on the face of the papers and of any authority on which either party intends to rely as far as can be possibly envisaged at that stage'.

See also: rule 3(a) ['Practice Directions'].

[325] See *The State v Dakoa* (2009) N3586, [2009] PGNC 8.

See however: *The State v Robin Erick* (2006) N3023, [2006] PGNC 41; *The State v Ereman Donald Kanailom* (2008) N3273, [2008] PGNC 8 and *The State v Richard Saku and others (No. 2)* (2006) N3283.

[326] See *The State v Dakoa* (2009) N3586, [2009] PGNC 8.

See however: *The State v Robin Erick* (2006) N3023, [2006] PGNC 41; *The State v Ereman Donald Kanailom* (2008) N3273, [2008] PGNC 8 and *The State v Richard Saku and others (No. 2)* (2006) N3283.

See also: Order 2, Division 1, rules 3(a) and 6(h) of the *Criminal Practice Rules 1987* ['Practice Directions'].

- the constitutional right of an accused person to a fair trial; and
- the need to ensure that the trial is conducted fairly from the perspective of both the prosecution and defence.[327]

[3.2.2] DISTRICT COURT

In the District Court when it is sought to have a 'voir dire proceedings' conducted an accused person must:

- make application to the Court to hold the 'voir dire proceedings';
- outline the issues to be explored; and
- show, to whatever extent the Court may reasonably require, that there is indeed a significant issue to be tried.[328]

[3.3] GROUNDS TO CHALLENGE ADMISSIBILITY[329]

The admissibility of confessional evidence must be considered:

- in the circumstances in which it was made; and
- by reference to the age, background and psychological condition of the accused person.[330]

---

[327] See *The State v Dakoa* (2009) N3586, [2009] PGNC 8.

[328] See *Lars, Da Silva and Kalanderian* (1991) 73 A Crim R 91.

[329] See also: *R v Baldry* (1852) 2 Den 430, (1852) 169 ER 568; *R v Kassulke* [2004] QCA 175; *R v Fraser* [2004] QCA 92; *R v Baefaka* [1983] SILR 26; *R v Prager* [1972] 1 WLR 260, [1972] 1 All ER 1114, (1972) 56 Cr App R 151; *R v Isequilla* (1975) 60 Cr App R 52; *R v Voisin* (1918) 13 Cr App R 89 at 94; *R v Rennie* (1982) 74 Cr App R 207, [1982] 1 All ER 385, [1982] 1 WLR 64, [1982] Crim LR 110; *R v Joyce* (1957) 42 Cr App R 19; *R v Smith* (1959) 43 Cr App R 121; *R v Houghton* (1978) 68 Cr App R 197; *R v Challinor and Cross* (1983) 76 Cr App R 229; *R v Gardner and Hancox* (1915) 11 Cr App R 265 and *R v Pilley* (1922) 16 Cr App R 138.

[330] See *Collins v R* (1980) 31 ALR 307 at 343, [1980] FCA 72.

CONFESSIONAL EVIDENCE

Confessional evidence may be excluded[331] because:

- of the issue of voluntariness[332], including non-compliance with the Judges Rules which is related to an accused person's right to silence;

- of the issue as to whether it was improperly or unfairly obtained[333], including non-compliance with sections 37 ['Protection of the Law'] and 42 ['Liberty of the Person'] of the *Constitution of the Independent State of Papua New Guinea*.

  However, failure to comply with the provisions of section 42(2) does not for that reason alone render a confession inadmissible.[334]

  Although unreliability is an important aspect of the unfairness discretion, it is not exclusive[335]; and

- of the exercise of the public policy discretion.

  The discretion to exclude a confession on public policy grounds takes into account:

  - the need to bring to conviction those who commit offences; and

  - the public interest in the protection of individuals from improper or unlawful treatment[336]; or

---

331 Refer also to the chapter titled 'Discretion To Exclude Relevant Evidence'.

332 See *Uda Liki Gasika v The State* [1983] PNGLR 58 at 60.

333 See *Uda Liki Gasika v The State* [1983] PNGLR 58 at 60.

334 See *SCR No. 1 of 1977; Re Rights of Person Arrested or Detained* [1977] PNGLR 362, [1977] PGSC 15.

335 See *R v Swaffield; Pavic v R* (1998) 192 CLR 159, (1998) 72 ALJR 339, (1998) 151 ALR 98, [1998] HCA 1.

336 See *R v Ireland* (1970) 126 CLR 321 at 334, [1970] ALR 727, (1970) 44 ALJR 263, [1970] HCA 21; *Bunning v Cross* (1978) 141 CLR 54 at 72, (1978) 19 ALR 641, [1978] HCA 22; *R v Foster* (1993) 67 ALJR 550 at 554, (1993) 113 ALR 1 at 7, (1993) 66 A Crim R 112, [1993] HCA 80; *R v Pollard* (1992) 176 CLR 177 at 196, (1992) 110 ALR 385, (1992) 67 ALJR 173, (1992) 64 A Crim R 393; *Cleland v R* (1982) 151 CLR 1, (1982) 43 ALR 619, [1982] HCA 67; *R v Swaffield; Pavic v R* (1998) 192 CLR 159 at 175-181, 190-191 and 211-14, (1998) 72 ALJR 339, (1998) 151 ALR 98, [1998] HCA 1; *McDermott v R* (1948) 76 CLR 501; *Van der Meer v R* (1988) 62 ALJR 656 at 660, (1988) 82 ALR 10, [1988] HCA 56; *R v Stead* (1992) 62 A Crim R 40 at 48-49 and *R v O'Neill* [1996] 2 Qd R 326, (1995) 81 A Crim R 458.

- its 'probative value[337]' is small and the undue prejudice that is likely to be suffered is substantial[338].

However, it is not always possible to treat voluntariness, reliability and unfairness to an accused person and public policy considerations as discrete issues.[339]

The failure by an accused person to complain when given the opportunity does not necessarily outweigh any of the factors to be considered when determining the admissibility of confessional evidence.[340]

Whilst a Court is not obliged to give reasons for making a ruling on the admissibility of confessional evidence there may be occasions where good practice requires a reasoned ruling, such as where there is:

- a question of law; or

- the exercise of its discretion.[341]

The ruling in a 'voir dire proceedings' is however not necessarily final. It may be reviewed at later stages of the trial if:

- further evidence emerges that raises a doubt as to its admissibility[342]; or

- the Court has had a change of mind.[343]

---

[337] Refer also to the chapter titled 'Weight'.

[338] See *R v Swaffield; Pavic v R* (1998) 192 CLR 159 at 183-184 and 191-193, (1998) 72 ALJR 339, (1998) 151 ALR 98, [1998] HCA 1 and *R v Morris* (1995) 78 A Crim R 465.

[339] As observed by Toohey, Gaudron and Gummow JJ in *R v Swaffield; Pavic v R* (1998) 192 CLR 159, (1998) 72 ALJR 339, (1998) 151 ALR 98, [1998] HCA 1.

[340] See *R v Karo Moro* [1975] PNGLR 14.

[341] See *Wallace and Fuller v R* [1997] 1 Cr App R 396.

[342] See *R v John Theodore Mumford* (1953) No. 48 and *The State v John Michael Awa; The State v Eric Steven Gituthe; The State v Degemba Michael; The State v John Michael Awathe; The State v Harry Ewag* (2000) N2012.

See also: *R v Watson* [1980] 2 All ER 293, (1980) 70 Cr App R 273; *Ajodha v The State* [1982] AC 204 at 223, [1981] 2 All ER 193; *MacPherson v R* (1991) 147 CLR 512 at 536-547, (1981) 37 ALR 81, [1981] HCA 46 and *R v Stat-Bhambra* (1989) 88 Cr App R 55.

[343] See *R v Watson* [1999] 3 NZLR 257.

CONFESSIONAL EVIDENCE

The normal practice is that all evidence taken in a 'voir dire proceedings' becomes evidence on the trial with the exception of such portions as may be validly objected to by the defence.[344]

However, if the evidence that an accused person gives during the course of a 'voir dire proceedings' is not to be treated as part of the defence case, the prosecution is not permitted to lead such evidence as part of its case, irrespective of the outcome of the admissibility of the confessional evidence. Furthermore, whilst an accused person may give evidence, he or she has the right to silence in respect of the substantive trial.[345]

[3.4] VOLUNTARINESS[346]

[3.4.1] STATUTORY PROVISION

Section 28 of the *Evidence Act* (Ch. 48) ['Confessions Induced by Threats'] states:

> 'A confession that is tendered in evidence in any criminal proceedings shall not be received in evidence if it has been induced by a threat or promise by a person in authority; and a confession made after an such threat or promise shall be deemed to have been induced by it unless the contrary is shown'.[347]

---

[344] See *R v Amo and Amura* [1963] PNGLR 22; *The State v Kusap Kei Kuya* [1983] PNGLR 263 at 270; *The State v Paro Wampa and five others (No. 2)* [1987] PNGLR 281 at 284-285; *The State v Raphael Walimini* (2004) N2627 and *The State v William Nanua Kapris and others* (2011) N4232, [2011] PGNC 24.

See however: *R v Amo and Amuna* [1963] PNGLR 22 at 26-27.

[345] See *Wong Kam-Ming v R* [1979] 2 WLR 81, (1979) 69 Cr App R 47, [1980] AC 247, [1979] Crim LR 168.

[346] See also: *R v Hall* (1853) 2 Leach 559; *Cleland v R* (1982) 151 CLR 1, per Deane J at 18, (1982) 43 ALR 619, [1982] HCA 67; *R v Shard Amad Ali* [1999] NZCA 242; *R v Nanisen* [1971] NZLR 269 at 274; *R v Stephens* [2003] NZCA 57; *Van der Meer v R* (1988) 62 ALJR 656, (1988) 82 ALR 10, [1988] HCA 56; *Woon v R* (1964) 109 CLR 529; *Ajodha and others v The State* [1981] 3 WLR 1, (1981) 73 Cr App R 129, [1982] AC 204; *R v Mushtaq* [2005] UKHL 25; *Thongiai v R* [1997] UKPC 31 and *Kaitavu v R* [1987] FJCA 6, [1987] SPLR 125.

[347] This section does not derogate from the common law relating to the admissibility of confessional evidence which remains applicable except insofar as the section applies, see *Attorney-General (NSW) v Martin* (1909) 9 CLR 713, [1909] HCA 74; *McDermott v R* (1948) 76 CLR 501, per Dixon J at 512 and *R v Silva* (1912) St R Qd 198 at 215.

[3.4.2] GENERAL PRINCIPLES

A confession can be admitted only if it is shown to voluntarily made.[348]

This does not mean that it was volunteered.[349]

The rational basis for the rule excluding a confession that is not 'voluntary' is a combination of:

- the potential unreliability of a confession that is involuntary; and
- the common law privilege against self-incrimination.[350]

In the absence of evidence to the contrary, it is presumed that an 'admission against interest' was made voluntarily.[351]

An involuntary confession is inadmissible not because the law presumes it to be untrue, but because of the danger that such a confession might be unreliable.[352]

---

[348] See *R v Ula* [1975] PNGLR 123, [1975] PGSC 39.

See aso: *R v Swaffield; Pavic v R* (1998) 192 CLR 159, (1998) 72 ALJR 339, (1998) 151 ALR 98, [1998] HCA 1; *McDermott v R* (1948) 76 CLR 501 at 511-512; *R v Lee* (1950) 82 CLR 133 at 144, [1950] HCA 25 and *Collins v R* (1980) 31 ALR 257 at 304, [1980] FCA 72.

[349] See *The State v Kwambol Embogol* (1977) N91.

[350] As Deane J noted in *Cleland v R* (1982) 151 CLR 1, (1982) 43 ALR 619, [1982] HCA 67.

[351] See *Hough v Ah Sam* (1912) 15 CLR 452, per Barton J at 457, [1912] HCA 78 and *R v Williams* (1992) 8 WAR 265, per Rowland and Owen JJ at 271.

[352] See *R v Warickshall* [1783] EngR 60, (1783) 1 Leach 263, 168 ER 234; *R v Baldry* (1852) 2 Den 430 at 445, (1852) 169 ER 568 at 574 and *R v Scott* (1856) 1 Dears & Bell 47 at 58, [1856] EngR 19, 169 ER 909 at 913-914.

See also: *R v Swaffield; Pavic v R* (1998) 192 CLR 159, (1998) 72 ALJR 339, (1998) 151 ALR 98, [1998] HCA 1; *Sinclair v R* (1946) 73 CLR 316 at 335, per Dixon J, [1946] HCA 55 and *Cleland v R* (1982) 151 CLR 1 at 27-28, (1982) 43 ALR 619, [1982] HCA 67.

CONFESSIONAL EVIDENCE

In order for a confession to be admissible it must be made voluntarily by the accused person which is:

> Out of the exercise of a free choice to speak or be silent.[353]

An accused person must appreciate that:

- he or she is under no obligation to speak; and
- he or she is free to speak or not to speak.[354]

Therefore, voluntariness includes the right not to:

- give information to the police; or
- answer questions, ie., the right to silence.[355]

That right is reflected in the administering of a caution in compliance with the Judges Rules.[356]

---

[353] See *Uda Like Gasika v The State* [1983] PNGLR 58 at 60; *The State v Dakoa* (2009) N3586, [2009] PGNC 8; *R v Kuras* [1964] PNGLR 18; *R v Kar Moro and 16 others* [1975] PNGLR 14; *The State v John Julio and others (No. 1)* (1996) N1446 and *R v Sirakuras* [1964] PNGLR 18 at 19.

See also: *Ibrahim v R* [1914] AC 599, [1914] UKPC 1; *R v Rennie* [1982] 1 WLR 64, [1982] 1 All ER 385, (1982) 74 Cr App R 207, [1982] Crim LR 110; *Wendo v R* (1963) 109 CLR 559, [1963] HCA 19; *R v Lee* (1950) 82 CLR 133 at 149, [1950] HCA 25; *Duke v R* (1989) 180 CLR 508, (1989) 63 ALJR 139 at 141; *R v Hagan* [1966] Qd R 219; *Kaitavu v R* [1987] FJCA 6, [1987] SPLR 125 and *R v Swaffield; Pavic v R* (1998) 192 CLR 159, (1998) 72 ALJR 339, (1998) 151 ALR 98, [1998] HCA 1.

[354] See *R v Emanuel Patrick Domara* (1953) No. 43; *The State v William Nanua Kapris and others* (2010) N4139, [2010] PGNC 146; *The State v Dakoa* (2009) N3586, [2009] PGNC 8 and *R v Kuras* [1964] PNGLR 18.

[355] See *Boudreau v R* [1949] SCR 262; *R v Fitton* [1956] SCR 958; *R v Esposito* (1985) 24 CCC (3d) 88 and *R v Singh* [2007] 3 SCR 405, 2007 SCC 48, 285 DLR (4th) 583, [2008] 1 WWR 191, 225 CCC (3rd) 103, 51 CR (6th) 199, 163 CRR (2d) 280, 73 BCLR (4th) 1.

[356] See *Boudreau v R* [1949] SCR 262; *R v Fitton* [1956] SCR 958; *R v Esposito* (1985) 24 CCC (3d) 88 and *R v Singh* [2007] 3 SCR 405, 2007 SCC 48, 285 DLR (4th) 583, [2008] 1 WWR 191, 225 CCC (3rd) 103, 51 CR (6th) 199, 163 CRR (2d) 280, 73 BCLR (4th) 1.

CONFESSIONAL EVIDENCE

The absence of a proper caution is a matter to be taken into account in determining whether a voluntary statement is 'voluntary' in the sense of being made in the exercise of a free choice to speak or be silent.[357]

However, it is compulsion or pressure that offends against the common law, not necessarily the absence of a caution.[358]

An accused person must not be overborne[359] by a person in authority[360], and therefore confessional evidence must not be attained as a consequence of:

---

[357] See *The State v Kiki Hapea* [1985] PNGLR 6; *The State v Kwambol Embogol* (1977) N91; *R v Demana-Harina* [1965-66] PNGLR 144 and *The State v Peter Joseph Hayden* [1976] PNGLR 509.

[358] See also: *R v Ginitu Ileandi* [1967-68] PNGLR 496 at 503 and *The State v Kuya* [1983] PNGLR 263, (1983) N431, [1983] PGNC 37.

[359] See *The State v William Nanua Kapris and others* (2010) N4139, [2010] PGNC 146; *R v Toronome-Tombarbui* [1963] PNGLR 55; *The State v Simon Tanuma* (1999) N1872; *The State v Towes Minmin* (2005) N2915, [2005] PGNC 63 and *The State v Richard Saku and others (No. 2)* (2006) N3283.

See also: *McDermott v R* (1948) 76 CLR 501, per Dixon J at 511; *Tofilau v R* (2007) 231 CLR 396, [2007] HCA 39 and *MacPherson v R* (1981) 147 CLR 512 at 519, (1981) 37 ALR 81, [1981] HCA 46.

[360] Where objection is made either under:

- section 28 of the *Evidence Act* (Ch. 48) ['Confessions Induced by Threats']; or
- the discretion of the Court,

the principles developed can only be applicable where the confession is made to, or is obtained by, a person in authority, see *The State v Canute Rambio* (1983) N410.

A 'person in authority' means generally speaking anyone who has authority or control over a suspect or over the proceedings or prosecution over him or her, see *Deokinanan v R* [1969] 1 AC 20, [1968] 2 All ER 346, per Viscount Dilhorne at 350.

See also: *Tofilau v R; Marks v R; Hill v R; Clarke v R* [2007] HCA 39; *R v Todd* (1910) 13 Man LR 364 and *R v Hodgson* [1998] 2 SCR 449, 163 DLR (4th) 577, 127 CCC (3d) 449, 18 CR (5th) 135, 113 OAC 97.

That term does not necessarily only include police and prosecutors, see *R v Thompson* [1893] 2 QB 12 and *R v Wilson* [1967] 2 QB 406.

See also: *Re Scofield* (1988) 37 A Crim R 197 at 200; *Jonkers v Police* (1996) 67 SASR 401 and *R v Dixon and Smith* (1992) 62 A Crim R 465 at 483.

As to whether a 'person in authority' is a witness to be called, see *The State v Canute Rambio* (1983) N410.

- any threat[361], whether:
  - physical; or
  - oral[362];
- any violence[363];
- any fear of prejudice[364];
- any duress[365];

---

[361] See

- *The State v Kabaia Tarangau and Melburne Israel* (2008) N3272, [2008] PGNC 9; *The State v Enana Idon* (2003) N2474; *R v Ginitu Ileandi and others* [1967-68] PNGLR 496 at 497; *The State v Joe Foe Leslie Leslie* (1996) N1552; *R v Toronome-Tombarbui* [1963] PNGLR 55; *R v Komi* [1967-68] PNGLR 265; *The State v Benjamin Garo* (1996) N1521; *The State v Avia Aihi and four others* (1979) N187A; *R v Gelu-Gaua* (1962) No. 256; *The State v Kiki Hapea* [1985] PNGLR 6 and *The State v John Ave Hubert Kuere and Mary Buku* (2004) N2622; and
- section 28 of the *Evidence Act* (Ch. 48) ['Confessions Induced by Threats'].

See also: *Ibrahim v R* [1914] AC 599, [1914] UKPC 1; *R v Fennel* (1881) 7 QBD 147 at 150-151; *R v Sang* (1979) 69 Cr App R 282, [1980] AC 402, [1979] 3 WLR 263, [1979] 2 All ER 1222, [1979] Crim LR 282, [1979] UKHL 3; *R v Lee* (1950) 82 CLR 133, [1950] HCA 25; *MacPherson v R* (1981) 147 CLR 512, per Gibbs CJ and Wilson J at 519, (1981) 37 ALR 81, [1981] HCA 46; *Tofilau v R* (2007) 231 CLR 396, [2007] HCA 39; *R v Lam Yip-ying* [1984] HKLR 419 and *R v Hurst* [1958] VR 396, [1958] VicRp 63.

[362] See *R v Loe (No. 1)* [1969-70] PNGLR 12.

[363] See *The State v John Ave Hubert Kuere and Mary Buku* (2004) N2622 and *The State v Enana Idon* (2003) N2474.

[364] See *The State v Enana Idon* (2003) N2474.

See also: *R v Warickshall* (1783) 1 Leach 263 at 263, 168 ER 234 at 234; *Ibrahim v R* [1914] AC 599 at 609-610, [1914] UKPC 1; *Commissioners of Customs and Excise v Harz and Power* [1976] AC 574; *McDermott v R* (1948) 76 CLR 501; *R v Voisin* [1918] 1 KB 531 at 537-538; *DPP v Ping Lin* [1976] AC 574, [1975] 3 WLR 419, [1975] 3 All ER 175, (1975) 62 Cr App R 14; *R v Rennie* (1982) 74 Cr App R 207, [1982] 1 All ER 385, [1982] 1 WLR 64, [1982] Crim LR 110; *Secretary for Justice v Lani Tat Ming and another* (2000) 3 HKCFAR 168; *R v Lam Yip Ying* [1984] HKLR 419; *Prosko v R* (1922) 63 SCR 226 and *R v Haughton and another* (1979) 68 Cr App R 197, per Lawton LJ at 204.

[365] See *The State v William Nanua Kapris and others* (2010) N4139, [2010] PGNC 146; *The State v Kwambol Embogol* (1977) N91 and *The State v John Ave Hubert Kuere and Mary Buku* (2004) N2622.

- any intimidation[366];
- any compulsion or pressure to answer questions.[367]

  It is necessary for a Court to examine the effect of the conduct of the police officers upon the will of the accused person in order to determine whether his or her will was overborne[368];
- any promise[369];
- any inducement.[370]

  The boundary between words that can be held to be an inducement and those that are not is often difficult to ascertain.[371]

  The old common law rule regarding inducements was no doubt to prevent an accused person from being entrapped into making an admission or statement by being led to believe that there was a stronger case against him or her than that which actually existed.[372]

---

[366] See *The State v William Nanua Kapris and others* (2010) N4139, [2010] PGNC 146; *The State v Kwambol Embogol* (1977) N91 and *The State v Enana Idon* (2003) N2474.

[367] See *The State v Peter Joseph Hayden (No. 2)* [1976] PNGLR 509 and *R v Ginitu Ileandi* [1967-68] PNGLR 496.

[368] See *Collins v R* (1980) 31 ALR 257, per Brennan J at 307, [1980] FCA 72; *R v Swaffield; Pavic v R* (1998) 192 CLR 159, (1998) 72 ALJR 339, (1998) 151 ALR 98, [1998] HCA 1 and *McDermott v R* (1948) 76 CLR 501, per Dixon J at 511.

[369] See *The State v KabaiaTarangau and Melburne Israel* (2008) N3272, [2008] PGNC 9; *The State v Enana Idon* (2003) N2474; *R v Gelu-Gaua* (1962) No. 256; *R v Toronome-Tombarbui* [1963] PNGLR 55 and *R v Komi* [1967-68] PNGLR 265.

See also:

- *Ibrahim v R* [1914] AC 599, [1914] UKPC 1; *R v Sang* (1979) 69 Cr App R 282, [1980] AC 402 at 445, [1979] 3 WLR 263, [1979] 2 All ER 1222, [1979] Crim LR 282, [1979] UKHL 3; *R v Lam Yip-ying* [1984] HKLR 419; *MacPherson v R* (1981) 147 CLR 512, (1981) 37 ALR 81, [1981] HCA 46 and *Tofilau v R* (2007) 231 CLR 396, [2007] HCA 39; and
- section 28 of the *Evidence Act* (Ch. 48) ['Confessions Induced by Threats'].

[370] See also: *R v Doyle; ex parte Attorney-General* [1987] 2 Qd R 732 at 747.

[371] See *Cleary v R* [1963] 48 Cr App R 116.

[372] See *The State v August Toiamia* (1978) N145.

An inducement may take many forms, including fear of prejudice or hope of advantage exercised by or held out by the person in authority.[373]

Whilst an inducement may be so vague that no reasonable person would be influenced by it, a Court must remember that not all accused persons are reasonable men or women and may be ignorant and terrified by the predicament in which they find themselves.[374]

The defence does not have to show that the inducement actually induced the confession in a causative sense; all that is necessary for the defence to show is that:

- the inducement preceded the confession; and
- the inducement had not been removed[375];

- any hope of advantage[376], including:
    - an accused person being told that if he or she confessed the investigating officer would make things easier in court[377];
    - an accused person being told that if he or she confessed he or she would be given bail[378]; and

---

[373] See *The State v August Toiamia* (1978) N145.

[374] See *R v Joseph Kom* [1967-68] PNGLR 265.

[375] See *The State v August Toiamia* (1978) N145.

[376] See *The State v Enana Idon* (2003) N2474.

See also: *Ibrahim v R* [1914] AC 599 at 609-610, [1914] UKPC 1; *Commissioners of Customs and Excise v Harz and Power* [1976] AC 574; *R v Fennel* (1881) 7 QBD 147 at 150-151; *McDermott v R* (1948) 76 CLR 501; *R v Voisin* [1918] 1 KB 531 at 537-538; *DPP v Ping Lin* [1976] AC 574, [1975] 3 WLR 419, [1975] 3 All ER 175, (1975) 62 Cr App R 14.; *R v Rennie* (1982) 74 Cr App R 207, [1982] 1 All ER 385, [1982] 1 WLR 64, [1982] Crim LR 110; *Secretary for Justice v Lani Tat Ming and another* (2000) 3 HKCFAR 168; *R v Lam Yip Ying* [1984] HKLR 419; *Prosko v R* (1922) 63 SCR 226 and *R v Haughton and another* (1979) 68 Cr App R 197, per Lawton LJ at 204.

[377] See *R v John Lee* [1969-70] PNGLR 12.

See also: *R v Northam* (1967) 52 Cr App R 97.

[378] See *R v Zavecka* (1970) 54 Cr App R 202.

- an accused person being told that if he or she confessed he or she would not be prosecuted[379];

- any oppression[380], ie., conduct that tends to sap and does sap the will of an accused person so that he or she provides a confession[381], including:

  - the nature of the questioning.

    However, the use of a raised voice and limited bad language, though not condoned by the Royal Papua New Guinea Constabulary or the Bougainville Police Service does not necessarily amount to oppression[382], and nor does the use of hostile and aggressive questioning[383];

  - the period of questioning;

  - the environment in which questioning takes place; and

  - the characteristics of the accused person[384].

---

[379] See *R v Boughton* (1911) 6 Cr App R 8.

[380] See *The State v August Toiamia* (1978) N145.

See also: *Ibrahim v R* [1914] AC 599 at 609-610, [1914] UKPC 1; *McDermott v R* (1948) 76 CLR 501; *R v Voisin* [1918] 1 KB 531 at 537-538; *DPP v Ping Lin* [1976] AC 574, [1975] 3 WLR 419, [1975] 3 All ER 175, (1975) 62 Cr App R 14; *R v Rennie* (1982) 74 Cr App R 207, [1982] 1 All ER 385, [1982] 1 WLR 64, [1982] Crim LR 110; *Secretary for Justice v Lani Tat Ming and another* (2000) 3 HKCFAR 168; *R v Lam Yip Ying* [1984] HKLR 419 and *Prosko v R* (1922) 63 SCR 226.

[381] See *R v Prager* [1972] 1 WLR 260, [1972] 1 All ER 1114, (1971) 56 Cr App R 151.

See also: *R v Li Wai-Fat* [1977] WLR 531 and *R v Fulling* [1987] QB 426, [1987] 2 WLR 923, [1987] 2 All ER 65, [1987] Crim LR 492, (1987) 85 Cr App R 136, per Lane LCJ at 142.

[382] See *R v Emmerson* (1991) 92 Cr App R 284, [1991] Crim LR 194; *R v Heaton* [1993] Crim LR 593; *R v Beales* [1991] Crim LR 118 and *R v Paris* (1993) 97 Cr App R 99.

[383] See *R v L* [1994] Crim LR 839.

[384] See New Zealand Law Commission, 1992, 'Criminal Evidence: Police Questioning', Preliminary Paper 21, page 77.

- any persistent importunity or sustained or undue insistence or pressure[385]; and
- whether the accused person was so intoxicated that he or she was deprived of his or her understanding as to what he or she was confessing.[386]

The question of voluntariness is to be determined by asking whether, on the 'balance of probabilities', whether the accused person was so intoxicated at the time of his or her interview that he or she was incapable of:

- appreciating that he or she had a free choice as to whether to speak or remain silent; or
- understanding the questions being asked and provide reasonable responses to those questions.[387]

Therefore, the confession of an accused person who is intoxicated is not necessarily inadmissible.[388]

The effects of alcoholic liquor vary, to a very significant extent, from person to person. Questions of fact and degree will arise in determining whether a confession made by an accused person who is intoxicated, to some extent, was voluntary.[389]

---

[385] See *The State v William Nanua Kapris and others* (2010) N4139, [2010] PGNC 146; *The State v Kwambol Embogol* (1977) N91; *The State v Dakoa* (2009) N3586, [2009] PGNC 8; *R v Kuras* [1964] PNGLR 18; *The State v John Ave and two others* (2004) N2622; *The State v Raphael Walimini* (2004) N2621; *The State v Joanes Mesak* (2005) N2853; *The State v Ereman Donald Kanailom* (2008) N3273, [2008] PGNC 8; *The State v KabaiaTarangau and Melburne Israel* (2008) N3272, [2008] PGNC 9 and *The State v Richard Saku and others* (2006) N3283.

See also: *McDermott v R* (1948) 76 CLR 501, per Dixon J at 511; *R v Swaffield; Pavic v R* (1998) 192 CLR 159, (1998) 72 ALJR 339, (1998) 151 ALR 98, [1998] HCA 1; *Tofilau v R* [2007] HCA 59 and *Naniseni v R* [1971] NZLR 269.

[386] See *Commonwealth v Howe* (1857) 9 Gray 110.

See also: *Sinclair v R* (1946) 73 CLR 316, per Dixon J at 336, [1946] HCA 55.

[387] See *The State of Western Australia v Silich* [2011] WASCA 135; *R v Buchanan* [1966] VR 9 at 15, [1966] VicRp 3 and *R v Smith* (1992) 58 SASR 491, per Perry J at 498.

[388] See *R v Ostojic* (1978) 18 SASR 188 and *R v Williams* (1992) 8 WAR 265 at 277.

[389] See *R v Ostojic* (1978) 18 SASR 188 at 196-197.

The proper approach in determining whether a confession was 'voluntary' is to examine:

- the view point of the accused person[390].

  The state of mind of the interviewing police officers is irrelevant[391]; and

- the circumstances of the particular case[392], including whether there was sufficient lapse of time for the effect of the unlawful behaviour to dissipate, thereby rendering the subsequent admission 'voluntary'[393].

[3.5] JUDGES' RULES

[3.5.1] THE RULES

The Judges' Rules[394] are as follows:

'(1) **Preliminary Inquiries**

When a police officer is endeavouring to discover the author of a crime, there is no objection to putting questions in respect thereof to any person or persons, whether suspected or not, from whom he thinks that useful information can be obtained.

[For the purposes of these Rules, the words "crime" and "offence" are synonymous and include any offence for which a person may be apprehended or detained in custody: (1930 Circular).]

---

390 See *Deokinanan v R* [1969] 1 AC 20.

See also: *Collins v R* (1980) 31 ALR 257 at 307, [1980] FCA 72.

391 See *DPP v Ping Lin* [1976] AC 574, [1975] 3 WLR 419, [1975] 3 All ER 175, (1975) 62 Cr App R 14.

392 See *R v Lee* (1950) 82 CLR 133 at 144, [1950] HCA 25; *R v Jeffries* (1947) 47 SR (NSW) 284, per Street J at 311-314 and *R v Isequilla* [1975] 1 All ER 77 at 82.

393 See *The State v Goi Mubin* [1990] PNGLR 99 and *The State v William Nanua Kapris and others* (2010) N4139, [2010] PGNC 146.

394 Referred to as the old Judges' Rules as set out in (1930) 24 QJP pages 150-154.

These rules apply in Papua New Guinea, see *The State v Kiki Hapea* [1985] PNGLR 6 at 8 and *State v Kwainfelin* [1986] PNGLR 106, [1986] PGNC 34.

See however: *The State v Goli Golu* [1979] PNGLR 11 in which the new Judges' Rules were applied.

(2) Questions after decision to arrest

When a police officer has made up his mind to charge a person with a crime, he should first caution such person before asking any questions or any further questions, as the case may be.

(3) Questions to persons in custody

Persons in custody should not be questioned without the usual caution being first administered.

[Rule 3 was never intended to encourage or authorise the questioning or cross-examination of a person in custody after he/she has been cautioned: (1930 Circular).]

(4) Statement volunteered

If a prisoner wishes to volunteer any statement the usual caution should be administered. It is desirable that the last two words ("against you") of such caution should be omitted, and that the caution should end with the words "be given in evidence".

(5) Form of caution

The caution to be administered to a prisoner when he is formally charged should therefore be: "Do you wish to say anything in answer to the charge? You are not obliged to say anything unless you wish to do so but whatever you say will be taken down in writing and may be given in evidence." Care should be taken to avoid any suggestion that his answer can only be used in evidence against him, as this may prevent an innocent person making a statement which might assist to clear him of the charge.

[As regards any difficulties that may have arisen as to the proper form of caution:

(a) at any time before the formal charge is made; and

(b) immediately before the formal charge is made,

the Judges say –

"With regard to the form of caution it is obvious that the words in Rule (5) are only applicable when the formal charge is being made and can have no application when a violent or resisting prisoner is being taken to the police station. In any case, before the formal charge is made, the usual caution is, or should be 'You are not obliged to say anything, but anything you say may be used in evidence'." (1930 Circular)]

(6) Statement made after caution

A statement made by a prisoner before there is time to caution him is not rendered inadmissible in evidence merely by reason of no caution having been given, but in such a case he should be cautioned as soon as possible.

(7) No cross-examination upon voluntary statement

A prisoner making a voluntary statement must not be cross-examined, and no questions should be actually said. For instance, if he has mentioned an hour without saying whether it was morning or evening or has given a day of the week and day of the month which do not agree, or has not made it clear to which individual or what place he intended to refer in some part of the statement, he may be questioned sufficiently to clear up the point.

(8) Statements from several persons accused of same offence

When two or more persons are charged with the same offence, and statements are taken separately from the persons charged, the police should not read these statements to the other person charged, but each of such persons should be furnished by the police with a copy of such statements and nothing should be said or done by the police to invite a copy. If the person charged desires to make a statement in reply the usual caution should be administered.[395]

(9) Statements to be read over and signed

Any statement made in accordance with the above rules should whenever possible, be taken down in writing and signed by the person making it after it has been read to him and he has been invited to make any correction he may wish'. (emphasis added)

[3.5.2] GENERAL PRINCIPLES

The Judges' Rules are used as a means of enabling the Courts to indicate to the police the kind of standard of practice and behaviour that the Courts think is appropriate.[396]

The Judges Rules have been referred as administrative directions, and not rules of law.[397]

---

[395] See *R v Ginitu Ileandi and others* [1967-68] PNGLR 496; *R v Amo and Amuna* [1963] PNGLR 22 and *R v Skelly* [1965-66] PNGLR 105 at 108.

[396] See *R v Demana-Harina* [1965-66] PNGLR 144 at 145.

[397] See *Peart v R* [2006] 1 WLR 970, [2006] UKPC 5 and *Nimrod Miguel v The State* [2011] UKPC 14.

CONFESSIONAL EVIDENCE

In *Fred Bukoya v The State*[398] the Supreme Court stated:

> 'Many cases in this jurisdiction have long recognised the applicability of the Judges Rules, and in particular, that a person taken into custody must be given to understand that he is under no compulsion to speak, that anything he says should be said voluntarily, but that anything he does say may be taken down and given in evidence in compliance with Rule 5 [...]:
>
> The Judges Rules are in addition to the constitutional right not to bear evidence against oneself (*Constitution* section 37 (10).
>
> Whether the Judges Rules are:
>
> - part of the underlying law of Papua New Guinea: see the *State v Goli Golu* [1979] PNGLR 11 (Saldahana J.) and *State v Win Kwainfelin* PNGLR 106 (Pratt J.);
>
> - not part of the underlying law[399] but only a rule which judges can referred to in determining if a statement was made voluntarily: see the *State v Kiki Hapea* [1985] PNGLR 6 (McDermott J.) and doubtful as to whether they are part of the underlying law of Papua New Guinea: See *State v Mana Turi* [1986] PNGLR 221;
>
> - to be treated as a reference to the Judges Rules of the United Kingdom 1912 or 1964[400]: see the *State v Win Kwainfelin* [1986] PNGLR 106, *State v Mana Turi* [1986] PNGLR 121 and the *State v Kiki Hapea* [1985] PNGLR 6;
>
> - to be continued to be referred to at all, or in the light of the *Constitution* section 37 (1), section 42 (2), (3) and (4) the judges of Papua New Guinea should formulate their own rules: see *State v Kiki Hapea* [1985] PNGLR 6 (McDermott J.);
>
> are not issues which have been settled by this Court. There has been no argument before us on these matters which must be left for another day'.

---

[398] (2007) SC887.

The Judges' Rules have also been referred to as only a guide, see *R v Demana-Harina* [1966-67] PNGLR 144 at 145.

[399] See also: *R v Gelu-Gauna* (1962) No. 256.

Refer also to the section titled 'Underlying Law' in the chapter titled 'Sources Of Law' in the text titled 'Injia on Criminal Practice and Procedure in Papua New Guinea and the Pacific'.

[400] See also: *R v Demana* [1965-66] PNGLR 144, [1965] PGSC 11.

Once an accused person is being asked to incriminate himself or herself a caution ought to be administered[401], but not necessarily in precise terms[402].

The purpose of a caution includes reminding an accused person of his or her right to silence.[403]

The caution should be very carefully explained to an accused person and the accused person may be asked to explain in his or her own words as to what he or she understood by the caution.[404]

A caution must really relieve the mind of an accused person from the anxiety and doubts that might well have been in his or her mind. The police should be very, very careful to make it clear to an accused person that it really is a matter of indifference to them whether he or she speaks or not; it is up to the accused person.[405]

---

[401] See *R v Sparks* [1991] Crim LR 128.

See also: *The State v Karura Peter* (1983) N438(M).

[402] See *The State v Kwambol Embogol* (1977) No. 91.

[403] See *Hall v R* [1971] 1 WLR 298, per Lord Diplock at 301.

[404] See *The State v Lakio Tambai* (1980) N235 and *R v Fari Pako* (1962) No. 259.

[405] See *R v Ato-Mumu* (1967) No. 447.

[3.6] RIGHT TO SILENCE[406]

The expression 'the right to silence' is often used to express compendiously the rejection by the common law of inquisitorial procedures made familiar by the Courts of Star Chamber and High Commission in the United Kingdom.[407]

The historical component of the right of silence should not be ignored. In days gone by people literally shed their blood and sacrificed their freedom in the name of the ideals embodied in the right of silence.[408]

The right to silence has been described as referring to 'a disparate group of immunities, which differ in nature, origin, incidence and importance'.[409]

The right of silence, however, has not always been fully acknowledged.[410]

---

[406] As to the right to silence generally, see also: *Mule v R* (2005) 199 CLR 620 at 630, (2005) 221 ALR 85, (2005) 79 ALJR 1573, [2005] HCA 49; *RPS v R* (2000) 199 CLR 620, [2000] HCA 3; *R v Brophy* (1981) 73 Cr App R 287, per Lord Fraser at 291; *R v DAH* [2004] QCA 419; *R v Vannatter* [1999] QCA 104; *R v Coyne* [1996] 1 Qd R 512 at 519; *R v Reeves* (1992) 29 NSWLR 109 at 115; *Kim Kae Jun and the Crew of the Vessel No. 1 New Star v DPP and the Commissioner of Police* [1999] SBHC 151; *Cleland v R* (1982) 151 CLR 1, per Dawson J at 30-31, (1982) 43 ALR 619, [1982] HCA 67; *R v Broyles* [1991] 3 SCR 595; *R v Herbert* [1990] 2 SCR 151 at 180-181 and 186; *Massiah v United States* (1963) 377 US 201; *Miranda v Arizona* (1966) 384 US 436; *Police v Afoa* [1994] WSSC 3; *R v Anderson (M)* [1988] QB 678, [1988] 2 All ER 549, (1988) 87 Cr App R 349; *Maxwell v DPP* (1934) 24 Cr App R 152, [1935] AC 309; *Jones v DPP* [1962] 1 All ER 569, (1962) 46 Cr App R 129, [1962] 2 WLR 575, [1962] AC 635; *Weissensteiner v R* (1993) 178 CLR 217, (1993) 68 ALJR 23; *Republic v Agege* [1989] NRSC 1 and *Kanaveilomani* (1994) 72 A Crim R 492.

Refer also to the section titled 'The Defence Case' in the chapter titled 'Court Procedure' in the text titled 'Injia on Criminal Practice and Procedure in Papua New Guinea and the Pacific'.

[407] See *Environment Protection Authority v Caltex Refining Co Pty Ltd* (1993) 178 CLR 477 at 526, [1993] HCA 74; *Rees v Kratzmann* (1965) 114 CLR 63 at 80; *Sorby v The Commonwealth* (1983) 152 CLR 281 at 317, [1983] HCA 10; *Azzopardi v R* (2001) 205 CLR 50 at 91 and *X7 v Australian Crime Commission* [2013] HCA 29.

[408] See New Zealand Law Commission, 1992, 'Criminal Evidence: Police Questioning', Preliminary Paper 21, page 13.

[409] See *R v Director of Serious Fraud Office; ex parte Smith* [1993] AC 1, per Lord Mustill at 30.

[410] See *R v Beljajev* [1984] Vic Rp 57, [1984] VR 657 at 662 and *Petty and Maiden v R* (1991) 173 CLR 95, per Brennan J at 107, [1991] HCA 34.

CONFESSIONAL EVIDENCE

The right to silence is akin to the privilege against self-incrimination.[411]

The right to silence is based on the policy of the common law according to Blackstone[412] that a suspect's 'fault [is] not to be wrung out of himself, but rather to be discovered by other means, and other men'.[413]

The right of silence in its broadest sense reflects the principle that, in the absence of the manifestation in a statute of a clear legislative intention to the contrary[414], all citizens are free to:

- remain silent; and
- decline to provide the authorities with information.[415]

---

[411] See *The State v Joseph Fron* (2011) N4552, [2011] PGNC 223 and *SCR No. 2 of 1990; Re s333 Income Tax Act 1959 (Amended)* [1991] PNGLR 211.

Refer also to the section titled 'Privilege Against Self-Incrimination' in the chapter titled 'Witnesses' in the text titled 'Injia on Criminal Practice and Procedure in Papua New Guinea and the Pacific'.

[412] See Blackstone's Commentaries, vol. IV, p. 296.

[413] See *Rees v Kratzmann* (1965) 114 CLR 63, per Windeyer J at 80, [1965] HCA 49.

[414] See:

- *R v Scott* (1856) Dears & B 47; *Petty and Maiden v R* (1991) 173 CLR 95, [1991] HCA 34 and *Commissioner of Taxation v De Vonk* (1995) 61 FCR 564, per Foster J at 569.
- section 136 of the *Customs Act* (Ch. 101) ['Power to Question'];
- section 78 of the *Firearms Act* (Ch. 310) ['Information to be Supplied']; and
- section 31 of the *Motor Traffic Act* (Ch. 243) ['Failure to Assist in Identification of Offending Driver'].

See also: *R v Director of Serious Fraud Office; ex parte Smith* [1993] AC 1, per Lord Mustill at 40.

[415] See New Zealand Law Commission, 1992, 'Criminal Evidence: Police Questioning', Preliminary Paper 21, page 10.

CONFESSIONAL EVIDENCE

The 'right to silence' follows from the fundamental principles that:

- the prosecution must prove a charge 'beyond reasonable doubt[416]'; and
- no person is required (with a few exceptions) to prove his or her innocence.[417]

The 'right to silence' encompasses:

- the privilege that all people enjoy from being compelled to answer questions about an alleged offence[418] on pain of punishment the answers to which may incriminate them[419];
- the right to decide whether to give evidence[420];
- the entitlement of all people to be treated in a lawful and proper manner[421];

---

[416] Refer also to the chapter titled 'Proof Of Issues' in the text titled 'Injia on Criminal Practice and Procedure in Papua New Guinea and the Pacific'.

[417] See *Petty v R* (1991) 173 CLR 95, per Gaudron J at 128-129.

Refer also to the chapter titled 'Proof Of Issues' in the text titled 'Injia on Criminal Practice and Procedure in Papua New Guinea and the Pacific'.

[418] See *R v Sang* (1979) 69 Cr App R 282, [1980] AC 402, [1979] 3 WLR 263, [1979] 2 All ER 1222, [1979] Crim LR 282, [1979] UKHL 3; *Glennon v R* (1994) 179 CLR 1 at 8 and *R v Swaffield; Pavic v R* (1998) 72 ALJR 339 at 431, (1998) 192 CLR 159, (1998) 151 ALR 98, [1998] HCA 1.

See however:

- section 136 of the *Customs Act* (Ch. 101) ['Power to Question'];
- section 78 of the *Firearms Act* (Ch. 310) ['Information to be Supplied']; and
- section 31 of the *Motor Traffic Act* (Ch. 243) ['Failure to Assist in Identification of Offending Driver'].

Refer also to the section titled 'Privilege Against Self-Incrimination' in the chapter titled 'Witnesses' in the text titled 'Injia on Criminal Practice and Procedure in Papua New Guinea and the Pacific'.

[419] See *R v Director of Serious Fraud Office; ex parte Smith* [1993] AC 1 at 30-31 per Lord Mustill.

[420] See *R v Director of Serious Fraud Office; ex parte Smith* [1993] AC 1 at 30-31 per Lord Mustill.

Refer also to the subsection titled 'Right To Decide Whether To Give Evidence' in the section titled 'The Defence Case' in the chapter titled 'Court Procedure' in the text titled 'Injia on Criminal Practice and Procedure in Papua New Guinea and the Pacific'.

[421] See *R v Swaffield; Pavic v R* (1998) 72 ALJR 339 at 431, (1998) 192 CLR 159, (1998) 151 ALR 98, [1998] HCA 1.

- the immunity from the drawing of adverse inferences from an accused person's refusal to answer questions[422];

- the immunity, possessed by persons who have been charged with a criminal offence, from having questions material to the offence addressed to them by police officers or persons in a similar position of authority[423]; and

- the immunity, at least in certain circumstances, possessed by accused persons undergoing trial, from having adverse comment made on any failure:

    - to answer questions before the trial; or

    - to give evidence at the trial[424].

There is nothing about the 'right to silence' that does not entitle an accused person to change his or her mind about answering all or a limited number of questions.[425]

Provided an accused person makes a conscious decision to continue with an interview and there is no suggestion of:

- intimidation;

- persistent importunity; or

- sustained or undue insistence or pressure

---

[422] See *R v Swaffield; Pavic v R* (1998) 72 ALJR 339 at 431, (1998) 192 CLR 159, (1998) 151 ALR 98, [1998] HCA 1.

Refer also to the section titled 'The Defence Case' in the chapter titled 'Court Procedure' in the text titled 'Injia on Criminal Practice and Procedure in Papua New Guinea and the Pacific'.

[423] See *R v Director of Serious Fraud Office; ex parte Smith* [1993] AC 1, per Lord Mustill at 30-31.

[424] See *R v Director of Serious Fraud Office; ex parte Smith* [1993] AC 1, per Lord Mustill at 30-31.

Refer also to the subsection titled 'Right To Decide Whether To Give Evidence' in the section titled 'The Defence Case' in the chapter titled 'Court Procedure' in the text titled 'Injia on Criminal Practice and Procedure in Papua New Guinea and the Pacific'.

[425] See *R v Crooks* [1999] QCA 194, per Atkinson J.

then the interview can continue.[426]

Until there is evidence to the contrary, the only inference that can be safely drawn from silence at a police station is that an accused person was exercising his or her right to silence in accordance with the warning given to him or her by the police officer conducting the interview. Why an accused person exercised that right cannot be inferred from silence.[427]

[3.7] IMPROPERLY OR UNFAIRLY OBTAINED

[3.7.1] GENERAL PRINCIPLES

A Court has a discretion to exclude an accused person's voluntary confession if it would be unfair to the accused person to admit the confession into evidence. The purpose of this discretion is to protect the rights and privileges of the accused person, including his or her procedural rights.[428]

In considering whether a confessional statement should be excluded:

- the question is not whether the police have acted unfairly; but
- the question is whether it would be unfair to the accused person to use his or her statement against him or her.[429]

---

[426] See *R v Ireland* (1970) 126 CLR 321 at 332, [1970] ALR 727, (1970) 44 ALJR 263, [1970] HCA 21 and *R v Clark* (1997) 97 A Crim R 414 at 418-420.

[427] See *Fred Bukoya v The State* (2007) SC887.

See also: *Petty v R* (1991) 173 CLR 95; *Harman v The State of Western Australia* [2004] WASCA 230; *Glennon v R* (1994) 179 CLR 1; *Chau Chi-Hung v R* [1982] HKCA 215; *R v Coyne* [1996] 1 Qd R 512 at 519; *R v Gilbert* (1978) 66 Cr App R 237 and *Lee Fuk Hing v HKSAR* [2004] HKCFA 79.

[428] See *R v Swaffield; Pavic v R* (1998) 72 ALJR 339, (1998) 192 CLR 159 at 171-175, 189-190 and 209, (1998) 151 ALR 98, [1998] HCA 1.

[429] See *Van Der Meer v R* (1988) 62 ALJR 656 at 665, (1988) 82 ALR 10, [1988] HCA 56; *McDermott v R* (1948) 76 CLR 501 at 513-515; *R v Lee* (1950) 82 CLR 133 at 154, [1950] HCA 25; *Duke v R* (1989) 63 ALJR 139, per Brennan J at 141, [1989] HCA 1; *Collins v R* (1980) 31 ALR 257, per Muirhead J at 277 and per Brennan J at 313, [1980] FCA 72; *Bunning v Cross* (1978) 141 CLR 54 at 72, (1978) 19 ALR 641, [1978] HCA 22; *Cleland v R* (1982) 151 CLR 1 at 18, (1982) 43 ALR 619, [1982] HCA 67 and *Pollard v R* (1992) 176 CLR 177 at 196, (1992) 110 ALR 385, (1992) 67 ALJR 173, (1992) 64 A Crim R 393.

It is a question of degree in each case, and it is for the presiding judge or magistrate to determine, in the light of all the circumstances, whether:

- the statements or admissions of the accused person have been extracted from him or her under conditions which render it unjust to allow his or her own words to be given in evidence against him or her[430]; and

- whether it would be unfair to the accused to admit the evidence because of unreliability arising from the means by which, or the circumstances in which, it was procured[431].

The discretion to exclude a voluntary confession on the ground of unfairness:

- is not limited to cases in which the confession has been procured by unlawful or improper conduct on the part of police; but

- extends to all cases in which admission of the evidence would be unfair to the accused person.[432]

A Court has a broad discretion to exclude confessional evidence if it considers that:

- such evidence was improperly or unfairly obtained;

- it would be unfair to an accused person to admit such evidence; or

- it possibly considers that such evidence should be rejected as a measure of judicial control of the investigation of offences.[433]

---

[430] See *R v Jeffries* (1947) 47 SR (NSW) at 312, (1947) 64 WN 71.

[431] See *Van der Meer v R* (1988) 62 ALJR 656 at 666, (1988) 82 ALR 10 at 26, [1988] HCA 56.

[432] See *R v Williams* (1992) 8 WAR 265, per Rowland and Owen JJ at 273.

[433] See *R v Wendo* [1963] PNGLR 217 at 232.

The primary issue in the exercise of this discretion is:

> Whether the admission of the confession that has been improperly or unfairly obtained would be unfair to the accused person in the sense of jeopardising his or her right to a fair trial.[434]

The test of 'unfairness' is not a game governed by a sportsman's code of fair play.[435]

Unfairness is to be judged against and only against what is required to secure a fair trial.[436]

What is unfair also needs to be determined by:

> the circumstances of each case together with a consideration of factors,

such as the age, education, sophistication, intelligence and background of the accused person.[437]

However, the term 'unfairness' lacks precision and demands an evaluation of all of the relevant circumstances.[438]

An objection grounded on unfairness requires a Court to take a broader view of all the circumstances in which the confessional evidence was made. A Court makes an assessment as to whether:

- any of the constitutional rights of the accused person were breached.[439]

---

[434] See *R v Duke* (1989) 180 CLR 508, (1989) 63 ALJR 139 at 141; *Ridgeway v R* (1995) 29 ALR 41, (1995) 69 ALJR 484 at 493, [1995] HCA 66; *R v Swaffield; Pavic v R* (1998) 72 ALJR 339, (1998) 192 CLR 159 at 171-175, 189-190 and 209, (1998) 151 ALR 98, [1998] HCA 1; *R v Lee* [1950] CLR 133 at 150-151 and 154, [1950] HCA 25; *Cleland v R* (1982) 43 ALR 619, (1982) 151 CLR 1 at 18, 30 and 36, [1982] HCA 67; *Van der Meer v R* (1988) 62 ALJR 656 at 666, (1988) 82 ALR 10, [1988] HCA 56; *McDermott v R* (1948) 76 CLR 501 and *R v Foster* (1993) 67 ALJR 550 at 559, 563 and 564, (1993) 113 ALR 1 at 7, (1993) 66 A Crim R 112, [1993] HCA 80.

[435] See *R v Sang* (1979) 69 Cr App R 282, [1980] AC 402 at 456, [1979] 3 WLR 263, [1979] 2 All ER 1222, [1979] Crim LR 282, [1979] UKHL 3 and *R v Swaffield; Pavic v R* (1998) 192 CLR 159, per Brennan CJ at 185-186, (1998) 72 ALJR 339, (1998) 151 ALR 98, [1998] HCA 1.

[436] See *R v Sang* (1979) 69 Cr App R 282, [1980] AC 402 at 456, [1979] 3 WLR 263, [1979] 2 All ER 1222, [1979] Crim LR 282, [1979] UKHL 3 and *R v Scott* [1989] AC 1242 at 1256.

[437] See *The State v Kwambol Embogol* (1977) N91 and *The State v Jeffery Harold Malepo (No. 1)* (1996) N1448.

[438] See *R v Swaffield; Pavic v R* (1998) 192 CLR 159, (1998) 72 ALJR 339, (1998) 151 ALR 98, [1998] HCA 1.

[439] See *The State v Dakoa* (2009) N3586, [2009] PGNC 8 and *The State v Mana Turi* [1986] PNGLR 221.

However, a failure to comply with all or any of those constitutional provisions does not for that reason alone render an admission made by an accused person inadmissible[440]; or

- whether there was any other impropriety in the way that the police investigated the case or dealt with the accused person.

  When considering that the test to be applied as to whether a confession was made voluntarily is whether the accused person was overborne in the sense that the confession was not made out of the exercise of a free choice to speak or be silent[441], the issues of impropriety include:

  - whether the accused person was suffering any illness[442];

  - whether there was overly persistent questioning.[443]

    However, a police officer is under a duty to ascertain the facts and is not bound to accept the first answer given by an accused person.[444]

    Furthermore, it is not improper for the police to persist in questioning an accused person after:

    - the accused person gives an indication that he or she does not wish to answer any more questions; or

---

[440] See *Constitutional Reference No. 1 of 1977* [1977] PNGLR 362; *The State v Silih Sawi* [1983] PNGLR 234 at 237; *Maxwell Arthur Schliebs v Singh* [1981] PNGLR 364 and *The State v Wangabin Tonieng and others* (1986) N542.

[441] See *Uda Like Gasika v The State* [1983] PNGLR 58 at 60; *The State v Dakoa* (2009) N3586, [2009] PGNC 8; *R v Kuras* [1964] PNGLR 18; *R v Kar Moro and 16 others* [1975] PNGLR 14 and *The State v John Julio and others (No. 1)* (1996) N1446.

See also: *Ibrahim v R* [1914] AC 599, [1914] UKPC 1; *R v Rennie* [1982] 1 WLR 64, [1982] 1 All ER 385, (1982) 74 Cr App R 207, [1982] Crim LR 110; *Wendo v R* (1963) 109 CLR 559, [1963] HCA 19; *R v Lee* (1950) 82 CLR 133 at 149, [1950] HCA 25; *Duke v R* (1989) 180 CLR 508, (1989) 63 ALJR 139 at 141; *R v Hagan* [1966] Qd R 219 and *Kaitavu v R* [1987] FJCA 6, [1987] SPLR 125.

[442] See *The State v Joseph Maino* [1977] PNGLR 216 at 218.

[443] See *The State v Canute Rambio* (1983) N410.

[444] See *R v Clarke* (1997) 97 A Crim R 414 at 419; *R v Wyatt* [1972] VR 902 at 905 and *R v Pritchard* [1991] 1 VR 84 at 91-94.

    - the accused person had refused to answer questions.[445]

  Questioning is also not to be regarded as unfair merely because it is persistent. It is however a question of degree as to whether such questioning is overly persistent, and therefore unfair[446];

  - the length of period in custody whilst not being charged before being questioned[447];

- whether there was evidence of extortion[448];
- whether the accused person was suffering from exhaustion or tiredness[449];
- whether the accused person denies that he or she made any confession, and therefore alleges a fabrication by the investigating officer[450]; and
- whether there was a fraudulent misrepresentation[451].

---

[445] See *R v Robinson* (1996) 89 A Crim R 42 at 52; *R v Clarke* (1997) 97 A Crim R 414 and *R v Hart* [1979] Qd R 8 at 13.

[446] See *R v Clarke* (1997) 97 A Crim R 414 at 419-420; *R v Wyatt* [1972] VR 902 at 905 and *R v Pritchard* [1991] 1 VR 84 at 91-94.

[447] See *The State v Joanes Mesak* (2005) N2853 and *The State v Dakoa* (2009) N3586, [2009] PGNC 8.

[448] See *R v Ginitu Ileandi and others* [1967-68] PNGLR 496 at 497; *The State v Joe Foe Leslie Leslie* (1996) N1552 and *The State v Canute Rambio* (1983) N410.

[449] See *The State v Joseph Maino* [1977] PNGLR 216 at 218 and *R v Amo and Amuna* [1963] PNGLR 22.

[450] See *The State v Wally Kason* (1996) CR No. 1481 of 1996; *The State v Eddie Sam* (2004) N2521 and *The State v John Yambra Pai* (1986) N535.

See also: *MacPherson v R* (1981) 147 CLR 512, per Gibbs CJ and Wilson J at 522, (1981) 37 ALR 81, [1981] HCA 46 and *Ajodha and others v The State* (1981) 3 WLR 1, (1981) 73 Cr App R 129, [1982] AC 204, per Lord Bridge at 220.

[451] See *The State v Canute Rambio* (1983) N410.

See also: *R v Linnane* (1979) 32 SASR 72.

[3.7.2] RIGHT TO COMMUNICATE

CONSTITUTIONAL PROVISION

Section 42(2) of the *Constitution of the Independent State of Papua New Guinea* ['Liberty of the Person'] states (in part):

> 'A person who is arrested or detained –
>
> (b) shall be permitted whenever practicable to communicate without delay and in private with a member of his family or a personal friend, and with a lawyer[452] of his choice (including the Public Solicitor[453] if he is entitled to legal aid); and
>
> (c) shall be given adequate opportunity to give instructions to a lawyer of his choice in the place in which he is detained'.

---

[452] The term 'lawyer' is defined as meaning:

> 'a person who has been admitted to practice as a lawyer under an Act of the Parliament', ie., the *Lawyers Act 1986*, see section 8 ['Principles of Interpretation'] and Schedule 1.2.2 ['Meaning of Certain Expressions'] of the *Constitution of the Independent State of Papua New Guinea.*

[453] The 'Public Solicitor' is the person occupying the office established by section 176 of the *Constitution of the Independent State of Papua New Guinea* ['Establishment of Offices'].

See also:

- section 177 of the *Constitution of the Independent State of Papua New Guinea* ['Functions of the Public Prosecutor and the Public Solicitor'];
- sections 128 ['Bougainville Public Prosecutor and Bougainville Public Solicitor'] and 129 ['Functions of the Bougainville Public Prosecutor and the Bougainville Public Solicitor'] of the *Constitution of the Autonomous Region of Bougainville*;
- section 59 of the *District Courts Act* (Ch. 40) ['Legal Representation']; and
- section 2 of the *Public Solicitor (Charges) Act* (Ch. 337) ['Charge for Legal Services'].

Refer also to the subsection titled 'Office Of The Public Solicitor' in the section titled 'Right To Representation' in the chapter titled 'Rights Of An Accused Person' in the text titled 'Injia on Criminal Practice and Procedure in Papua New Guinea and the Pacific'.

CONFESSIONAL EVIDENCE

STATUTORY PROVISION

Section 18 of the *Arrest Act* (Ch. 339) ['Duties of Officer-in-Charge of Station'] states (in part):

> '(1) Where a person has been arrested and taken to a police station, the officer-in-charge of the police station[454] shall –
>
> (a) promptly inform the person arrested or cause him to be informed in language he understands of –
>
> (iii) his right, immediately and in private –
>
> (B) to give instructions to a lawyer[455] of his choice, including the Public Solicitor if he is entitled to legal aid; and
>
> (2) The officer-in-charge of a police station shall at all times permit persons arrested or detained at the police station –
>
> (a) whenever practicable, without delay and in private to communicate with –
>
> (ii) a lawyer of his choice, including the Public Solicitor if he is entitled to legal aid; and
>
> (b) to give instructions to a lawyer of his choice, including the Public Solicitor if he is entitled to legal aid'.

---

[454] The term 'officer-in-charge' is defined in section 1(1) of the *Arrest Act* (Ch. 339) in relation to a police station at a particular time, as meaning:
'the police officer who is in charge of the police station at that time'.

[455] The term 'lawyer' is defined in section 3(1) of the *Interpretation Act* (Ch. 2) as meaning:
'a person who has been admitted to practice as a lawyer under the *Lawyers Act 1986*'.

CONFESSIONAL EVIDENCE

GENERAL PRINCIPLES[456]

Section 42 of the *Constitution of the Independent State of Papua New Guinea* ['Liberty of the Person'] is a beneficial provision and should be construed liberally in favour of the citizen.[457]

The Courts have to be careful to ensure that section 42(2) is a meaningful right for all persons[458], and not 'mere ritualistic verbiage'[459].

Section 42(2) applies to all persons:

- arrested; or
- detained

for any offence, and not just indictable offences.[460]

If a suspect wants to consult a legal representative he or she should be able to do so early in an investigation.[461]

---

[456] See also: *R v Kingston* (1948) 32 Cr App R 183; *Williams v R* (1986) 161 CLR 278 at 400; *Pollard v R* (1992) 176 CLR 177, (1992) 110 ALR 385, (1992) 67 ALJR 173, (1992) 64 A Crim R 393; *R v Harris* [1985] Crim LR 244; *R v Bridges* [1991] SCR 190; *Ravuwai v The State* [2006] FJCA 51; *McKinnon v R* [2005] NZCA 94 and *R v McClure* [2001] 1 SCR 445, 195 DLR (4th) 513, 151 CCC (3d) 321, 40 CR (5th) 1, 80 CRR (2d) 217, 142 OAC 201.

[457] See *The State v Konts Kot* (1987) N623 and *The State v John Koga Ivoro* (1989) N772.

[458] See *The State v John Koga Ivoro* (1989) N772.

[459] See *The State v Silih Sawi* [1983] PNGLR 234 at 237.

[460] See *Gamunu Nonoga and others v Constable Kila Lakana* (1984) N475(M).

[461] See *R v Lemsatef* [1977] 1 WLR 812, per Lawton LJ at 815.

CONFESSIONAL EVIDENCE

As soon as an accused person is arrested[462] or detained[463]:

- his or her constitutional rights as provided for by section 42 must be carefully explained[464] before any questions are asked[465]; and
- he or she must be afforded those constitutional rights[466].

It must be explained to the accused person that:

- he or she has a right to see a relative or friend and a lawyer 'without delay'; and
- he or she did not have to go ahead with an interview until after he or she communicated with those persons.[467]

That right to consult applies equally to each of those persons.

---

[462] A person is 'arrested' when deprived totally of his or her personal liberty, or when his or her person is touched in such a way that he or she is made aware that he or she is under compulsion in relation to a criminal matter, see *SCR No 6 of 1987; The State v Songke Mai and Gai Avi* [1988-89] PNGLR 56 and *The State v Dakoa* (2009) N3586, [2009] PGNC 8.

A person 'who is helping the police with their investigations', or 'who agreed to come to the police station to give a statement', but in reality would not be allowed to leave has either been arrested, or is being held unlawfully, see *The State v John Koga Ivoro* (1989) N772.

Refer also to the section titled 'Arrest And Detain' in the chapter titled 'Police Powers' in the text titled 'Injia on Invetigatory Practice in Papua New Guinea and the Pacific'.

[463] See *The State v Paro Wampa* [1987] PNGLR 120.

[464] See *The State v Dakoa* (2009) N3586, [2009] PGNC 8.

It must be something 'more practical and useful than a mere mechanical caution', see *The State v Joseph Maino* [1977] PNGLR 216; *The State v Silih Sawi* [1983] PNGLR 234 and *The State v Dakoa* (2009) N3586, [2009] PGNC 8.

[465] See *The State v Paro Wamp and five others* (1987) N599 and *The State v Konts Kot* (1987) N623.

[466] See *The State v Dakoa* (2009) N3586, [2009] PGNC 8.

[467] See *The State v Paro Wampa* [1987] PNGLR 120 and *The State v Dakoa* (2009) N3586, [2009] PGNC 8.

CONFESSIONAL EVIDENCE

An accused person must be given a proper chance to decide whether he or she wishes to exercise that right[468], and if he or she does, a real opportunity to exercise that right in practice[469], whenever practicable[470]. Therefore, an accused person must be provided with the facilities to exercise those rights[471], such as:

- access to a telephone; or
- the person nominated being otherwise contacted.

It is not proper for an investigating officer to ask the question:

> "Do you wish to see the lawyer now or after the record of interview?"[472]

When an accused person is asked during the course of a record of interview whether or not he or she wishes to see a lawyer and the accused person says 'yes' the interviewing officer must then suspend the record of interview until genuine and practicable steps have been taken.[473]

However, an accused person may not be permitted to consult if it is not practicable.[474]

---

[468] See *Schliebs v Singh* [1981] PNGLR 364 and *The State v Dakoa* (2009) N3586, [2009] PGNC 8.

[469] See *Maxwell Arthur Schliebs v Singh* [1981] PNGLR 364; *The State v. Joseph Maino* [1977] PNGLR 216 at 218-221; *The State v Towes Minmin* (2005) N2915, [2005] PGNC 63; *The State v Dickia Leo Wargat* (2005) CR No. 1152 of 2003; *The State v Wangabin Tonieng and two others* (1986) N542; *The State v John Koga Ivoro* (1989) N772; *The State v Paro Wampa and five others* (1987) N599 and *The State v Albert Monja* (1987) N628.

[470] See *The State v Paro Wampa* [1987] PNGLR 120.

[471] See *The State v Towes Minmin* (2005) N2915, [2005] PGNC 63 and *The State v Dakoa* (2009) N3586, [2009] PGNC 8.

[472] See *SCR No 5 of 1987; In the Matter of The State v Songke Mai and Gai Avi* [1988-89] PNGLR 56, per Kapi DepCJ at 71.

[473] See *SCR No 5 of 1987; In the Matter of The State v Songke Mai and Gai Avi* [1988-89] PNGLR 56.

This principle applies equally to the taking of a 'voluntary statement'.

See also: *R v Taylor* [1993] 1 NZLR 647 and *R v Manninen* (1987) 41 DLR (4th) 301.

[474] See *SCR No 5 of 1987; In the Matter of The State v Songke Mai and Gai Avi* [1988-89] PNGLR 56, per Kapi DepCJ at 71.

What is 'practicable' is:

- a question of fact; and
- to be determined according to the facts of each case.[475]

Practicality is not assessed by reference to the exigencies of a criminal investigation; the right to personal liberty is not what is left over after the police investigation is finished.[476]

An accused person should be able to consult even in the early hours of the morning.[477]

If an accused person is arrested in office hours and the interview is commenced after hours then it is difficult to see why that interview should not be suspended if the accused person wishes to speak with a lawyer. Any attempt to delay or defer informing an accused person of his or her constitutional rights so as to limit his or her opportunities to exercise those rights should not be condoned.[478]

However, an accused person should not be able to delay an investigation in order to consult if the effect of such a consultation would cause:

- unreasonable delay[479]; or
- hindrance to the process of investigation or the administration of justice.[480]

---

[475] See *SCR No 5 of 1987; In the Matter of The State v Songke Mai and Gai Avi* [1988-89] PNGLR 56, per Kapi DepCJ at 71.

See also: *R v Etheridge* (1992) 9 CRNZ 268.

[476] See *SCR No 5 of 1987; In the Matter of The State v Songke Mai and Gai Avi* [1988-89] PNGLR 56 at 89.

[477] See *Schliebs v Singh* [1981] PNGLR 264 at 367 and *The State v Wangabin Tonieng and others* (1986) N542.

[478] See *The State v Anis* [1990] PNGLR 239 at 247.

[479] See *R v Te Kira* [1993] 3 NZLR 257, per Cooke P at 263.

[480] See *R v Lemsatef* [1977] 1 WLR 812, per Lawton LJ at 815 and *Driscoll v R* (1977) 137 CLR 517, per Barwick CJ at 522, (1977) 15 ALR 47, [1977] HCA 43.

An investigating officer must ensure that a suspect understands his or her constitutional right to a 'reasonable opportunity' to consult legal representation.[481] An issue to consider is whether there was:

- an emergency; or
- a circumstance of urgency

that necessitated that the conduct of the record of interview or the taking of the confessional statement could not be suspended until the legal representative was located.[482]

An accused person is entitled to consult his or her legal representative in private.[483]

A confession obtained after an accused person has been refused access to a legal representative may be ruled inadmissible by a court.[484]

[3.8] PUBLIC POLICY

The discretion to exclude a confession on public policy grounds takes into account:

- the need to bring to conviction those who commit offences; and
- the public interest in the protection of individuals from improper or unlawful treatment.[485]

---

481 See *R v Mallinson* [1993] 1 NZLR 528.

482 See *Police v Masame* [2007] WSSC 66.

483 See *Police v Kohler* [1993] 3 NZLR 129, per Cooke J at 132.

484 See *R v White* (1976) 13 SASR 276; *R v Stafford* (1976) 13 SASR 392; *R v Allan* [1977] Crim LR 163; *R v Borsellino* [1978] Qd R 507 and *R v Hart* [1979] Qd R 8.

485 See *R v Ireland* (1970) 126 CLR 321, per Barwick CJ at 334-335, [1970] ALR 727, (1970) 44 ALJR 263, [1970] HCA 21; *Bunning v Cross* (1978) 141 CLR 54 at 74, (1978) 19 ALR 641, [1978] HCA 22; *R v Foster* (1993) 67 ALJR 550 at 554, (1993) 113 ALR 1 at 7, (1993) 66 A Crim R 112, [1993] HCA 80; *R v Pollard* (1992) 176 CLR 177 at 196, (1992) 110 ALR 385, (1992) 67 ALJR 173 at 196, 203-204 and 206-209, (1992) 64 A Crim R 393; *Cleland v R* (1982) 151 CLR 1 at 19-20 and 23, (1982) 43 ALR 619, [1982] HCA 67; *R v Swaffield; Pavic v R* (1998) 192 CLR 159 at 175-181, 190-191 and 211-14, (1998) 72 ALJR 339, (1998) 151 ALR 98, [1998] HCA 1; *McDermott v R* (1948) 76 CLR 501; *Van der Meer v R* (1988) 62 ALJR 656 at 660, (1988) 82 ALR 10, [1988] HCA 56; *R v Stead* (1992) 62 A Crim R 40 at 48-49 and *R v O'Neill* [1996] 2 Qd R 326, (1995) 81 A Crim R 458.

CONFESSIONAL EVIDENCE

Under this exclusionary rule, a Court has a discretion to exclude confessional evidence:

- obtained by unlawful or improper means irrespective of whether the admission of the evidence would be unfair to the accused person[486]; and

- where it is satisfied that the confessional evidence is untrue[487].

This discretion should only be exercised in 'very exceptional[488]' or 'rare[489]' circumstances.

A confession should not be ruled inadmissible on merely a formal or technical ground.[490]

[3.9] PROCEDURE[491]

[3.9.1] INTRODUCTION

The procedure to be followed in a 'voir dire proceedings' should be as follows:

- The defence in the absence of the investigating and corroborating officers should specify the grounds upon which the admissibility of the confessional evidence is being challenged whether in the National Court or District Court.

- The prosecution then replies as to whether a 'voir dire proceedings' should be conducted when considering the grounds relied upon by the defence.

- The Court then rules on whether there is a need to conduct a 'voir dire proceedings'.

---

486 See *Cleland v R* (1982) 151 CLR 1 at 16 and 26-27, (1982) 43 ALR 619, [1982] HCA 67.

487 See *R v Court* [1837] EngR 230, (1837) 7 C & P 487, (1837) 173 ER 216 and *R v Baldry* (1852) 2 Den 430, (1852) 169 ER 568, per Campbell LCJ at 430 at 568.

See also: *Sinclair v R* (1946) 73 CLR 316, per Dixon J at 334, [1946] HCA 55.

488 See *Cleland v R* (1982) 151 CLR 1 at 9, (1982) 43 ALR 619, [1982] HCA 67 and *Collins v R* (1980) 31 ALR 257 at 317, [1980] FCA 72.

489 See *Cleland v R* (1982) 151 CLR 1 at 34, (1982) 43 ALR 619, [1982] HCA 67.

490 See *Lawrie v Muir* [1950] SLT 37 at 39-40.

See also: *R v Swaffield; Pavic v R* (1998) 192 CLR 159 at 177-178, (1998) 72 ALJR 339, (1998) 151 ALR 98, [1998] HCA 1; *Bunning v Cross* (1978) 19 ALR 641, (1978) 141 CLR 54 at 74-75, [1978] HCA 22 and *McDermott v R* (1948) 76 CLR 501 at 512-513.

491 See also: *The State v Kusap Kei Kuija* [1983] PNGLR 263 at 270.

- The prosecution should then call the investigating officer, followed by all other witnesses in order to prove that the confessional evidence was lawfully obtained, and therefore should be admitted.[492]

  Issues raised by the defence should be specifically addressed in examination-in-chief.

- The defence is obliged to put its case to the prosecution witnesses[493] in compliance with the rule in *Browne v Dunn*.[494]

  Such cross-examination, however, must be restricted to the issues concerning involuntariness and/or unfairness.[495]

- The defence may then call such witnesses as it thinks proper[496], including the accused person[497], on the issues raised on the challenge to the admissibility of the confessional evidence[498].

---

[492] See *Mecklina Kar Poning v The State* (2005) SC814; *The State v John Blasius* (2008) N3518, [2008] PGNC 169; *The State v Leo Aiyak* (1989) N799 and *The State v Kusap Kei Kuya* [1983] PNGLR 263.

[493] See *R v Gelu-Gaua* (1962) No. 265; *The State v Benjamin Garo* (1996) N1521 and *The State v Leo Aiyak* (1989) N799.

[494] See *The State v John Ave Hubert Kuere and Mary Buku* (2004) N2622; *The State v Joanes Mesak* (2005) N2853 and *The State v Ereman Donald Kanailom* (2008) N3273, [2008] PGNC 8.

Refer also to the subsection titled 'Rule In Browne v Dunn' in the section titled 'Cross-examination' in the chapter titled 'Examination Of Witnesses' in the text titled 'Injia on Criminal Practice and Procedure in Papua New Guinea and the Pacific'.

[495] See *The State v Kusop Kei Kuya* [1983] PNGLR 263 and *The State v John Yambra Pai* (1986) N535, [1986] PGNC 1.

[496] See *R v Gelu-Gaua* (1962) No. 265 and *The State v Benjamin Garo* (1996) N1521.

[497] See *R v Cowell* [1940] 2 All ER 599.

[498] See *Hassan v R* [1959] EACA 800 at 803.

CONFESSIONAL EVIDENCE

It is the election of the accused person as whether to give evidence at a 'voir dire proceedings'.[499]

However, an accused person cannot generally make an effective challenge to the admissibility of confessional evidence without giving evidence.[500] An accused person is therefore virtually compelled to:

- give evidence[501]; and
- call evidence[502].

The prosecution is not permitted to cross-examine an accused person as to:

- the truthfulness of his or her confession[503]; or
- his or her culpability[504].

---

[499] See *The State v Leo Aiyak* (1990) N799, [1990] PGNC 2.

See also: *Weissensteiner v R* (1993) 178 CLR 217, (1993) 68 ALJR 23 and *Azzopardi v R* (2001) 205 CLR 50, [2001] HCA 25.

See however: *R v Gelu-Gaua* (1962) No. 256.

[500] See *Wong Kam-ming v R* [1979] 2 WLR 81, (1979) 69 Cr App R 47, [1979] Crim LR 168, [1980] AC 247.

[501] See *The State v Leo Aijak* (1990) N799, [1990] PGNC 2.

See also: *R v Brophy* (1981) 2 All ER 705.

[502] See *The State v Leo Aijak* (1990) N799, [1990] PGNC 2.

[503] See *Uda Liki Gasika v The State* [1983] PNGLR 58; *The State v Bisket Uranguae Pokia* [1980] PNGLR 97 at 100 and *The State v Takiwa Pereya; The State v Pariake Walara* (2008) N3494, [2008] PGNC 144.

See also: *Wong Kam-ming v R* [1979] 2 WLR 81, (1979) 69 Cr App R 47, [1979] Crim LR 168, [1980] AC 247, per Lord Edmund Davies at 257.

[504] See *R v Minai* [1965-66] PNGLR 195.

The prosecution must also comply with the 'rule in *Browne v Dunn*'[505].

- The Court should then hear the submissions from the defence followed by the prosecution as whether to exercise its discretion to examine any confessional evidence in order to determine whether it will assist in determining the question of admissibility.[506]

  A Court may read confessional evidence in order to assist in assessing the credibility of the accused person and the witnesses called by the prosecution[507] and other witnesses called by the defence.

  Confessional evidence should not be read aloud by a witness to the Court prior to deciding the question of its admissibility.[508]

- The defence then addresses the Court followed by the prosecution regarding the admissibility of the confessional evidence.

- The Court then rules on the admissibility of the confessional evidence.

[3.9.2] VOLUNTARINESS

As to the issue of 'voluntariness':

- the defence must adduce evidence that on the 'balance of probabilities' supports the allegation of involuntariness[509]; and

---

[505] See *The State v Leo Aiyak* (1990) N799, [1990] PGNC 2.

As regards the law in relation to the 'Rule In Browne v Dunn', refer to the section titled 'Cross-examination' in the chapter titled 'Examination Of Witnesses' in the text titled 'Injia on Criminal Practice and Procedure in Papua New Guinea and the Pacific'.

[506] See *Uda Lili Gasika v The State* [1983] PNGLR 58 and *R v Suk Ula* [1975] PNGLR 123.

[507] See *R v Tovarula* [1973] PNGLR 140.

[508] See *Uda Lili Gasika v The State* [1983] PNGLR 58.

[509] See *The State v William Nanua Kapris and others* (2010) N4139, [2010] PGNC 146; *The State v Dakoa* (2009) N3586, [2009] PGNC 8; *The State v Lucas Soroken and others* (2006) N3029; *The State v David Yakuye Daniel* (2005) N2869, [2005] PGNC 89; *The State v Enana Idon* (2003) N2474; *The State v Allan Woila* [1978] PNGLR 99 and *The State v John Michael Awa and others* (2000) CR No. 905 of 1998.

- if so, the prosecution must negate the allegation/s 'beyond reasonable doubt'[510].

In determining whether confession evidence was obtained voluntarily it is a matter of assessing the surrounding circumstances:

> Was the confessional evidence obtained in the exercise of a free choice to speak or be silent[511],

by assessing the:

- demeanour[512];
- reliability; and
- credibility

of the witnesses[513]?

---

[510] See *The State v William Nanua Kapris and others* (2010) N4139, [2010] PGNC 146; *R v Wendo and others* [1963] PNGLR 217; *The State v Kiki Hapea* [1985] PNGLR 6; *The State v Dakoa* (2009) N3586, [2009] PGNC 8; *The State v John Michael Awa and others* (2000) CR No. 95 of 1998; *The State v Lucas Soroken and others* (2006) N3029; *The State v Allan Woila* [1978] PNGLR 99; *The State v Kusap Kei Kuya* [1983] PNGLR 263; *R v Kai Moro* [1975] PNGLR 14; *The State v Towes Minmin* (2005) N2915, [2005] PGNC 63; *The State v Joanes Mesak* (2005) N2853; *The State v John Ave, Hubert Kuere and Mary Buku* (2004) N2622; *The State v Raphael Walimini* (2004) N2621; *The State v Tobata Sebulon Martin and others* (2008) N3274, [2008] PGNC 7; *The State v Ereman Donald Kanailom* (2008) N3273, [2008] PGNC 8; *R v Fari Pako* (1962) No. 259; *The State v John Julio and others* (1996) N1446; *The State v Kabaia Tarangau and Melburne Israel* (2008) N3272, [2008] PGNC 9; *The State v John Blasius* (2008) N3518, [2008] PGNC 169; *The State v Towo Willy and six others* (2004) CR Nos. 342-351 of 2003; *The State v Kwanbol Embogol* (1977) N91; *The State v Benjamin Garo* (1996) N1521; *The State v Enana Idon* (2003) N2474; *R v Kari Pako* (1962) No. 259 and *R v Amo and Amuna* [1963] PNGLR 22.

See however: *R v Lee* (1950) 82 CLR 133 at 144, [1950] HCA 25; *MacPherson v R* (1981) 147 CLR 512, per Gibbs CJ and Wilson J at 522, (1981) 37 ALR 81, [1981] HCA 46; *Wendo v R* (1963) 109 CLR 559 at 572-573, [1963] HCA 19; *Cleland v R* (1982) 151 CLR 1 at 12 and 19, (1982) 43 ALR 619, [1982] HCA 67 and *Collins v R* (1980) 31 ALR 257 at 258, 271 and 310, [1980] FCA 72.

[511] See *The State v Kwambol Embogol* (1977) N91; *The State v Jeffery Harold Malepo (No. 1)* (1996) N1448; *The State v Benjamin Garo* (1996) N1521 and *The State v August Toiamia* (1978) N145.

[512] See *The State v Lakio Tambai* (1980) N235.

[513] Refer also to the section titled 'Court Decision' in the chapter titled 'Court Procedure' in the text titled 'Injia on Criminal Practice and Procedure in Papua New Guinea and the Pacific'.

Part of a confession may be excluded if, as a result of an imperative question, the accused person did not fully appreciate that he or she continued to have a free choice to speak or remain silent.[514]

[3.9.3] UNFAIRNESS

As to the issue of unfairness:

- the defence must adduce evidence[515] on the 'balance of probabilities'[516] that supports the allegation of unfairness, but the prosecution bears no specific onus[517], ie., that the investigating officer acted fairly or with propriety[518];
- a Court may reject a confession made voluntarily on the basis that it was unfairly obtained[519];
- in exercising the judicial discretion to exclude confessional evidence on the ground of unfairness, a Court should have regard to:
    - any proven breach of the constitutional rights as provided for by sections 37(1) ['Protection of the Law'] and 42(2)[520], (3) and (4) ['Liberty of the Person'] of the *Constitution of the Independent State of Papua New Guinea* judged according to the degree of seriousness or impropriety involved[521];

---

[514] See *R v William Taupa Tovarula and others* [1973] PNGLR 140.

[515] See *MacPherson v R* (1981) 147 CLR 512, per Gibbs CJ and Wilson J at 519-520, (1981) 37 ALR 81, [1981] HCA 46 and *Wendo v R* (1963) 109 CLR 559 at 565, [1963] HCA 19.

[516] See *The State v Kevin Evertius and Thomas Kindi* [1985] PNGLR 109.

[517] See *The State v William Nanua Kapris and others* (2010) N4139, [2010] PGNC 146; *Constitutional Reference No. 1 of 1977* [1977] PNGLR 362; *The State v Silih Sawi* [1983] PNGLR 234; *The State v Kevin Everitus and Thomas Kundi* [1985] PNGLR 109; *The State v Dakoa* (2009) N3586, [2009] PGNC 8 and *The State v John Koga Ivoro* (1989) N772.

[518] See *The State v William Nanua Kapris and others* (2010) N4139, [2010] PGNC 146.

[519] See *The State v Silih Sawi* [1983] PNGLR 234 at 237.

[520] See *Constitutional Reference No. 1 of 1977* [1977] PNGLR 362.

[521] See *The State v Mana Turi* [1986] PNGLR 221.

- any other proven impropriety that would render it unfair to admit the confessional evidence judged according to the degree of seriousness involved; and

- whether there is any evidence that suggests that the confession is unreliable[522],

whilst taking into consideration the reliability and credibility of the witness[523]; and

- a Court must weigh its disapproval of improper police conduct against the public interest in seeing that all relevant evidence for and against the accused person is before the Court[524].

In deciding whether to admit confessional evidence a Court should:

- firstly, consider the nature, seriousness and extent of the improprieties and breaches of the constitutional rights; and

- then secondly, decide whether in all of the circumstances it would be unfair to allow the confession to be adduced into evidence.[525]

[3.10] VOLUNTARINESS SUBMISSION

A submission at a 'voir dire proceedings' in relation to the issue of 'voluntariness' should cover the following:

1. The defence has raised the issue of voluntariness.

2. The defence must adduce evidence that on the 'balance of probabilities' supporting their allegation of involuntariness [see *The State v William Nanua Kapris and others* (2010) N4139].

---

522 See *R v Swaffield; Pavic v R* (1998) 192 CLR 159, (1998) 72 ALJR 339, (1998) 151 ALR 98, [1998] HCA 1; *Van der Meer v R* (1988) 62 ALJR 656 at 666 and 669, (1988) 82 ALR 10, [1988] HCA 56 and *Duke v R* (1989) 180 CLR 508 at 513, (1989) 63 ALJR 139.

523 See *The State v Lakio Tambai and two others* (1980) N235 and *The State v Towes Minmin* (2005) N2915, [2005] PGNC 63.

Refer also to the section titled 'Court Decision' in the chapter titled 'Court Procedure' in the text titled 'Injia on Criminal Practice and Procedure in Papua New Guinea and the Pacific'.

524 See *The State v Silih Sawi* [1983] PNGLR 234 at 237.

525 See *The State v William Nanua Kapris and others* (2010) N4139, [2010] PGNC 146 and *R v Skelly* [1965-66] PNGLR 105.

3. Section 28 of the *Evidence Act* (Ch. 48) states:

> 'A confession that is tendered in evidence in any criminal proceedings shall not be received in evidence if it has been induced by a threat or promise by a person in authority; and a confession made after an such threat or promise shall be deemed to have been induced by it unless the contrary is shown'.

4. In determining whether confession evidence was obtained voluntarily the Court should assess the surrounding circumstances, that is, whether the confessional evidence obtained in the exercise of a free choice to speak or be silent [see *The State v Kwambol Embogol* (1977) N91].

5. The prosecution has called [specify the names of the officers] who both gave evidence in order to negate the allegation/s 'beyond reasonable doubt' [see *R v Wendo and others* [1963] PNGLR 217].

6. Both officers gave evidence that the confessional evidence was obtained in compliance with the Judges Rules.

7. The defence called [specify the name of the witness/es] who gave evidence that the confessional evidence was obtained by means of:

7.1 a threat directed at the accused person.

It is alleged that [outline the allegation].

7.2 violence inflicted on the accused person.

It is alleged that [outline the allegation].

7.3 fear of prejudice.

It is alleged that [outline the allegation].

7.4 duress.

It is alleged that [outline the allegation].

7.5 intimidation.

It is alleged that [outline the allegation].

7.6 persistent importunity or sustained or undue insistence or pressure.

It is alleged that [outline the allegation].

7.7 a promise.

It is alleged that [outline the allegation].

7.8 an inducement.

It is alleged that [outline the allegation].

7.9 a hope of advantage.

It is alleged that [outline the allegation].

7.10 oppression.

It is alleged that [outline the allegation].

8. Both officers gave evidence and denied the allegations.

9. Both officers gave evidence that the following questions were asked[526]:

9.1 Question No. [insert number]

Do you agree that there was no threat made to you to provide the answers you have given?

The reply from the accused person was [insert the reply].

9.2 Question No. [insert number]

Do you agree that you were not assaulted in order to make you provide the answers you have given?

The reply from the accused person was [insert the reply].

9.3 Question No. [insert number]

Do you agree that there was no promise made to you to provide the answers you have given?

The reply from the accused person was [insert the reply].

10. Both officers gave evidence that the confessional evidence was adopted as follows:

[outline as how the confessional evidence was adopted]

---

[526] Refer also to the chapter titled 'Interviewing Suspects' in the text titled 'Injia on Investigatory Practice in Papua New Guinea and the Pacific'.

11. the accused person was so intoxicated that he or she was deprived of his or her understanding as to what he or she was confessing [see *Commonwealth v Howe* (1857) 9 Gray 110 and *Sinclair v R* (1946) 73 CLR 316, per Dixon J at 336, [1946] HCA 55]. [delete if not applicable]

The question of voluntariness is to be determined by asking whether, on the 'balance of probabilities', the accused person was so intoxicated at the time of his or her interview that he or she was incapable of appreciating that he or she had a free choice as to whether to speak or remain silent or to understand the questions being asked and provide reasonable responses to those questions [see *The State of Western Australia v Silich* [2011] WASCA 135; *R v Buchanan* [1966] VR 9 at 15 and *R v Smith* (1992) 58 SASR 491, per Perry J at 498].

Therefore, the confession of an accused person who intoxicated is not necessarily inadmissible [see *R v Ostojic* (1978) 18 SASR 188 and *R v Williams* (1992) 8 WAR 265 at 277].

The effects of alcoholic liquor vary, to a very significant extent, from person to person. Questions of fact and degree will arise in determining whether a confession made by an accused who is intoxicated, to some extent, was voluntary. [see *R v Ostojic* (1978) 18 SASR 188 at 196-197].

12. Both officers gave evidence that [outline their evidence in relation to this allegation].

13. An accused person cannot generally make an effective challenge to the admissibility of confessional evidence without giving evidence [see *Wong Kam-ming v R* [1979] 2 WLR 81, (1979) 69 Cr App R 47, [1979] Crim LR 168, [1980] AC 247]. [if applicable]

14. In order to determine whether the prosecution has negatived the allegation of voluntariness 'beyond reasonable doubt' the Court should assess the demeanour, reliability and credibility of the witnesses called by the prosecution and defence.

15. The Court should note that in this case the accused person chose not to give evidence and be cross-examined as to the allegation of voluntariness. [if applicable]

CONFESSIONAL EVIDENCE

[3.11] IMPROPERLY OR UNFAIRLY OBTAINED SUBMISSION

A submission at a 'voir dire proceedings' in relation to the issue as to whether confessional evidence was obtained 'improperly or unfairly' should cover the following:

1. The defence must adduce evidence that supports the allegation of unfairness [see *MacPherson v R* (1981) 147 CLR 512, per Gibbs CJ and Wilson J at 519-520, [1981] HCA 46 and *Wendo v R* (1963) 109 CLR 559 at 565, [1963] HCA 19] that the investigating officers did not act fairly and with propriety [see *The State v William Nanua Kapris and others* (2010) N4139] on the 'balance of probabilities' [see *The State v Kevin Evertius and Thomas Kindi* [1985] PNGLR 109].

2. However, the prosecution bears no specific onus [see *Constitutional Reference No. 1 of 1977* [1977] PNGLR 362].

3. The Court may reject a confession made voluntarily on the basis that it was unfairly obtained [see *The State v Silih Sawi* [1983] PNGLR 234 at 237].

4. The defence called [specify the name of the witness/es] who gave evidence that the confessional evidence was obtained unfairly by means because it is alleged that:

4.1 there had been a breach of the constitutional right/s of the accused person as provided for by sections 37(1) and/or 42(2), (3) and (4) of the *Constitution of the Independent State of Papua New Guinea* [see *The State v Dakoa* (2009) N3586, [2009] PGNC 8 and *The State v Mana Turi* [1986] PNGLR 221]. [delete what was not applicable]

It is alleged that [outline the allegation].

Any alleged breach of a constitutional right should however be judged according to the degree of seriousness or impropriety involved [see *The State v Mana Turi* [1986] PNGLR 221].

However, a failure to comply with all or any of those constitutional provisions does not for that reason alone render an admission made by an accused person inadmissible [see *Constitutional Reference No. 1 of 1977* [1977] PNGLR 362].

4.2 there was overly persistent questioning by the investigating officers after [an indication was made by the accused person that he or she did not wish to answer any more questions **or** the accused person had refused to answer questions] [see *R v Robinson* (1996) 89 A Crim R 42 at 52; *R v Clarke* (1997) 97 A Crim R 414 and *R v Hart* [1979] Qd R 8 at 13].

However, questioning is not to be regarded as unfair merely because it is persistent. It is however a question of degree as to whether such questioning is overly persistent and therefore unfair [see *R v Clarke* (1997) 97 A Crim R 414 at 419-420; *R v Wyatt* [1972] VR 902 at 905 and *R v Pritchard* [1991] 1 VR 84 at 91-94].

It is alleged that [outline the allegation].

4.3 the accused person was suffering an illness that adversely impacted on the ability of the accused person to chose whether to speak or be silent [see *The State v Joseph Maino* [1977] PNGLR 216 at 218].

It is alleged that [outline the allegation].

4.4 the accused person was held for a lengthy period in custody whilst not being charged and before being questioned [see *The State v Joanes Mesak* (2005) N2853 and *The State v Dakoa* (2009) N3586, [2009] PGNC 8].

It is alleged that [outline the allegation].

4.5 the alleged confession was obtained by means of extortion [see *R v Ginitu Ileandi and others* [1967-68] PNGLR 496 at 497 and *The State v Joe Foe Leslie Leslie* (1996) N1552].

It is alleged that [outline the allegation].

4.6 the accused person was suffering from exhaustion and/or tiredness that adversely impacted on the ability of the accused person to chose whether to speak or be silent [see *The State v Joseph Maino* [1977] PNGLR 216 at 218 and *R v Amo and Amuna* [1963] PNGLR 22].

It is alleged that [outline the allegation].

4.7 the accused person confessed as a consequence of a fraudulent misrepresentation [see *The State v Canute Rambio* (1983) N410].

It is alleged that [outline the allegation].

4.8 the accused person denies that he or she confessed and therefore alleges a fabrication by the investigating officers [see *The State v Wally Kason* (1996) CR No. 1481 of 1996; *The State v Eddie Sam* (2004) N2521 and *The State v John Yambra Pai* (1986) N535].

It is alleged that [outline the allegation].

5. The prosecution has called [specify the names of the officers] in order to negate the allegations of the defence.

6. In order to determine whether it was satisfied on the 'balance of probabilities' that it would be unfair to admit the confessional evidence a Court should take into consideration the demeanour, reliability and credibility of the witnesses [see *The State v Lakio Tambai and two others* (1980) N235 and *The State v Towes Minmin* (2005) N2915, [2005] PGNC 63].

7. If the Court is however satisfied on the 'balance of probabilities' that there was impropriety that would render it unfair to admit the confessional evidence then:

   - the Court should judge the impropriety according to the degree of seriousness involved; and

   - consider whether there is any evidence that suggests that the confession is unreliable [see *R v Swaffield; Pavic v R* (1998) 192 CLR 159, (1998) 72 ALJR 339, (1998) 151 ALR 98, [1998] HCA 1; *Van der Meer v R* (1988) 62 ALJR 656 at 666 and 669 and *Duke v R* (1989) 180 CLR 508 at 513, (1989) 63 ALJR 139].

8. A Court should weigh its disapproval of improper police conduct against the public interest in seeing that all relevant evidence for and against the accused person is before the Court [see *The State v Silih Sawi* [1983] PNGLR 234 at 237].

9. In deciding whether to admit confessional evidence a Court should consider the nature, seriousness and extent of the improprieties and breaches of the constitutional rights, and then decide whether in all of the circumstances it would be unfair to allow the confession to be adduced into evidence [see *The State v William Nanua Kapris and others* (2010) N4139 and *R v Skelly* [1965-66] PNGLR 105].

[4.0] ADOPTION

[4.1] INTRODUCTION

At common law an unsigned record of interview or voluntary statemenet is admissible as an exhibit to the extent that an accused person has 'adopted' it.[527]

---

[527] See *Stephens v R* (1985) 156 CLR 664 at 669; *Driscoll v R* (1977) 137 CLR 517 at 540, (1977) 15 ALR 47, [1977] HCA 43; *R v Todd* (1981) 72 Cr App R 299, [1981] Crim LR 621 and *R v Lapuse* [1964] VR 43.

[4.2] ADOPTED

Adoption includes[528]:

- an accused person signing or attesting his or her mark to a record of interview or voluntary statement as an acknowledgement as to the truth of its contents[529];

- an accused person attesting his or her mark to a record of interview or voluntary statement as an acknowledgement as to the truth of its contents after it has been read over to him or her[530], even though he or she may be illiterate[531]; and

- an accused person who has read out aloud a record of interview or voluntary statement or clearly demonstrates that it was read to him or her and states that it was true and correct.[532]

  In such circumstances that is considered equivalent to signing the record of interview or voluntary statement.[533]

[528] See however: *The State v Goi Mubin* [1990] PNGLR 99.

[529] See *R v Fenlon* (1980) 71 Cr App R 307, [1980] Crim LR 573; *R v Dillon* (1987) 85 Cr App R 29, [1984] Crim LR 100; *Dawson v R* (1961) 106 CLR 1 at 13; *R v Harris* (1970) 1 NSWLR 281 and *R v Clark* (1970) 1 NSWLR 289.

[530] See *Balo v R* [1975] PNGLR 378, [1975] PGSC 4 and *The State v Takiwa Pereya and The State v Pariake Walara* (2008) N3494, [2008] PGNC 144.

See also: *R v Lambe* (1791) 2 Leach 552, 168 ER 379; *R v Chappel* (1834) 1 M & ROB 396, 174 ER 136 and *R v Zema and Jeanes* [1970] VR 566 at 568-569.

[531] See *Gaio v R* (1960) 104 CLR 419, [1961] ALR 67, (1961) 34 ALJR 266 and *R v Salameh* (1985) 4 NSWLR 369, (1985) 20 A Crim R 183.

[532] See *R v Fenlon* (1980) 71 Cr App R 307, [1980] Crim LR 573 and *R v Dillon* (1987) 85 Cr App R 29, [1987] Crim LR 100.

[533] See *R v Fenlon* (1980) 71 Cr App R 307, [1980] Crim LR 573 and *R v Dillon* (1987) 85 Cr App R 29, [1987] Crim LR 100.

[4.3] UNADOPTED[534]

An 'unadopted' record of interview or voluntary statement may not be tendered as an exhibit by the prosecution[535], without the consent of:

- the defence; and
- the Court.

However, an investigating officer may use a record of interview or voluntary statement to refresh his or her memory in Court.[536]

A record of interview or voluntary statement is not adopted if:

- it is read out aloud by a police officer, and not the accused person, and the accused person refused to sign or acknowledge it[537]; and
- an accused person reads it over without comment[538].

A Court should give the most careful consideration to the question whether it is desirable in the interests of justice to exclude such confessional evidence.[539]

---

534 See also: *R v Sekhon* (1987) 85 Cr App R 19, [1987] Crim LR 693 and *R v Virgo* (1978) 67 Cr App R 323, [1978] Crim LR 557.

535 See *R v Fenlon* (1980) 71 Cr App R 307, [1980] Crim LR 573 and *R v Dillon* (1987) 85 Cr App R 29, [1987] Crim LR 100.

See however: *The State v Benjamin Garo* (1996) N1521.

536 See *R v Layer* (1792) 8 MOD 82 at 89, 88 ER 64 at 69-70 and *R v Jones* (1783) 1 Lavin 46, 168 ER 954.

See also: *Driscoll v R* (1977) 137 CLR 517 at 541, (1977) 15 ALR 47, [1977] HCA 43.

537 See *R v Kerr (No. 1)* [1951] VR 211 and *R v Lapuse* [1964] VR 43.

538 See *R v Vandine* [1968] 1 NSWLR 417.

539 See *The State v Benjamin Garo* (1996) N1521 and *The State v Goi Mubin* [1990] PNGLR 99.

See also: *Driscoll v R* (1977) 137 CLR 517, (1977) 15 ALR 47, [1977] HCA 43.

CONFESSIONAL EVIDENCE

[5.0] USE OF AN INTERPRETER[540]

An interpreter is only to be considered as a 'translating machine' and his or her translation must be accurate and interpreted faithfully.[541]

If the services of an interpreter are used to interpret a conversation with an accused person, he or she must be called to give evidence.[542]

The interpreter should also initial or sign the record of interview or voluntary statement in the presence of the accused person.[543]

In circumstances in which an interpreter is used to ask questions and record answers, both:

- the interpreter; and
- the interviewing officer

are permitted to give such evidence.[544]

Where confessional evidence has been recorded in a language different to the accused person's own language and has been read back to the accused person in his or her own language, then the accused person's signature is more than an acknowledgement of the translation, but is acknowledgement of the truth of the document, and hence such a document is admissible as evidence.[545]

---

[540] Refer also to the section titled 'Right To An Interpreter' in the chapter titled 'Rights Of An Accused Person' in the text titled 'Injia on Criminal Practice and Procedure in Papua New Guinea and the Pacific'.

[541] See *Gaio v R* (1960) 104 CLR 419, [1961] ALR 67, (1961) 34 ALJR 266.

[542] See *R v Attard* (1958) 43 Cr App R 90; *Webb and Hay v R* (1994) 181 CLR 41 at 79-80; *Bannon v R* (1995) 185 CLR 1; *R v Robinson and Tiplady* (1985) 123 LSJS 37; *R v Korwin-Drozynski* [1963] Qd R 362; and *Re Van Beelan* (1974) 9 SASR 163.

[543] See *The State v Lakio Tambai and two others* (1980) N235.

[544] See *Gaio v R* (1960) 104 CLR 419, [1961] ALR 67, (1961) 34 ALJR 266.

[545] See *Fande Balo v R* [1975] PNGLR 378 and *R v Aivei Ieme* [1973] PNGLR 1.

CONFESSIONAL EVIDENCE

If an interpreter repeated in one language to the investigating officer what an accused person said in the other language, the evidence of the officer as to the verbal statements of the accused person would be admissible. The evidence of the officer in such circumstances does not constitute 'hearsay evidence[546]'.[547]

---

[546] Refer also to the chapter titled 'Hearsay Evidence'.

[547] See *R v Gabi Kopa* [1964] PNGLR 257.

DEMONSTRATION OR RE-ENACTMENT

A demonstration or re-enactment at the scene of an offence, ie., crime scene, by an accused person may be beneficial in order to clarify what occurred.

It is highly desirable for an investigating officer when completing the taking of confessional evidence to ask the suspect to accompany him or her back to the crime scene for the purposes of clarification, amplification or demonstration, if required.[548]

However, prior to the conduct of such a demonstration or re-enactment an accused person must be warned that he or she does not have to participate.[549]

An accused person should be questioned in a record of interview as to what he or she did at the demonstration or re-enactment.

However, if the record of interview is ruled to be inadmissible then the evidence of the demonstration or re-enactment will also be ruled as inadmissible.[550]

A demonstration or re-enactment should be conducted prior to an accused person being formally charged.

If an accused person is placed in custody after being formally charged then permission of the District Court is required in order to remove him or her to conduct a demonstration or re-enactment.[551]

---

[548] See *R v Suk Ula and others* [1975] PNGLR 123.

[549] See *R v Suk Ula and others* [1975] PNGLR 123.

[550] See *Lam Chi-Ming and others v R* (1990) 93 Cr App R 358.

[551] See *R v Suk Ula and others* [1975] PNGLR 123.

See also: *R v Bruce* [1965] QWN 48; *Williams v R* (1986) 161 CLR 278 and *Mc Aneny v Kearney; ex parte Kearney* [1966] Qd R 306.

DOCUMENTARY EVIDENCE

[1.0] INTRODUCTION

The importance of documentary evidence cannot be overestimated. In criminal cases, parties often resort to documents to prove many issues.[552]

When seeking to tender any document, like any evidence, the prosecution or defence must consider its admissibility.

It is not permissible as a general principle to:

> prove a fact against an accused person by producing a document in which that fact is recorded

without calling the maker of the document to say that what he or she wrote in the document represents a true statement of fact.[553]

Authenticity is an aspect of relevance.[554]

Whilst many documents indicate their authenticity on their face, the common law rule of admissibility requires that before a document is received in evidence its authenticity must be shown by evidence extrinsic to the document itself. The indications on the face of the document are not on their own regarded as sufficient to demonstrate the authenticity aspects of relevance.[555]

Unless a document is authentic - that is unless:

- it was written by its supposed author; and
- it is genuinely what it:
  - purports; or
  - is asserted to be,

---

[552] See New Zealand Law Commission, 1999, 'Evidence. Volume 1: Reform of the Law and Evidence. Volume 2: Evidence Code and Commentary', Report 55, page 135.

[553] See *R v Gillespie and Simpson* (1967) 57 Cr App R 172, [1967] Crim LR 238.

[554] See New Zealand Law Commission, 1994, 'Evidence Law: Documentary Evidence and Judicial Notice – A Discussion Paper', Preliminary Paper 22.

[555] See New Zealand Law Commission, 1994, 'Evidence Law: Documentary Evidence and Judicial Notice – A Discussion Paper', Preliminary Paper 22.

it is, in most cases, irrelevant although it may have some connection to the case.[556]

The authorship of private documents can be proven by:

- the admissible testimony of the author[557];
- the admissible hearsay statement of the author[558];
- the evidence of a witness who observed the author write the document[559];
- the evidence of a witness who:
  - had regularly corresponded with the author; and
  - is able to recognise the handwriting of the author to the satisfaction of the Court[560]; and

---

[556] See New Zealand Law Commission, 1994, 'Evidence Law: Documentary Evidence and Judicial Notice – A Discussion Paper', Preliminary Paper 22.

[557] See New Zealand Law Commission, 1994, 'Evidence Law: Documentary Evidence and Judicial Notice – A Discussion Paper', Preliminary Paper 22.

Refer also to the section titled 'Formal Admission' in the chapter titled 'Court Procedure' in the text titled 'Injia on Criminal Practice and Procedure in Papua New Guinea and the Pacific'.

[558] See New Zealand Law Commission, 1994, 'Evidence Law: Documentary Evidence and Judicial Notice – A Discussion Paper', Preliminary Paper 22.

Refer also to the chapter titled 'Hearsay Evidence'.

[559] See *R v O'Brien* (1912) 7 Cr App R 29 and *R v McCartney and Hansen* (1928) 20 Cr App R 179.

See also: New Zealand Law Commission, 1994, 'Evidence Law: Documentary Evidence and Judicial Notice – A Discussion Paper', Preliminary Paper 22.

[560] See *R v O'Brien* (1912) 7 Cr App R 29.

See also: New Zealand Law Commission, 1994, 'Evidence Law: Documentary Evidence and Judicial Notice – A Discussion Paper', Preliminary Paper 22.

Refer also to the chapter titled 'Opinion Evidence'.

- the opinion evidence of a handwriting expert evidence which involves a comparison between:
    - the document in question; and
    - a document known to have been written by the relevant person.[561].[562]

Furthermore, the common law provides that where a witness sees a person sign a document in a particular name, that is sufficient evidence it was signed by the relevant person, unless, perhaps, the name is very common.[563]

A Court must be satisfied 'beyond reasonable doubt' that any disputed writing is genuine.[564]

A document that is otherwise inadmissible cannot be made admissible in evidence simply by putting it to an accused person in cross-examination[565].[566]

[2.0] BEST EVIDENCE AND SECONDARY EVIDENCE RULES[567]

Where the contents of a document are to be proved, the law of evidence requires that:

- the original must be produced; or
- its absence explained.

---

[561] See *R v Rickard* (1918) 13 Cr App R 140; *R v Tilley and Tilley* (1961) 45 Cr App R 360 at 364 and *R v Smith* (1968) 52 Cr App R 648, [1968] Crim LR 674.

See also: New Zealand Law Commission, 1994, 'Evidence Law: Documentary Evidence and Judicial Notice – A Discussion Paper', Preliminary Paper 22.

Refer also to the chapter titled 'Opinion Evidence'.

[562] Refer also to the section titled 'Handwriting Evidence' in the chapter titled 'Identification Evidence'.

[563] See *Jones v Jones* (1841) 9 M & W 75 and *Roden v Ryde* (1843) 4 QB 626.

[564] See *R v Ewing* [1983] QB 1039, (1983) 77 Cr App R 47.

[565] Refer also to the section titled 'Cross-examination' in the chapter titled 'Examination Of Witnesses' in the text titled 'Injia on Criminal Practice and Procedure in Papua New Guinea and the Pacific'.

[566] See *R v Treacy* [1944] 2 All ER 229, (1944) 30 Cr App R 93 at 96.

[567] Refer also to the chapter titled 'Best Evidence And Secondary Evidence Rules'.

DOCUMENTARY EVIDENCE

This is usually called 'the secondary evidence rule'.[568]

Primary evidence may be defined as:

- the best evidence; or

- that kind of proof which, under any possible circumstances, affords the greatest certainty of the fact in question;

whereas secondary evidence is 'all evidence falling short of this'.[569]

The admissibility of secondary evidence, ie., a copy of an original document, has been considered in the courts. If a copy or a copy of a copy is sought to be tendered there must be evidence so that it is proved to be a true copy of the original.[570]

The 'secondary evidence rule' may be seen as the last vestige of the 'best evidence rule', now largely obsolete.[571]

The only remaining instance of that rule is:

> If an original document is available it must be produced and a witness cannot give secondary evidence by producing a copy, if the original is available[572],

subject to statutory exceptions[573].

---

[568] See New Zealand Law Commission, 1994, 'Evidence Law: Documentary Evidence and Judicial Notice – A Discussion Paper', Preliminary Paper 22.

[569] See New Zealand Law Commission, 1994, 'Evidence Law: Documentary Evidence and Judicial Notice – A Discussion Paper', Preliminary Paper 22.

[570] See *R v Collins* (1960) 44 Cr App R 170 at 174.

Refer also to the chapter titled 'Best Evidence and Secondary Evidence Rules'.

[571] See New Zealand Law Commission, 1994, 'Evidence Law: Documentary Evidence and Judicial Notice – A Discussion Paper', Preliminary Paper 22.

[572] See *Garton v Hunter* [1969] 2 QB 37 at 44.

See also: *Kajala v Noble* (1982) 75 Cr App R 149, per Ackner LJ at 152.

[573] See:
- section 55 ['Secondary Evidence of Registered Deed or Document, etc.']; and
- Division 6 of Part IV ['Photographic and Machine Reproductions']

of the *Evidence Act* (Ch. 48).

DOCUMENTARY EVIDENCE

[3.0] REAL EVIDENCE

In order to seek to tender a document 'used' by an accused person as 'real evidence', it is necessary to prove some connection between the accused person and the document, such as proving that the accused person:

- was the author[574];
- was aware of the document;
- had exercised some control over it; or
- was some other way connected with it.[575]

[4.0] PUBLIC DOCUMENT[576]

The common law has long recognised the inconvenience that would result if a party was required to produce in court the original of a public document.[577]

During the 19th century, the English courts recognised that most public documents should be held admissible as evidence of the truth of their contents, thus constituting another extremely important exception to the hearsay rule. This exception is clearly based on both:

- reliability; and
- convenience.[578]

---

[574] Refer also to the section titled 'Handwriting Evidence' in the chapter titled 'Identification Evidence'.

[575] See *Howey v Bradley* [1970] Crim LR 223.

See also: *R v Horne* [1992] Crim LR 304.

[576] See also: *Myers v DPP* (1964) 48 Cr App R 348, [1965] AC 1001, [1964] 2 All ER 881, [1964] 3 WLR 145.

[577] See New Zealand Law Commission, 1994, 'Evidence Law: Documentary Evidence and Judicial Notice – A Discussion Paper', Preliminary Paper 22.

[578] See Law Reform Commission of Ireland, 2010, 'Hearsay in Civil and Criminal Cases', Chapter 3.

Factors which assist in determining whether a document is 'public' include:

- whether there is a strict duty to inquire into all of the circumstances recorded[579];
- whether it concerns a public matter[580];
- whether the document is to be retained and is open for public inspection[581]; and
- whether it was produced by a public official who:
    - was under a duty to make inquiry; or
    - had personal knowledge of the matters stated, recorded or reported in the document for the use of the members of the public[582].

Such a document is admitted as proof of its contents as an exception to the 'hearsay rule[583]'.[584]

Such a document may speak for itself without the need to call any witness to verify the truthfulness of its contents.[585]

---

579 See New Zealand Law Commission, 1994, 'Evidence Law: Documentary Evidence and Judicial Notice – A Discussion Paper', Preliminary Paper 22.

580 See New Zealand Law Commission, 1994, 'Evidence Law: Documentary Evidence and Judicial Notice – A Discussion Paper', Preliminary Paper 22.

581 See New Zealand Law Commission, 1994, 'Evidence Law: Documentary Evidence and Judicial Notice – A Discussion Paper', Preliminary Paper 22.

582 See *Sturla v Freccia* [1880] 5 App Cas 623 at 623.

583 Refer also to the chapter titled 'Hearsay Evidence'.

584 See *Lilley v Pettit* [1946] KB 401, [1946] 1 All ER 593.

See also:

- section 5 ['Acts of Parliament, etc'];
- section 6 ['Regulations, etc']; and
- sections 38 to 51 ['Proof and Evidence in Certain Cases']

of the *Evidence Act* (Ch. 48).

585 See *R v Patel* (1981) 73 Cr App R 117, [1981] 3 All ER 94, [1981] Crim LR 250.

The rationale for the exception was that the truthfulness of the statement could be presumed from:

- the nature of the document; and
- the manner in which it was made.

The weight to be given to each of the criteria depends on the type of document.[586]

It would be both impractical and unnecessary to require the statement maker to be a witness since that person could not generally be expected to recollect of the matters described in the document.

[5.0] PRIVATE DOCUMENT

[5.1] INTRODUCTION

In ordinary circumstances, the form and content of a document and the circumstances in which it was made enable an inference of personal knowledge to be shown.[587]

The issue of admissibility when seeking to tender a 'private document' for the purpose of proving its contents is governed by the 'hearsay rule[588]'.

Therefore, the principle question to be asked is:

> 'For what purpose is the document sought to be admitted?'

If a document is sought to be admitted so as to prove the truth of its contents,

> then it must fall within an exception to the 'hearsay rule[589]',

otherwise a witness will need to be called who was responsible for preparing the document.

---

[586] See New Zealand Law Commission, 1994, 'Evidence Law: Documentary Evidence and Judicial Notice – A Discussion Paper', Preliminary Paper 22.

[587] See *McKay v Hutchins and Fire and All Risks Insurance Co Ltd* [1990] 1 Qd R 533 and *Ritz Hotel Ltd v Charles of the Ritz Ltd (Nos. 15 & 16)* (1988) 14 NSWLR 107.

[588] Refer also to the chapter titled 'Hearsay Evidence'.

[589] Refer also to the chapter titled 'Hearsay Evidence'.

The following are however exceptions to that requirement:

- a statement of a dead witness[590];
- a statement of an insane witness[591];
- a statement of a witness who is too ill to travel[592];

---

[590] See section 102 of the *District Courts Act* (Ch. 40) ['Statements of Witnesses Dead, etc'].

As regards the law in relation to a 'Dying Declaration', refer to the chapter titled 'Hearsay Evidence'.

Refer also to:
- the section titled 'Admission Of Evidence Without The Calling Of A Witness' in the chapter titled 'Court Procedure' in the text titled 'Injia on Criminal Practice and Procedure in Papua New Guinea and the Pacific'; and
- the section titled 'Depositions' in the chapter titled 'Hearsay Evidence'.

[591] See section 102 of the *District Courts Act* (Ch. 40) ['Statements of Witnesses Dead, etc'].

As regards the competency of a mentally-ill witness to give evidence, refer to the section titled 'Competency And Compellability' in the chapter titled 'Witnesses' in the text titled 'Injia on Criminal Practice and Procedure in Papua New Guinea and the Pacific'.

Refer also to:
- the section titled 'Admission Of Evidence Without The Calling Of A Witness' in the chapter titled 'Court Procedure' in the text titled 'Injia on Criminal Practice and Procedure in Papua New Guinea and the Pacific'; and
- the section titled 'Depositions' in the chapter titled 'Hearsay Evidence'.

[592] See section 102 of the *District Courts Act* (Ch. 40) ['Statements of Witnesses Dead, etc'].

As regards the competency of a mentally-ill witness to give evidence, refer to the section titled 'Competency And Compellability' in the chapter titled 'Witnesses' in the text titled 'Injia on Criminal Practice and Procedure in Papua New Guinea and the Pacific'.

Refer also to:
- the section titled 'Admission Of Evidence Without The Calling Of A Witness' in the chapter titled 'Court Procedure' in the text titled 'Injia on Criminal Practice and Procedure in Papua New Guinea and the Pacific'; and
- the section titled 'Depositions' in the section titled 'Hearsay Evidence'.

- a statement of a witness who is unwilling to travel[593];
- a statement of a witness who is being intentionally prevented from giving evidence[594];
- a confessional statement[595];
- video-taped evidence[596];
- evidence by affidavit;
- a bank record; and
- a business record.

---

[593] See section 102 of the *District Courts Act* (Ch. 40) ['Statements of Witnesses Dead, etc'].

As regards the competency of a mentally-ill witness to give evidence, refer to the section titled 'Competency And Compellability' in the chapter titled 'Witnesses' in the text titled 'Injia on Criminal Practice and Procedure in Papua New Guinea and the Pacific'.

Refer also to:

- the section titled 'Admission Of Evidence Without The Calling Of A Witness' in the chapter titled 'Court Procedure' in the text titled 'Injia on Criminal Practice and Procedure in Papua New Guinea and the Pacific'; and
- the section titled 'Depositions' in the chapter titled 'Hearsay Evidence'.

[594] See section 102 of the *District Courts Act* (Ch. 40) ['Statements of Witnesses Dead, etc'].

Refer also to:

- the section titled 'Admission Of Evidence Without The Calling Of A Witness' in the chapter titled 'Court Procedure' in the text titled 'Injia on Criminal Practice and Procedure in Papua New Guinea and the Pacific'; and
- the section titled 'Depositions' in the chapter titled 'Hearsay Evidence'.

[595] Refer also to the chapter titled 'Confessional Evidence'.

[596] See section 37C of the *Evidence Act* (Ch. 48) ['Video-taped Evidence'].

[5.2] BANKER'S BOOK[597]

Section 1 of the *Evidence Act* (Ch. 48) ['Interpretation'] states:

'"bank" means a person, partnership or company engaged in the ordinary business of banking by receiving deposits and issuing bills or notes payable to the bearer at sight or on demand, and includes a government savings bank established under a law'.

Section 91 ['Entries in Bankers' Books'] states:

'Subject to this Part, a copy of an entry in a banker's book is, in all legal proceedings, prima facie evidence of the entry and of the matters, transactions and accounts recorded in the book'.

Section 92 ['Documents Purporting to be Copies of Entries'] states:

'A copy of an entry in a banker's book is not admissible in evidence under this Part unless an officer of the bank testifies orally or by affidavit that –

(a) he has compared the copy with the original entry; and

(b) the copy is a correct copy of an entry that was made in the usual and ordinary course of business in a book that, at the time when the entry was made, was one of the ordinary books of the bank; and

(c) the book is in the custody or control of the bank'.

Section 93 ['Production of Books by Bankers'] states:

'In any legal proceedings to which the bank is not a party, a banker or an officer of a bank is not compellable –

(a) to produce a banker's book the contents of which can be proved under this Part; or

(b) to appear as a witness to prove the matters, transactions, or accounts recorded in such a book;

unless otherwise ordered by the court or a Judge'.

Section 94 ['Inspection of Bankers' Books'] states:

'(1) On the application of any party to any legal proceedings, the court or a Judge may order –

[597] Refer also to the chapter titled 'Hearsay Evidence'.

(a) that the party be at liberty to inspect and take copies of entries in the books of a bank for any of the purposes of the proceedings; and

(b) that, on payment of the prescribed charge, the bank prepare and deliver to the party copies of such entries as are required for evidence in the proceedings.

(2) An order under Subsection (1) shall be served on the bank at least three clear days before it is to be obeyed, unless the court or Judge directs otherwise.

(3) The costs of an application to a court or Judge under this section, and the costs of anything done or to be done under an order of a court or Judge made under this section, are in the discretion of the court or Judge.

(4) Where costs referred to in Subsection (3) have been occasioned by a default or delay on the part of the bank, the court or Judge may order that the costs, or any part of them, be paid to any party by the bank.

(5) An order under Subsection (4) against a bank may be enforced as if the bank were a party to the proceedings'.

[5.3] BUSINESS RECORD[598]

Section 61 of the *Evidence Act* (Ch. 48) ['Business Records'] states:

'(1) In this section, "writing" includes a photographic reproduction or photostatic reproduction of a document[599].

(2) Subject to Subsection (3), a writing purporting to be a memorandum or record of an act, matter or event is admissible in evidence in a court as proof of the facts stated in if it appears to the court that –

(a) the memorandum or record was made in the regular course of a business[600] at or about the time of the doing or occurrence of the act, matter or event; and

---

[598] Refer also to the chapter titled 'Hearsay Evidence'.

[599] The term 'business' is defined in section 1 of the *Evidence Act* (Ch. 48) as including:
'a book, plan, paper, parchment or other material on which there is any writing that is marked with letters or marks denoting words or any other signs capable of carrying a definite meaning to persons conversant with them, and includes a part of a document'.

[600] The term 'business' is defined in section 1 of the *Evidence Act* (Ch. 48) as including:
'public administration and a business, profession, occupation, trade, undertaking or calling of any kind'.

(b) the source of information, and the method and time of the preparation of the memorandum or record, were such as to indicate its trustworthiness.

(3) Subsection (2) does not require a court to admit in evidence a writing if it appears to the court that the interests of justice would not be served by its admission.

(4) For the purposes of this section, a court, in considering whether a writing should be admitted in evidence, shall have regard to all relevant circumstances, including –

(a) the source from which the writing is produced; and

(b) the circumstances of its receipt and custody by the person producing it or by any person from whom it has been obtained for the purpose of producing it in evidence.

(5) In the exercise of the discretion of a court under this section, the court is not obliged to receive formal testimony but may inform itself in any way that it thinks fit and in particular by the affidavit, oath[601], affirmation or certificate of a person who professes to have knowledge of any of the matters to which the writing relates or of the circumstances relating to its preparation'.[602]

[5.4] COMPUTER RECORD

Pursuant to Division 5 of Part IV of the *Evidence Act* (Ch. 48) ['Computerised Information'] a computer record may be admissible as to the proof of its contents without the need to call evidence from a witness.[603]

[601] The term 'oath' is defined in section 3(1) of the *Interpretation Act* (Ch. 2) as including:
'the making of a solemn declaration or affirmation'.

[602] As regards a reproduction of a business document if the original has been destroyed, lost or otherwise unavailable, see section 72 of the *Evidence Act* (Ch. 48) ['Reproductions of Business Documents Destroyed, Lost or Unavailable'].

[603] Refer also to the chapter titled 'Hearsay Evidence'.

[5.5] DOCUMENTARY MEDICAL EVIDENCE

[5.5.1] INTRODUCTION[604]

Section 102 of the *District Courts Act* (Ch. 40) ['Statements of Witnesses Dead, etc'] refers to a 'person registered under the *Medical Registration Act 1980' and* section 37 of the *Evidence Act* (Ch. 48) ['Evidence of Scientific Examination'] refers to the term 'medical practitioner'.

Whilst the term 'medical practitioner' is not defined in the *Evidence Act* (Ch. 48), it is defined in section 3(1) of the *Interpretation Act* (Ch. 2) as meaning:

> 'a person registered, provisionally registered or temporarily registered as a medical practitioner under the *Medical Registration Act 1980*'.

The term 'registered medical practitioner' is defined in section 1 of the *Medical Registration Act 1980* as meaning:

> 'a person whose name appears on a register kept under Section 11(1)(a)'.

Section 11(1) ['Registers to be Kept'] states (in part):

> 'The Medical Registrar shall keep separate registers of persons approved by the Board for –
>
> (a) registration as medical practitioners under Section 22'.

Section 22 ['Approval of Registration'] states:

> 'Where, by personal interview or by any other means, the Board is satisfied that an applicant for registration, or provisional registration, as a medical practitioner –
>
> (a) is of good character and a fit and proper person to be registered, or provisionally registered, as a medical practitioner; and
>
> (b) possesses the minimum qualifications for registration, or provisional registration, set out in Section 23 or 24,
>
> the Board may approve the registration, or provisional registration, of the applicant as a medical practitioner'.

---

[604] Refer also to:
- the chapter titled 'Medical Evidence'; and
- the section titled 'Common Law Exceptions' in the chapter titled 'Hearsay Evidence'.

DOCUMENTARY EVIDENCE

In compliance with sections 23 ['Minimum Qualifications for Registration'] and 24 ['Minimum Qualifications for Provisional Registration]' of the *Medical Registration Act 1980* a medical practitioner must:

- be duly registered as a medical practitioner;
- have acquired and completed the necessary studies in medicine and surgery; and
- have undergone clinical training at places as approved by the Papua New Guinea Medical Board.

[5.5.2] HOSPITAL PATIENT RECORD

Whilst a hospital patient record of a patient is a 'business record' for the purposes of section 61 of the *Evidence Act* (Ch. 48) ['Business Records'] it is not admissible, unless there is proof:

- as to how the document was made in accordance with section 61(2)(a);
- as to the trustworthiness of the source of information; and
- the method of preparation.[605]

Subject to satisfying that criteria to the satisfaction of the Court this provision only permits the tendering of the hospital patient record.

A hospital patient record may be tendered by a medical practitioner, health extension officer or a nurse.

[5.5.3] STATEMENT OF MEDICAL PRACTITIONER

Section 102 of the *District Courts Act* (Ch. 40) ['Statements of Witnesses Dead, etc'] permits the tendering of a statement of a medical practitioner duly registered under the *Medical Practitioners Act 1980* in the National Court with the consent of the Court.[606]

That section does not apply to a health extension officer or a nurse.

---

[605] See *Doa Kerua v The State* [1981] PNGLR 357.

[606] See *The State v Wailo (No. 2)* [1991] PNGLR 150, (1991) N1010, [1991] PGNC 83.

[5.5.4] AFFIDAVIT

STATUTORY PROVISION

Section 37 of the *Evidence Act* (Ch. 48) ['Evidence of Scientific Examination'] states:

'(1) An affidavit made by a medical practitioner who has made a medical, pathological or other scientific examination of a thing setting out –

(a) his qualifications; and

(b) that he has made the examination; and

(c) the facts that he has ascertained and the conclusions at which he has arrived as a result of the examination,

is admissible in evidence in any legal proceedings in a court.

(2) Without affecting the admissibility of an affidavit made under Subsection (1), that subsection does not prevent a court, where it is satisfied, on application, that the justice of the case warrants its doing so, from –

(a) requiring the medical practitioner who made the affidavit to attend and give evidence before the court if he is in the country and can be brought before the court without depriving the community or any part of the community of any essential service; or

(b) arranging for the taking of his evidence orally by way of commission or in any other manner.

(3) Where –

(a) a person is charged with an indictable offence; and

(b) evidence is given on affidavit under Subsection (1); and

(c) the deponent does not give evidence in person,

the court shall not dispose of the matter summarily except with the consent of the accused'.

DOCUMENTARY EVIDENCE

GENERAL PRINCIPLES

Section 37 of the *Evidence Act* (Ch. 48) ['Evidence of Scientific Examination'] enables the evidence of a medical practitioner to be given by the use of an affidavit, including a certified statement.[607]

The legal requirements of this section are as follows:

- the medical examination must have been conducted by a medical practitioner, ie., the medical practitioner's qualification and confirmation of registration;
- the medical practitioner's experience;
- that the medical practitioner had made the examination; and
- the facts that the medical practitioner has ascertained and the conclusions which he or she had arrived at as a result of the examination.

That section does not apply to a health extension officer or a nurse.

[607] See *The State v Paulin Taupin; The State v Jim Kandamain* (1995) N1323, [1995] PGNC 18.

EXHIBITS

[1.0] INTRODUCTION[608]

An exhibit is a silent witness.[609]

At a pre-trial review hearing both the prosecution and defence are to inform the National Court as to:

- the exhibits which are to be provided; and
- whether such exhibits are to be admitted by consent.[610]

A magistrate has the authority to:

- summons a person as a witness; and
- compel that person to bring and produce for the purpose of evidence all documents and writings in that person's possession or power.[611]

---

[608] As regards exhibit management and exhibit handling procedure, refer to the chapter titled 'Exhibits' in the text titled 'Injia on Investigatory Practice in Papua New Guinea and the Pacific'.

[609] See *Williams v R* [2005] NZCA 315, per Gendall J.

[610] Order 2, Division 1, rule 6(f) of the *Criminal Practice Rules 1987* ['Practice Directions'] states:

> 'At a hearing under this rule counsel shall inform the Court of exhibits which are to be provided and whether they are to be admitted by consent'.

See also: rule 3(a).

Refer also to:
- the chapter titled 'Documentary Evidence'; and
- the sections titled 'Formal Admission' and 'The Prosecution Case' in the chapter titled 'Court Procedure' in the text titled 'Injia on Criminal Practice and Procedure in Papua New Guinea and the Pacific'.

[611] See section 71 of the *District Courts Act* (Ch. 40) ['Production of Documents'].

Refer also to the section titled 'Attendance Of Witnesses' in the chapter titled 'Witnesses' in the text titled 'Injia on Criminal Practice and Procedure in Papua New Guinea and the Pacific'.

EXHIBITS

Where an exhibit is tendered in a Court and it appears to the Court that in the public interest that the exhibit should not be returned to its owner, the Court may order that the exhibit be forfeited, destroyed or otherwise dealt with.[612]

[2.0] CHECKING PROCEDURE

A prosecutor or defence legal representative is expected to:

- check the admissibility of any proposed exhibit;
- check to ensure the availability of any proposed exhibit; and
- ensure that any proposed exhibit can be produced by an appropriate witness.

A statement of a witness, including a police officer, should state immediately after referring to an exhibit:

> 'I now seek to produce [identify the exhibit] to the Court.
>
> Tendered and Marked as Exhibit No. ....'

Exhibits should be produced chronologically.

An exhibit such as clothing must be checked to ensure that it has not been cleaned after the commission of an offence. If it has then that should be explained to the Court by an appropriate witness.

[3.0] PRODUCTION IN COURT[613]

Whilst a witness can produce property to a Court, it is the Court that determines the admissibility of the property being produced.

---

[612] See section 628 of the *Criminal Code* (Ch. 262) ['Exhibits'].

However, that statutory provision only applies to the Code, see section 2 of the *Criminal Code Act* (Ch. 262) ['Establishment of the Criminal Code'].

[613] Refer also to the subsection titled 'Eliciting Evidence' in the section titled 'Examination-in-Chief' in the chapter titled 'Examination Of Witnesses' in the text titled 'Injia on Criminal Practice and Procedure in Papua New Guinea and the Pacific'.

See also: *R v Waterfield* [1975] 2 All ER 40, [1975] 1 WLR 711, (1975) 60 Cr App R 296.

It is therefore essential that the prosecution and defence understand that property can be tendered and admitted by a Court and marked either:

- as an exhibit; or
- for identification purposes only.

All property must be formally tendered by the prosecution or defence in order for it to become an exhibit. If it has not been formally tendered, it should not be considered as part of their case.

Property marked for identification purposes only is not an exhibit and therefore, cannot be relied on by the prosecution or defence.

In relation to a prosecution case the investigating officer should be the first witness called because that officer can in most cases produce most, if not all, of the exhibits to the Court. If however the investigating officer is only producing property which he or she has been told about by a witness and not identified by the accused person, then such property can only be produced for 'identification purposes only'.

For example, in offences involving violence:

- a weapon may be produced by a complainant and it can be tendered and marked as an 'exhibit' because the complainant may identify it as being the weapon used during the commission of the offence in question; and
- the investigating officer, if he or she is called before the complainant, can only produce the weapon for identification purposes only, if he or she did not observe the offence, unless the accused person has admitted and identified the weapon as the weapon used to that officer.

Otherwise, the prosecution would be relying on inadmissible evidence known as 'hearsay evidence[614]' because the investigating officer would have to rely on what he or she was told by the complainant.

[4.0] CONTINUITY OF POSSESSION

If any exhibit is to be admissible then the continuity of its possession must be proven.

---

[614] Refer also to the chapter titled 'Hearsay Evidence'.

EXHIBITS

The underlying purpose of testimony relating to the chain of custody or 'continuity of possession' is to prove that:

> the evidence which is sought to be tendered has not been altered, compromised, contaminated, substituted or otherwise tampered with, thus ensuring its integrity from collection to its production in court.[615]

Proof of continuity is not a legal requirement and gaps in continuity are not fatal to the prosecution's case, unless such gaps raise a reasonable doubt about the exhibit's integrity.[616]

However, not every person who had possession of an exhibit from the time of the commission of the offence until its production in court must be called to give evidence.[617]

The prosecution must prove that the exhibit:

- taken from a crime scene;
- transported to a police station and anywhere else for examination; and
- then produced in court

is the same exhibit and that it has not been contaminated.

Obviously, if a number of police officers had possession of an exhibit at the same time then only one of those officers would need to be called to give that evidence.

Proving continuity of possession is of particular importance if an exhibit needs to be analysed by an expert. In order for:

- the opinion evidence of an expert[618]; or
- a certificate issued under any statutory provision to be admissible

the prosecution must prove the continuity of possession from the possession of the accused person until the examination/analysis conducted by the expert.

---

[615] See *R v Larsen* 2001 BCSC 597, per Romilly J.

[616] See *R v Larsen* 2001 BCSC 597, per Romilly J.

[617] See *R v Stafford* [2009] QCA 407; *R v Butler* [2009] QCA 111; *R v Larsen* 2001 BCSC 597, per Romilly J and *Barry v New Zealand Police* [2008] NZHC 438.

[618] Refer also to the chapter titled 'Opinion Evidence'.

EXHIBITS

[5.0] MISSING EXHIBIT[619]

[5.1] STATUTORY PROVISIONS[620]

[5.1.1] SEARCH ACT

Section 12 of the *Search Act* (Ch. 341) ['Police to Maintain Record of Things Seized, etc'] states:

> 'Where any thing is seized by a policeman under this Act or is handed to a policeman, he shall enter in a permanent register of property –
>
> (a) a full description of the thing including where appropriate, a note of any identification marks; and
>
> (b) the time and date the thing was seized or received by him and in the case of things received by him the name and address of the person who handed the thing to him; and
>
> (c) the place and the person from whom the thing was seized; and
>
> (d) other details as are prescribed'.

Section 13 ['Possession of Certain Property'] states (in part):

> '(1) Where any thing is seized under this Act by a policeman or is handed to policeman, the thing shall be deemed to be in the possession of the State.
>
> (4) Anything referred to in Subsection (1), (2) or (3) may be retained in possession in accordance with that subsection for the purpose of examination and investigation and in the event that a person is charged with an offence in relation to that thing or in relation to which that thing is evidence the thing may, subject to any order to the contrary of a court, be retained in that possession until the charge and any subsequent proceedings on that charge have been determined'.

---

[619] Refer also to the subsection titled 'Eliciting Evidence' in the section titled 'Examination-in-Chief' in the chapter titled 'Examination Of Witnesses' in the text titled 'Injia on Criminal Practice and Procedure in Papua New Guinea and the Pacific.

See also: *Smakowski and Zestfair Ltd v Westminster City Council* [1990] Crim LR 419; *Hocking v Ahlquist Brothers Ltd* [1944] 1 KB 120, [1943] 2 All ER 722; *R v Robson and Harris* [1972] 2 All ER 699, [1972] 1 WLR 651, [1972] Crim LR 316; *Kajala v Noble* (1982) 75 Cr App R 149; *R v Wayte* (1983) 76 Cr App R 110; *Samuels v Stubbs* (1972) 4 SASR 200; *Grayden* (1988) 36 A Crim R 163 and *California v Trombetta* (1984) 467 US 479.

[620] Refer also to the section titled 'Search And Seize' in the chapter titled 'Police Powers' in the text titled 'Injia on Investigatory Practice in Papua New Guinea and the Pacific'.

[5.1.2] SEARCH REGULATION

Section 3 of the *Search Regulation* (Ch. 341) ['Register of Property'] states:

> 'A record of things seized by, or handed to, a policeman shall be kept in a register of property in Form 5'.

[5.2] DUTY TO RETAIN

It is part of ordinary human experience that documents and items, even those of great significance or intrinsic value, are not infrequently lost. The law has taken note of this over many centuries and is not so unrealistic as to consider that the loss of an original document or item of real evidence is fatal to any litigation based on it.[621]

However, if an exhibit is available it should be produced to the Court.[622]

The interest of the State in the person charged being brought to trial necessarily extends as well to:

> The preservation and retention of material evidence of his or her guilt or innocence for the purpose of the trial.[623]

Therefore, evidence relevant to the guilt or innocence of an accused person, including the preservation of articles which may give rise to the reasonable possibility of securing relevant evidence, must so far as necessary and practicable, be kept until the conclusion of a trial.[624]

Where an item is of real commercial value it cannot be expected that it be preserved for long periods pending trial just because there is a possibility that the accused person may wish to examine the item at some time before trial.[625] In such circumstances, a photograph should be taken.

---

[621] See *McFarlane v DPP* [2006] IESC 11.

[622] See *R v Kwaimanisi* [1995] SBHC 47.

[623] See *Dillon v O'Brien and Davies* [1887] 20 LRIR 300, per Palles CB and *R v Lushington; ex parte Otto* [1894] 1 QB 420.

[624] See *Braddish v DPP and another* [2002] 1 ILRM 151, [2001] IESC 45, [2001] 3 IR 127; *Robert Murphy v DPP* [1989] ILRM 71, per Lynch J at 76 and *Dunne v DPP* [2002] IESC 27, [2002] 2 IR 305, [2002] 2 ILRM 241.

[625] See *R v Roberts* (1999) 106 A Crim R 67 and *Takiveikata v The State* [2008] FJHC 315.

[5.3] EVIDENCE IN LIEU

If an exhibit cannot be:

- located, it cannot be said that there has been any withholding of evidence[626]; and

- tendered then an explanation must be given for the non-production by a witness.[627]

  Such an explanation may be given by person who saw the exhibit before it went missing as to:

  - what it looked like; and

  - what was done to locate it.

In order to determine whether the explanation of the prosecution was satisfactory, a Court should analyse the circumstances surrounding the loss of the evidence.[628]

The two relevant considerations are:

- whether the evidence has been lost because of acts or omissions by the police involving bad faith[629]; and

- whether it is probable that the evidence would have been of real assistance to the defence in the circumstances of the particular case because it would have contributed to creating a reasonable doubt.[630]

---

[626] See *R v Katonwualiku* [2000] NZCA 208.

[627] See *Birch v The State* [1979] PNGLR 75.

See also: *Butera v DPP (Victoria)* (1987) 62 ALJR 7 and *R v La* (1997) 116 CCC (3d) 97.

[628] See *R v La* (1997) 116 CCC (3d) 97.

[629] In *Arizona v Youngblood* (1988) 488 US 51 Rehnquist CJ stated:

> 'We therefore hold that unless a criminal accused person can show bad faith on the part of the police, failure to preserve potentially useful evidence does not constitute denial of due process of law'.

[630] See *R v Harmer* [2003] NZCA 126.

On appeal, the issue is whether the unavailability of the evidence to the defence appears to have given rise to a miscarriage of justice.[631]

If not, the witness may then give secondary evidence in describing the missing exhibit.[632]

A copy of a record of interview is admissible provided that:

- the original is missing; and
- the original cannot with reasonable diligence be located.[633]

There will be no violation of an accused person's right to a fair trial, unless the accused person establishes that the non-disclosure has:

- probably prejudiced; or
- had an adverse effect on

his or her ability to make full answer and defence.[634]

A carbon copy of the original document may be ruled to be admissible.[635]

In order for a Court to admit a photocopy the prosecution must prove:

- that the original existed which would have been admissible in itself[636];
- that the copy is a true and faithful copy of the original;

---

[631] See *R v Harmer* [2003] NZCA 126.

Refer also to the chapter titled 'Appeals' in the text titled 'Injia on Criminal Practice and Procedure in Papua New Guinea and the Pacific'.

[632] See *Butera v DPP (Victoria)* (1987) 62 ALJR 7 at 9.

[633] See *The State v Wangabin Tonieng, Thomdai Lamasis and Bamba Makis* (1986) N542, [1986] PGNC 5.

[634] See *R v La* (1997) 116 CCC (3d) 97.

[635] See *Durston v Mercuri* (1969) VR 507; *Buckley v Macken* [1961] 1 NZLR 46; *Hay v Mitchell* (1973) 2 NSWLR 736 and *R v Collins* (1960) 44 Cr App R 170.

[636] Refer also to the chapter titled 'Documentary Evidence'.

- that the original is:
    - lost; or
    - destroyed;
- that a diligent search was made for it, and
- that there is evidence as to:
    - how the original was kept before it was lost; and
    - how the copy was made.[637]

In order for a submission that a permanent stay should be imposed as a consequence of a missing exhibit an accused person must be able to show on the 'balance of probabilities' that:

> There is a permanent defect which goes to the root of the trial of such a nature that nothing that the Court can do in the conduct of the trial can relieve against its unfair consequences.[638]

However, trials involve the reconstruction of events, and it happens on occasions that relevant material is not available; documents, recordings and other things may be lost or destroyed and witnesses may die. The fact that a Court is called upon to determine issues of fact upon less than all of the material which could relevantly bear upon the matter does not make the trial unfair.[639]

---

[637] See *R v Vincent Lobendahn* (1972) 17 FLR 1 and *The State v Kanito Matanigasau* [2003] FJHC 103.

[638] See *Z v DPP* [1994] ILRM 481, per Hamilton P.

See also: *McNamara and McNamara* [1998] Crim LR 278; *Holmden v Bitar* (1987) 27 A Crim R 255, (1987) 47 SASR 509; *R v Beckford* [1996] 1 Cr App R 94; *R v Chu Kam-to and Wong Yuk-lan* [1995] 1 HKCLR 179, [1994] 1 HKC 775; *HKSAR v Cheung Wai* [1998] 4 HKC 249; *R v Medway* [2000] Crim LR 415; *Altaf v Crown Prosecution Service* [2007] EWCA (Crim) 691; *Takiveikata v The State* [2008] FJHC 315 and *R (on the application of Ebrahim) v Feltham Magistrates' Court and another and Mouat v DPP* [2001] 1 WLR 1293, [2001] 1 All ER 831, per Brooke LJ at 836.

Refer also to the chapter titled 'Abuse Of Process' in the text titled 'Injia on Criminal Practice and Procedure in Papua New Guinea and the Pacific'.

[639] See *R v Edwards* (2009) 83 ALJR 717, [2009] HCA 20.

FORENSIC EVIDENCE

[1.0] INTRODUCTION

In order to determine what has occurred it may be necessary to secure and preserve:

- the crime scene; and
- any secondary crime scene.

For the safety and security of the public and in order to establish a safe and effective operational environment, it is at times necessary to isolate and contain an incident.

Isolation and containment are necessary to:

- separate and protect the public from the incident; and
- preserve the continuity of any evidence at the scene.

As soon as possible after arriving at a crime scene it is the responsibility of the First Response Officer to ensure that the scene is protected and therefore, preserved.

Upon concluding that an offence has been committed the scene is to be treated as a crime scene.

The investigating officer will have to then determine whether there is the potential for forensic evidence to be collected:

- at the crime scene; and
- from the suspect[640].

Until that evidence is collected the crime scene must remain protected and preserved.

[2.0] ROLE OF THE SCENES-OF-CRIME OFFICER

A Scenes-of-Crime Officer is responsible at a crime scene for:

- the collection of physical and trace evidence;
- the collection of comparative samples, as required; and

[640] See section 22 of the *Arrest Act* (Ch. 339) ['Medical Examination'].

- making an assessment as to whether particular forensic specialists should attend the crime scene.

However, a Scenes-of-Crime Officer will not necessarily be available and in such circumstances the evidence should still be collected.[641]

[3.0] TYPES OF EVIDENCE

[3.1] INTRODUCTION

An investigating officer needs to understand the types of evidence that may be present at a crime scene.

[3.2] PHYSICAL EVIDENCE

The term 'physical evidence' is used to describe:

> any item, large or small, in any state (solid, liquid or gas) and in any condition (living, dead or inanimate, for example, plants).

Therefore, physical evidence can take any form.

[3.3] TRACE EVIDENCE

The term 'trace evidence' is used to describe:

> physical evidence that is very small, such as hairs, fibres and paint particulars.

Such evidence is normally invisible to the naked eye.

In the case of an offender, it is very good evidence because the offender does not realise it is there and therefore, will not attempt to dispose of it.

Generally trace evidence can be obtained from the clothing of the offender.

---

[641] Refer also to the chapter titled 'Exhibits'.

[4.0] EVIDENTIARY VALUE

All forensic evidence is of evidentiary evidence.

The value of forensic evidence is however determined by how useful it is in:

- verifying that an offence has been committed;
- identifying the person responsible; and
- exonerating any other person who may be under suspicion.

A Court must however be satisfied not only as to its relevancy, but also its reliability.[642]

[5.0] BIOLOGICAL EVIDENCE

[5.1] BLOOD

In most crimes of violence, such as a homicide offence, sexual offence and an offence involving a shooting or serious assault, blood will be either from the victim or the offender or both.

Blood can be used to:

- determine the sequence of events at a crime scene; and
- tie a suspect to a particular crime scene.

Sometimes the location of a bloodstain at a crime scene is obvious, while at other times a detailed search is required using chemical screening tests for blood.

These tests can be carried out by a crime scene examiner or a biologist from the National Forensic Science Centre.

With blood splatter, contact smears or pools of blood are present at a crime scene. An interpretation of the events that caused them should be attempted.

Blood splatter interpretation is conducted by staff at the National Forensic Science Centre.

[642] See *Daubert v Merrell Dow Pharmaceuticals Inc* (1993) 509 US 579, [1993] USSC 99.

The types of information that can be obtained from blood splatter are as follows:

- the origin of blood (whether from the victim or the offender);
- the distance between the impact area and its origin at the time of the commission of the offence;
- the type and direction of impact;
- the number of blows struck;
- the position of the victim during blows;
- the movement and direction of the offender and victim during the commission of the offence and after; and
- which hand the blows were struck with.

Blood typing or grouping is conducted by the forensic scientists at the National Forensic Science Centre.

To identify the origin of the blood, a comparison sample must be obtained from:

- the suspect[643]; and
- the victim.

[5.2] HAIR

Hairs are found at any crime scene, from homicides to break and enters.

At the point of entry to a crime scene there may be a few strands of hair caught on the window or on a shrub outside.

Hairs most commonly found at a crime scene are those from the head and pubic region.

Forensic scientists at the National Forensic Science Centre are, to a limited degree, able to distinguish animal hair from human hair and, in most cases, determine from what part of the body the hair comes from.

[643] See section 22 of the *Arrest Act* (Ch. 339) ['Medical Examination'].

[5.3] SALIVA

Saliva is an excellent source of DNA.

DNA stands for deoxyribonucleic acid and is found in most of the body's cells.

The probability of two people having the same DNA profile is statistically almost incomprehensible.

However, the extraction of DNA from blood, semen or other bodily tissue is a very complex process and can be very expensive.

DNA analysis is currently not yet available in Papua New Guinea. Any inquiries for such testing should be made through the National Forensic Science Centre.

[5.4] SEMINAL FLUID

Although blood is the most commonly encountered physiological fluid at a crime scene, seminal fluid is a close second largely due to its high incidence at offences of a sexual nature.

Seminal fluid consists of a highly proteinaceous serum that contains a large number of spermatozoa.

Seminal stains will occur on the clothing of a victim and offender, especially the underclothing and on the bedding or surface where the sexual act occurred.

There may be sample on the victim that may be taken by a medical practitioner.

In all cases, where possible, the entire exhibit should be collected and transported to the National Forensic Science Centre.

The identification of seminal fluid is only a reliable indication of recent sexual activity.

[5.5] OTHER BIOLOGICAL EVIDENCE

Other biological evidence that may be useful as evidence includes skin, muscle, fat, organs, intestines and bones.

Limited tests can be carried out at the National Forensic Science Centre and tests on stomach contents, liver, kidneys, etc will have to be carried out overseas.

[6.0] CHEMICAL EVIDENCE

[6.1] ACCELERANTS

Accelerants are flammable liquids used by arsonists to accelerate the spread of a fire.

The examination of a fire scene by a forensic officer is to determine:

- the origin of the fire; and
- the cause of the fire.

Once the forensic officer has determined the origin of the fire, samples of debris are collected from that area.

These samples are subjected to laboratory tests at the National Forensic Science Centre.

The presence of flammable liquids in fire debris as well as other indicators present at a crime scene may be evidence to support the offence.

[6.2] EXPLOSIVES

Determining the size of an explosion scene can be quite difficult because the radius of interest is not always obvious.

During an explosion the explosive substance generates a fireball of expanding burning gas.

The blast can carry with it small particles of unexploded matter.

Depending on the explosive used, this unexploded matter has often been located on lightweight materials, such as fibres.

Blank and background samples and swabs need to be collected for analysis at the National Forensic Science Centre.

[6.3] GLASS

Glass comparisons are commonly used in cases of break and enter and wilful damage.

When a person breaks a glass window, either:

- with their body; or
- with an instrument,

glass is transferred to their clothing and shoes.

A comparison glass sample must be collected from the broken window or object.

If more than one window or item is broken, separate samples of glass must be collected from all possible sources.

Glass can be analysed by scientific officers using a GRIM (glass refractive index management machine) that measures the refractive index and a SEM (scanning electron microscope) that measures elemental composition.

However, such examinations are currently not yet available in Papua New Guinea.

[6.4] GREASE AND OIL

Grease and oil can be associated with a stolen vehicle and arson.

It is possible to give evidence, with absolute confidence, that two oils are different and of different origins.

The extent to which two oils can be said to be different depends on a large number of variables.

The presence of unburnt oil can be of real use depending on sample preservation and sampling.

Limited examination facilities are available at the National Forensic Science Centre.

[6.5] GUNSHOT RESIDUE

In cases of shootings it is important to establish who fired the weapon.

When a firearm is discharged there are vaporized constituents of the priming composition, referred to as 'gunshot residue', that may be on the hands or clothing of the offender.

However, gunshot residue tests are currently not yet available in Papua New Guinea.

[6.6] PAINT

Paint comparison is useful in the investigation of cases of break and enter and wilful damage.

Paint transfer can occur from a door to a wrench (break and enter) or from a paint can to a wall (wilful damage).

Paint samples transfer can occur as a consequence of a smear, gaze, chip or spray.

A comparison (control) sample must be collected from the suspected source.

Paint samples are compared by staff at the National Forensic Science Centre microscopically.

Whilst such an examination is unable to prove that the paint chip on a wrench came from a particular door it can confirm whether paint of the same elemental composition as that on the door was found on the wrench.

Laboratory examination consists of microscopic examination, and in the case of a paint chip, layer number and type.

Whilst such an examination cannot be conducted at the National Forensic Science Centre it can be conducted at the UPNG Chemistry Department.

[6.7] SEXUAL LUBRICANT

Lubricants used in conjunction with an offence of a sexual nature, takes many forms and can be located in various places.

Some common lubricants include baby oil and vaseline.

In order to link people with this evidence there is the need for a comparative analysis. Preserving a crime scene, includes the victim and suspect.

Their clothing is required for such an analysis.

Whilst such a comparative analysis is currently not yet available in Papua New Guinea, evidentiary material should always be taken possession of.

[7.0] IMPRESSION EVIDENCE

[7.1] IMPERFECTIONS

Minute imperfections can be seen on a variety of objects, such as shoes or tools.

These imperfections will produce markings on other surfaces during normal use.

These markings are often characterised by the type of object used and, in many cases, are unique to that object.

Microscopic imperfections are the result either of manufacture, or random or accidental damage during use.

In order to leave a mark, the object must be harder than the surface on which it is applied.

[7.2] TYPES OF MARKS

[7.2.1] INTRODUCTION

There are two types of marks:

- compression; and
- scraping.

[7.2.2] COMPRESSION MARKS

Compression marks are left when an object is simply pressed into a surface capable of showing up the impression.

Examples of compression marks, include:

- footwear impressions;
- toolmarks;
- toothmarks;
- tyremarks; and

- impressions on a typed document.

[7.2.3] SCRAPING MARKS

Scraping marks are made by pressure combined with movement of the object across a surface.

The resulting mark possesses microscopic striations from the object.

Examples of scraping marks include:

- toolmarks with movement, such as tyre lever scratch marks on a safe; and
- ballistics, ie., marks on projectile fired from a firearm.

[7.3] FOOTWEAR IMPRESSIONS

Impressions of footwear at a crime scene may or may not be visible to the naked eye.

In some situations strong oblique light can help to see footwear impressions more clearly.

Shoe impressions can be found on counters, tables, chairs or papers.

A shoe impression in soil or fine powder on a smooth surface can be lifted with an electrostatic dust lifter, preserving the entire impression.

Such an examination can be carried out at the National Forensic Science Centre.

[7.4] TOOL MARKS

A tool can be identified as an individual tool by surface features, the result of the manufacturing process, wear and damage.

When a tool is applied to a surface it may leave a mark that has its own distinct features.

For example, during a break and enter, a screwdriver is used to jimmy open an aluminum window leaving a scratch or score mark on the metal frame. A cast of this mark, made using impression material suitable for forensic applications, can be taken and held for later comparison. If the screwdriver is found in the possession of a suspect, it can be used to produce test marks. Casts of these test marks can then be compared to the exhibit cast by means of a comparison microscope. This can identify the screwdriver as the tool used in the break and enter.

These same principles can be applied by the toolmark examiner to the identification of a wide variety of tools, including pliers, bolt cutters and knives.

Such examinations can be conducted at the National Forensic Science Centre.

[7.5] TOOTH MARKS

Tooth marks are mainly compression marks (although striation marks can occur) that occur in foodstuffs, such as apples, cheese, chewing gum or bread, or on the skin of a victim or offender.

The relative position of teeth, their width, the distance between teeth, the ridges on the edge of the teeth and any unusual characteristics can show in a bite mark.

It is sometimes possible to positively identify an offender from a bite mark.

Such an examination may be arranged with the assistance of the National Forensic Science Centre.

[7.6] TYRE MARKS

Tyre impressions left at a crime scene can provide information similar to that provided by footwear comparisons.

In most cases the characteristics of the tyre can be determined.

Such examinations can be carried out at the National Forensic Science Centre.

[7.7] TYPED-DOCUMENT IMPRESSIONS

An examination of a typed document is done at the Document Examination Centre of the National Forensic Science Centre.

The individual marks made by a typewriter may be unique to that particular typewriter.

These marks can show up on a typed document.

In some cases, the make and model of the typewriter can be determined from the typed document.

The document examiner will, in most cases, need the suspect typewriter for comparison.

Fingerprint examination can also be conducted on the typed document.

Usually this is done after the examination by the document examiner because the fingerprinting process may obscure the document to some extent.

[7.8] BALLISTICS[644]

[7.8.1] MARKS

The manufacturing process of firearm components, such as the barrel, firing pin, extractor and ejector, leave microscopic surface markings.

These markings have been found to be unique to each weapon, showing significant variation even between weapons manufactured consecutively.

When a round of ammunition is fired, marks corresponding to the microscopic marks on the weapon, may be left on the carriage case or projectile.

Accidental damage and wear may add to or alter the weapon's fingerprint over time.

When it is necessary to establish whether or not a particular weapon has been used in a shooting, the firearm examiner will compare the exhibit cartridge case or projectile to those test fired from the suspect weapon. These comparisons are carried out using a comparison microscope. This instrument allows two objects to be viewed simultaneously so that microscopic marks caused by firing can be compared and assessed. By this means a suspect weapon can be positively identified or excluded from an investigation.

[644] Refer also to the section titled 'Gunshot Residue' in this chapter.

The ballistics experts at the National Forensic Science Centre perform many other functions, not just the identification of a firearm. A ballistics expert may be involved in crime scene interpretation and determining the sequence of events at a crime scene.

This is done through:

- the use of chemical screening tests for lead or copper projectiles;
- calculating trajectories by means of the relative locations of areas of gunshot damage and/or the appearance of areas of gunshot damage;
- calculating the relative position of offenders and victims, by blood splatter interpretation, including blood splatter on the clothing of an offender and location of cartridge cases; and
- determining the type of weapon used by identifying cartridge cases or projectiles from the appearance of wounds or property damage.

[7.8.2] FUNCTION TESTING OF A FIREARM

Allegations are frequently made about the functioning or safety aspects of a firearm involved in a shooting offence.

It may be suggested that:

- the firearm discharged when dropped or struck; or
- the components of the firearm may have malfunctioned.

A firearms examiner can perform tests on the firearm in order to determine whether it is prone to fire without operating the trigger.

Extensive test firing may be conducted to establish the frequency and nature of any malfunction.

[7.8.3] RANGE DETERMINATION

When a firearm is discharged, unburnt propellant powder, primer particles and soot emerge from the barrel along with the projectile.

Due to the small size of the individual particles they have a relatively short range (between 30 centimetres and 3 metres).

As a result, their presence in the vicinity of a wound or other gunshot damage may be used to determine the range from which the shot was fired.

In making this determination a firearms examiner will fire the suspect firearm against targets from varying ranges.

These range determinations are essential in cases where the range is a critical factor, such as when a shot is alleged to have been fired in the course of a struggle.

[8.0] FINGERPRINTS[645]

[8.1] INTRODUCTION

Fingerprint evidence can be of prime importance to an investigating officer.

Its ability to positively identify people who have come into contact with:

- surfaces at a crime scene; or
- objects connected to the crime scene

is widely acknowledged.

Fingerprints should be taken for comparison purposes.

[8.2] STATUTORY PROVISION

Section 21 of the *Arrest Act* (Ch. 339) enables a police officer to take the fingerprints and palm prints of any person on a charge of committing an offence.

[645] Refer also to the section titled 'Fingerprint Evidence' in the chapter titled 'Identification Evidence'.

FORENSIC EVIDENCE

[8.3] GENERAL PRINCIPLES

The evidence of fingerprints or palm prints alone is sufficient evidence of identity to support a conviction, subject to:

- their location; and
- the circumstances of the case.[646]

The fact of the individuality of the corrugations of the skin on the fingers of the human hand is recognised as to require very little, if any, evidence of it.[647]

A fingerprint is, therefore, in reality an unforgeable signature.[648]

A Court may take 'judicial notice[649]' that no two people have identical fingerprints.[650]

If there are fewer than eight similar ridge characteristics, it is highly unlikely that a Court will exercise its discretion to admit such evidence and, save in wholly exceptional circumstances, the prosecution should not seek to adduce such evidence.

If there are eight or more similar ridge characteristics, a Court may exercise its discretion in favour of admitting the evidence.

How the discretion is exercised will depend on all the circumstances of the case, including in particular:

- the expertise of the fingerprint expert;
- the experience of the fingerprint expert;

---

[646] See *R v Koito-Gaocatal* [1967–1968] PNGLR 217, [1967] PGSC 26; *The State v Jack Kumul Ure Kore* (1999) N1856 and *The State v Jupui Kapera* (1986) N567.

See also: *Blacker v R* (1910) 10 CLR 604; *R v Castleton* (1910) 3 Cr App R 74 and *R v Court* (1960) 44 Cr App R 242.

[647] See *Parker v R* (1912) 14 CLR 681.

[648] See *Parker v R* (1912) 14 CLR 681.

[649] Refer also the section titled 'Judicial Notice' in the chapter titled 'Court Procedure' in the text titled 'Injia on Criminal Practice and Procedure in Papua New Guinea and the Pacific'.

[650] See *The State v Jupui Kapera* (1986) N567.

- the number of similar ridge characteristics;
- whether there are dissimilar characteristics;
- the size of the print relied on, in that the same number of similar ridge characteristics may be more compelling in a fingerprint of print than in an entire print; and
- the quality and clarity of the print on the item relied on, which may involve, for example, consideration of possible injury to the person who left the print, as well as factors such as smearing or contamination.[651]

[9.0] MECHANICAL EXAMINATION

In cases of 'Dangerous Driving' and 'Driving Without Due Care And Attention' arrangements should be made to have the vehicle driven by the offender mechanically examined for defects.[652]

[10.0] PHOTOGRAPHIC EVIDENCE

Photographs are the best means of providing a description of a crime scene to a Court.

It does not matter who takes a photograph.

The issue of admissibility is:

> whether the witness who is seeking to tender the photograph as an exhibit is able to give evidence as to what the photograph depicts.

---

[651] See *R v Koito-Gaocatal* [1967–1968] PNGLR 217, [1967] PGSC 26.

See also: *R v Buckley* (1999) 163 JP 561.

[652] As regards the law in relation to the offences of 'Dangerous Driving' and 'Driving Without Due Care And Attention', refer to the chapter titled 'Traffic Offences' in the text titled 'Injia on Criminal Offences in Papua New Guinea and the Pacific'.

FORENSIC EVIDENCE

[11.0] HANDWRITING EVIDENCE[653]

[11.1] STATUTORY PROVISION

Section 31 of the *Evidence Act* (Ch. 48) states:

> 'A comparison of a disputed hand-writing with a sample of hand-writng proved, to the satisfaction of the court, to be genuine may be made by witnesses, and the hand-writings and the testimony of the witnesses respecting them may be submitted to the court as evidence of the genuineness or otherwise of the hand-writing in dispute'.

[11.2] GENERAL PRINCIPLES[654]

The issue whether an accused person is the author of a particular document can be proved by:

- an admission by the accused person;
- a witness who observed the accused person write the document[655];
- the evidence of a witness who had regularly corresponded with the accused person and who is able to recognise the handwriting of the accused person to the satisfaction of the Court[656]; or
- the opinion evidence of a handwriting expert[657].

---

[653] Refer also to the section titled 'Handwriting Evidence' in the chapter titled 'Identification Evidence'.

[654] See also: *R v Smith (Hereford) (a)* (1909) 3 Cr App R 87 at 90.

[655] See *R v O'Brien* (1912) 7 Cr App R 29 and *R v McCartney and Hansen* (1928) 20 Cr App R 179.

[656] See *R v O'Brien* (1912) 7 Cr App R 29.

[657] See *R v Rickard* (1918) 13 Cr App R 140; *R v Tilley and Tilley* (1961) 45 Cr App R 360 at 364 and *R v Smith* (1968) 52 Cr App R 648, [1968] Crim LR 674.

Refer also to the chapter titled 'Opinion Evidence'.

FORENSIC EVIDENCE

The Court must be satisfied 'beyond reasonable doubt[658]' that the disputed writing is genuine.[659]

A document examiner at the National Forensic Science Centre is competent to:

- make a determination as to whether a document is forged; and

- make a determination as to who is the author of a particular document, provided a suitable comparative document is provided.

Although expert evidence is not essential for a Court to come to a conclusion on a comparison of disputed handwriting, a Court must warn itself of the dangers involved in proceeding without expert testimony.[660]

A photocopy of a disputed writing may be used for the purpose of comparison, if there is evidence that the original has been lost.[661]

[12.0] CANNABIS IDENTIFICATION

[12.1] INTRODUCTION[662]

In general cannabis and marijuana refer to the same thing.[663] The substance taken out of a cannabis plant is a drug and a part of a cannabis plant in its natural state is also a dangerous drug. Marijuana is just another name for cannabis.[664]

---

[658] Refer also to the chapter titled 'Proof Of Issues' in the text titled 'Injia on Criminal Practice and Procedure in Papua New Guinea and the Pacific'.

[659] See *R v Ewing* [1983] QB 1039, (1983) 77 Cr App R 47.

[660] See *The State v Baine* [1990] 1 PNGLR 1 and *R v Magalu* [1974] PNGLR 188, [1974] PGSC 21.

See also: *R v Derrick* (1910) 5 Cr App R 162.

See however: *R v O'Sullivan* (1969) 53 Cr App R 274 and *R v Tilley and Tilley* (1961) 45 Cr App R 360.

[661] See *Lockheed Arabia v Owen* [1993] 3 WLR 468, (1993) 3 All ER 641, [1993] QB 806.

[662] As regards the law in relation to 'Drug Offences', refer also to the chapter titled 'Drug Offences' in the text titled 'Injia on Criminal Offences in Papua New Guinea and the Pacific'.

[663] See *Mickey Wassey v The Police* (2005) N2922, [2005] PGNC 70.

[664] See *Angel Anis v Jayjay Waiyo* (1990) N18.

FORENSIC EVIDENCE

A marijuana plant is in fact a plant of the genus cannabis from the flowers and leaves of which is derived the hallucinogenic drug variously known as Indian Hemp, hashish, bhang, ganga, charas, churrus, marijuana or pot. It is usually prepared in the form of cigarettes, known as 'reefers'. This narcotic is a dangerous drug.[665]

[12.2] PROOF

[12.2.1] INTRODUCTION

There is no provision in the *Dangerous Drugs Act* (Ch. 228) that permits the tendering of a certificate.

The prosecution may either:

- rely on an admission by the accused person;
- rely on a Formal Admission[666];
- call the analyst to give evidence[667];
- rely on the tendering of an affidavit[668] subject to the provisions of sections 34 ['Evidence by Affidavit'] and 35 ['Affidavit Evidence on Notice'] cof the *Evidence Act* (Ch. 48) with the consent of the accused person and the Court; or
- rely on the opinion evidence of a suitably qualified police officer by virtue of his or her personal and professional experience in dealing with the alleged dangerous drug.

---

[665] See *Richard Cheong v Vincent Nemil* [1981] PNGLR 472 at 473.

[666] Refer also to the section titled 'Formal Admission' in the chapter titled 'Court Procedure' in the text titled 'Injia on Criminal Practice and Procedure in Papua New Guinea and the Pacific'.

[667] In that regard contact the Forensic Biology Section, National Forensic Science Centre at Port Moresby or the Papua New Guinea Forest Research Institute at Lae.

[668] Refer also to the Appendix.

[12.2.2] AFFIDAVIT

An affidavit from an analyst must state:

- his or her qualifications for identifying cannabis and its derivatives;
- the recognised method or methods used for such identification;
- the steps taken on the particular occasion; and
- the results, some conclusion as to what it was in the material subjected to analysis which constituted the cannabis and in particular the quantity of cannabis identified should have been clearly stated.[669]

However, for an affidavit from an analyst to be admissible the prosecution must prove continuity of the dangerous drug from:

- the position where it was located;

to

- when it was analysed.

The prosecution must therefore be able to prove which person/s had possession of the dangerous drug between those locations.

[12.2.3] OPINION EVIDENCE

In order for the prosecution to rely on the opinion evidence[670] of a police officer as to the identification of cannabis the following questions need to be addressed in their statement:

What do you believe it is?

Professional Experience

How long have you been a police officer?

Have you previously arrested accused persons in relation to cases involving marijuana under section 3 of the *Dangerous Drugs Act* (Ch. 228) in which the accused persons were convicted?

---

[669] See *Maxwell Arthur Schliebs v H Singh* [1981] PNGLR 264 at 371.

[670] Refer also to the section titled 'Lay Person' in the chapter titled 'Opinion Evidence'.

How many cases were there approximately?

Is what that is alleged to be in the possession of the accused person the same leafy material as those cases involving marijuana which those accused persons were convicted?

Are there any similar characteristics between the marijuana in those cases and the case involving this accused person?

What are those characteristics?

Personal Experience

Have you observed any person consume marijuana in your presence in your personal life?

Why do you believe that it was marijuana?

How was it consumed?

Were you able to observe what was being consumed?

Are there any similar characteristics between the marijuana consumed in those circumstances and the case involving this accused person?

What are those characteristics?

HEARSAY EVIDENCE

[1.0] INTRODUCTION

One of the most far-reaching exclusionary rules of evidence is the rule against hearsay, or the 'hearsay rule' as it is often called.[671]

As a general matter, it excludes evidence which is not given orally by a witness at trial and based on that witness's own knowledge of events.[672]

Hearsay evidence is an exception to the general rule that all evidence that is 'relevant[673]' is admissible.[674]

The origins of the need to exclude hearsay may be traced back to the early 13th century.[675]

The common law has long insisted that the person with immediate knowledge of a fact in issue should testify to that fact under oath in the presence of the Court, and be subject to cross-examination by the opposing party.[676]

It is a settled principle that hearsay evidence is inadmissible[677], unless it is an exception to the hearsay rule.

However, as Lord Reid said in *Myers v DPP*[678]:

> 'By the nineteenth century many exceptions had become well established; but again in most cases we do not know how or when the exceptions came to be recognised'.

---

[671] See New Zealand Law Commission, 1989, 'Hearsay Evidence An Options Paper', Preliminary Paper 10, page 1.

[672] See New Zealand Law Commission, 1989, 'Hearsay Evidence An Options Paper', Preliminary Paper 10, page 2 and New Zealand Law Commission, 1991, 'Hearsay Law: Hearsay – A Discussion Paper', Preliminary Paper 15.

[673] Refer also to the chapter titled 'Relevance'.

[674] See Hearsay in Criminal Proceedings [2009] HKLRC 1 at section 1.1.

[675] See Law Reform Commission of Ireland, 2010, 'Hearsay in Civil and Criminal Cases', Introduction.

[676] See New Zealand Law Commission, 1989, 'Hearsay Evidence An Options Paper', Preliminary Paper 10, page 2.

[677] See *Ishmael Pavo Wrahuhan v The State* (2007) SC895, [2007] PGSC 27.

[678] [1965] AC 1001 at 1020.

HEARSAY EVIDENCE

As stated by Jeffreys LCJ in *R v Braddon and Speke*[679]:

> 'If she were here herself, if she did say it, and would not swear to it, we could not hear her; how then can her saying be evidence before us?'

However, it is difficult to make any general statement about the law of hearsay which is entirely accurate.[680]

Hearsay evidence is any statement of fact other than one made, of his or her own knowledge, by a witness in the course of oral testimony.[681]

Hearsay evidence may also be described as:

- an oral or written assertion[682], express or implied[683], by a person other than the person who made it, as evidence of any fact or opinion so asserted, expressed or implied[684]; or

- testimony given by a witness concerning words spoken, statements made or documents generated by a person who is not produced in court as a witness is inadmissible if the testimony is presented to prove the truth of the facts which the witness asserts[685].

---

[679] (1684) 9 State Trials 1127 at 1189.

[680] See *Myers v DPP* [1965] AC 1001, per Lord Reid at 1019, (1964) 48 Cr App R 348, [1964] 2 All ER 881, [1964] 3 WLR 145 and *R v Starr* [2000] 2 SCR 144, 190 DLR (4th) 591, [2000] 11 WWR 1, 147 CCC (3d) 449, 36 CR (5th) 1, 148 ManR (2d) 161.

See also: *Mawaz Khan v R* [1967] AC 454 at 459, [1967] 1 All ER 80 at 81.

[681] See *R v Horncastle and others* [2009] UKSC 14.

[682] See Law Reform Commission of Ireland, 2010, 'Hearsay in Civil and Criminal Cases', Chapter 2.

There are however some exceptions in respect to documentary evidence.

[683] An implied assertion is a statement by conduct that is not tendered to prove the truth of its contents but is taken to allow an inference to be drawn from it, see Law Reform Commission of Ireland, 2010, 'Hearsay in Civil and Criminal Cases', Chapter 2.

As regards the admissibility of implied assertions, see *R v Kearley* [1992] 2 AC 228; *Pollitt v R* (1992) 174 CLR 558; *Walton v R* (1989) 166 CLR 283 and *Lord Advocate's Reference (No. 1 of 1992)* [1992] SCCR 724 at 741.

[684] See *R v Kearley* [1992] 2 AC 228 at 254 and 259 and *R v Sharp* [1988] 1 WLR 7 at 11.

[685] See *Cullen v Clarke* [1963] IR 368 at 378.

HEARSAY EVIDENCE

The hearsay rule applies only to out-of-court statements tendered for the purpose of directly proving that the facts are as asserted in the statement.[686]

The hearsay rule has little to do with common sense.[687]

As stated by Lord Griffiths in *R v Kearley*[688]:

> '... most layman if told that the criminal law of evidence forbade them even to consider such evidence as we are debating in this appeal would reply "Then the law is an ass".'

The hearsay rule does not forbid the proof of what somebody said out of Court.[689]

What it does forbid is the proof of a fact by telling what somebody said about that fact out of Court.[690]

It is duty of a Court to ensure that hearsay evidence is not admitted, irrespective of whether there is any objection as to its admissibility[691], including during the course of a committal proceedings[692], unless it is covered by an exception.

Hearsay evidence is inadmissible whether it assists the prosecution or defence.[693]

---

686 See *Walton v R* (1989) 166 CLR 283; *Wong Wai-man and others v HKSAR* (2000) 3 HKCFAR 322 at 327 and *HKSAR v Or Suen Hong* [2001] 2 HKLRD 669 at 678.

687 As Diplock LJ pointed it out in *Jones v Metcalfe* [1967] 1 WLR 1286.

688 [1992] 2 All ER 344, (1992) 95 Cr App R 88, [1992] 2 WLR 656, [1992] Crim LR 797, [1992] AC 228 at 236-237.

689 See *Kamleh v R* (2005) 79 ALJR 541 at 544.

690 See *Kamleh v R* (2005) 79 ALJR 541 at 544.

691 See *Yandasingi v The State* [1995] PNGLR 268, [1995] PGSC 22.

692 See *R v Burusep* [1963] PNGLR 181, [1963] PGSC 3.

693 See *R v Horncastle and others* [2009] UKSC 14.

HEARSAY EVIDENCE

The reasons for the exclusion of hearsay evidence are as follows:

- it is not the best evidence[694];

- the absence of an oath or solemn declaration or affirmation when the statement was made[695];

- the inability of the Court to assess the demeanour, and therefore the credibility of the person who made the statement when the statement was made[696];

- the inability of the Court to ensure that the witness actually said what is claimed[697]; and

- the lack of contemporaneous cross-examination by the opponent.[698]

  Confrontation and the opportunity for cross-examination is of central significance to the common law adversarial system of trial.[699]

Therefore, the fundamental issue in respect to hearsay evidence is:

Its reliability.[700]

---

[694] See *Teper v R* [1952] AC 480, per Lord Normand at 486.

Refer also to the chapter titled 'Best Evidence and Secondary Evidence Rules'.

[695] See *R v B (KG)* [1993] 1 SCR 740, per Lamer CJ at 764; *Teper v R* [1952] AC 480, per Lord Normand at 486 and *R v Starr* [2000] 2 SCR 144, 190 DLR (4th) 591, [2000] 11 WWR 1, 147 CCC (3d) 449, 36 CR (5th) 1, 148 ManR (2d) 161.

[696] See *R v B (KG)* [1993] 1 SCR 740, per Lamer CJ at 764 and *Teper v R* [1952] AC 480 at 488.

[697] See *R v B (KG)* [1993] 1 SCR 740, per Lamer CJ at 764 and *Teper v R* [1952] AC 480 at 488.

[698] See *R v B (KG)* [1993] 1 SCR 740, per Lamer CJ at 764; *Teper v R* [1952] AC 480 at 488; *R v Starr* [2000] 2 SCR 144, 190 DLR (4th) 591, [2000] 11 WWR 1, 147 CCC (3d) 449, 36 CR (5th) 1, 148 ManR (2d) 161 and *R v Blastland* [1986] AC 41, per Lord Bridge at 53-54.

See also: section 37(4)(f) of the *Constitution of the Independent State of Papua New Guinea* ['Protection of the Law'].

Refer also to the section titled 'Cross-examination' in the chapter titled 'Examination Of Witnesses' in the text titled 'Injia on Criminal Practice and Procedure in Papua New Guinea and the Pacific'.

[699] See *Lee v R* (1998) 72 ALJR 1484.

[700] See *R v Horncastle and others* [2009] UKSC 14; *R v Blastland* [1986] AC 41, per Lord Bridge at 53-54 and *Pollitt v R* (1992) 174 CLR 558 at 620.

HEARSAY EVIDENCE

The admissibility of hearsay evidence should be treated with caution if it relates to an assertion that may have been:

- invented; or
- fabricated.[701]

However, the hearsay rule should not be applied inflexibly.[702]

When considering the dangers for which the rule seeks to prevent, a Court should decide whether to admit the evidence based on its:

- reliability[703] which involves an inquiry into the circumstances in which the hearsay statement was made.[704]

  The hearsay evidence must have sufficient apparent reliability, either inherent or circumstantial, or both, to justify its admission in spite of the dangers against which the hearsay rule is designed to guard. The expression 'apparent reliability' is used to signify that the Court is the gatekeeper and decides whether to admit the evidence or not. If the evidence is admitted, the Court, as trier of fact, must decide how reliable the evidence is and therefore what 'weight[705]' should be placed on it. If a sufficient threshold level of apparent reliability is not reached, the hearsay evidence should not be admitted. The inability of a primary witness to give evidence is not good reason to admit unreliable hearsay evidence[706];

---

[701] See Law Reform Commission of Ireland, 2010, 'Hearsay in Civil and Criminal Cases', Chapter 5.

[702] See *Walton v R* (1989) 63 ALJR 226, per Mason CJ at 229 and *Daylight* (1989) 41 A Crim R 354.

[703] See *R v Horncastle and others* [2009] UKSC 14; *R v Blastland* [1986] AC 41, per Lord Bridge at 53-54; *Pollitt v R* (1992) 174 CLR 558 at 620; *Walton v R* (1989) 63 ALJR 226, per Mason CJ at 229; *Daylight* (1989) 41 A Crim R 354; *R v Khan* [1990] 2 SCR 531; *R v Smith* [1992] 2 SCR 915, (1992) 15 CR (4th) 133; *R v O'Brien* [1978] 1 SCR 591; *R v Baker* [1989] 1 NZLR 738; *R v Bain* [1996] 1 NZLR 129 and *R v Khelawon* [2006] 2 SCR 787, 2006 SCC 57.

[704] See New Zealand Law Commission, 1999, 'Evidence. Volume 1: Reform of the Law and Evidence. Volume 2: Evidence Code and Commentary', Report 55, page 14.

[705] Refer also to the chapter titled 'Weight'.

[706] See *R v Manase* [2001] 2 NZLR 197.

- necessity [707] which involves an inquiry into the availability of the maker of the statement[708];

- relevance.[709]

  This is not strictly a requirement directed to this exception to the hearsay rule. Rather it is an affirmation and a reminder of the overriding criterion for the admissibility of all and any evidence. It is a self-contained issue. The evidence in question either has sufficient relevance or it does not. The same test applies as would have applied to the primary (ie non-hearsay) evidence[710];

- inability.

  This requirement will be satisfied when the primary witness is unable for some reason to be called to give the primary evidence. If the primary witness is personally able to give that evidence, it will seldom, if ever, be appropriate to admit hearsay evidence simply because the witness would prefer not to face the ordeal of giving evidence or would find it difficult to do so. To adopt that approach would be to tilt the balance too far against the accused or opposite party who is thereby deprived of the ability to cross-examine[711]; and

- probative value[712].

---

[707] See *R v Khan* [1990] 2 SCR 531; *R v Smith* [1992] 2 SCR 915, (1992) 15 CR (4th) 133; *R v O'Brien* [1978] 1 SCR 591; *R v Baker* [1989] 1 NZLR 738; *R v Bain* [1996] 1 NZLR 129 and *R v Khelawon* [2006] 2 SCR 787, 2006 SCC 57.

[708] See New Zealand Law Commission, 1999, 'Evidence. Volume 1: Reform of the Law and Evidence. Volume 2: Evidence Code and Commentary', Report 55, page 14.

[709] Refer also to the chapter titled 'Relevance'.

[710] See *R v Manase* [2001] 2 NZLR 197.

[711] See *R v Manase* [2001] 2 NZLR 197.

[712] See *Walton v R* (1989) 63 ALJR 226, per Mason CJ at 229 and *Daylight* (1989) 41 A Crim R 354.

Refer also to the chapter titled 'Weight'.

However, the evidence of a statement made to a witness by a person who is not called to give evidence is not hearsay, and is admissible, when it is led:

> Not to establish the truth of the statement, but only to establish the fact that it was made.[713]

Irrespective, the 'weight[714]' to be given to such evidence is less easy to appraise than that of evidence delivered by a witness face-to-face, and subject to testing by cross-examination[715].[716]

[2.0] TEST TO BE APPLIED

The test that should be applied when considering the admissibility of any conversation is as follows:

> 'In determining whether evidence is "hearsay", it is necessary to determine the purpose for which the evidence is sought to be admitted.[717]
>
> If the prosecution or defence relies on the evidence as being the truth of what is contained in the statement, it is "hearsay" if the witness who gives the evidence in the witness box does not have direct knowledge of the evidence contained in the statement'.

Direct knowledge refers to the reception of evidence through the witness's own senses. For example, 'A' observes a murder being conducted. 'A' then goes and tells 'B' what happened. Any account given by 'B' to a Court about the conversation would be 'hearsay' because 'B' is unable to be cross-examined as to the truth of the conversation, ie., what actually occurred.

---

713 See *The State v Kapil Omba* (2010) N4130; *The State v John Wanjil* [1997] PNGLR 64 and *Jack Gopave v Francis Kugame* (2003) N2482.

See also: *Subramanian v Public Prosecutor* [1956] 1 WLR 965 at 970; *Guy and Finger v R* [1978] WAR 125; *R v Murphy* [1985] 4 NSWLR 42 at 61; *HKSAR v Wong Wai-man* [2000] 1 HKLRD 473 at 479 and *R v Baltzer* (1974) CCC (2d) 118.

714 See also the chapter titled 'Weight'.

715 Refer also to the section titled 'Cross-examination' in the chapter titled 'Examination Of Witnesses' in the text titled 'Injia on Criminal Practice and Procedure in Papua New Guinea and the Pacific'.

716 See *R v Horncastle and others* [2009] UKSC 14.

717 See also: *Oei Hengky Wiryo v HKSAR* [2007] 1 HKLRD 568, per McHugh NPJ at 584.

Therefore, a fundamental feature in determining the admissibility of hearsay evidence is to ask the following question:

> What is the 'purpose' for which the conversation is adduced?[718]

The hearsay rule only applies to out-of-court statements tendered for the 'purpose' of:

> Directly proving that the facts are as asserted in the statement.[719]

If the original evidence was given not to prove the truth of what another had said, but to show why the witness had acted in the way he or she did then it is not hearsay.[720]

In order for a sketch plan to be admissible a witness seeking to tender it must have direct knowledge of all the information contained in the plan.[721]

Hearsay evidence that is favourable to the defence does not render it admissible.[722]

[3.0] EXCEPTIONS TO THE HEARSAY RULE

[3.1] INTRODUCTION

There are exceptions to the rule against hearsay whereby the witness who gives the evidence may not be able to be cross-examined as to the truthfulness of such evidence.

Such exceptions are in two categories:

- common law exceptions[723]; and
- statutory exceptions.

---

[718] See *R v Starr* [2000] 2 SCR 144, 190 DLR (4th) 591, [2000] 11 WWR 1, 147 CCC (3d) 449, 36 CR (5th) 1, 148 ManR (2d) 161.

[719] See *Wong Wai-man and others v HKSAR* (2000) 3 HKCFAR 322 at 327; *HKSAR v Or Suen Hong* [2001] 2 HKLRD 669 at 678 and *Walton v R* (1989) 166 CLR 283, per Mason CJ at 288.

[720] See *Salafilamo v R* [1995] SBCA 8.

[721] See *Hiki v R* (Solomon Islands Criminal Appeal Case No. 9 of 1979).

[722] See *Leung Foon v The Republic of Nauru* [1969-1982] NLR 26, [1974] NRSC 6.

[723] In *R v Smith* (1992) 75 CCC (3d) 257 the Supreme Court of Canada at 267 reaffirmed its previous proposition that the Canadian courts would not follow the traditional practice of excluding hearsay evidence, unless it falls within one of the stated exceptions.

[3.2] COMMON LAW EXCEPTIONS

[3.2.1] CONFESSIONAL EVIDENCE

What an accused person admits or confesses[724] to be true may reasonably be presumed to be.[725]

A statement of fact which suggests an inference as to any fact that is relevant and which is adverse to the interests of the person responsible for the statement, referred to an 'admission against interest', is generally admissible against that person although it is 'hearsay' and is usually described as an 'admission'.[726]

[3.2.2] FRESH COMPLAINT[727]

A 'fresh complaint', also referred to as 'recent complaint', is admissible to prove:

- that the behaviour of a prosecutrix/complainant was consistent with his or her story; and
- that he or she did not consent.[728]

Such a complaint does not however prove the truth of his or her story.[729]

---

[724] By a strict application of the law there is a difference between an admission and a confession, see Law Reform Commission of Ireland, 2010, 'Hearsay in Civil and Criminal Cases', Chapter 3.

Refer also to the chapter titled 'Confessional Evidence'.

[725] See *Slatterie v Pooley* (1840) 151 ER 579, per Viscount Parke at 581.

See also:
- *Bannon v R* (1995) 132 ALR 87; *Pollit v R* (1992) 174 CLR 558, [1992] HCA 35; *Osifelo v R* [1995] SBCA 3 and *Mule v R* (2005) 79 ALJR 1573, [2005] HCA 49; and
- New Zealand Law Commission, 1992, 'Criminal Evidence: Police Questioning', Preliminary Paper 21, page 74.

[726] See *Commissioners of Customs and Excise v Harz* [1967] 1 AC 760, per Thesiger J at 786.

[727] Refer also to the section titled 'Suspect Witness' in the chapter titled 'Witnesses' in the text titled 'Injia on Criminal Practice and Procedure in Papua New Guinea and the Pacific'.

[728] See *R v Lillyman* [1896] 2 QB 167, [1895-9] All ER 586.

[729] See *R v Lillyman* [1896] 2 QB 167, [1895-9] All ER 586.

The doctrine of 'recent complaint' is an exception to the rule against prior consistent statements and the rule against hearsay.[730]

The 'purpose' of such a complaint is:

- not to prove the truth of the complaint, ie., that the accused person committed the offence; but

- to corroborate the evidence of the complainant that he or she was the victim of a sexual offence[731].[732]

[3.2.3] MEDICAL EVIDENCE[733]

A medical practitioner[734], health extension officer or nurse is able to give evidence of what a complainant said during the course of an examination.

---

[730] See *Suresh v R* (1998) 72 ALJR 769, [1998] HCA 23 and *R v Bertrand* (2008) 20 VR 222, [2008] VSCA 182.

[731] Refer also to the section titled 'Sexual Offence Victim' in the chapter titled 'Victims Of Crime' in the text titled 'Injia on Investigatory Practice in Papua New Guinea and the Pacific'.

[732] See *The State v Michael Rave, James Maien and Phillip Baule* [1983] PNGLR 85; *The State v Stuart Hamilton Merriam* [1994] PNGLR 104 and *Peter Townsend v George Oika* [1981] PNGLR 12.

See also: *Jones v R* (1997) 143 ALR 52; *Suresh v R* (1996) 16 WAR 23 and *R v Robertson; ex parte Attorney-General* [1991] 1 Qd R 262, (1990) 45 A Crim R 408.

Refer also to the section titled 'Suspect Witness' in the chapter titled 'Witnesses' in the text titled 'Injia on Criminal Practice and Procedure in Papua New Guinea and the Pacific'.

[733] See also: *Gordon v R* (1982) 41 ALR 64; *R v Thomson* [1912] 3 KB 19, (1912) 7 Cr App R 276; *R v Blastland* [1986] AC 41, [1985] 3 WLR 345, [1985] 2 All ER 1095, (1985) 81 Cr App R 266, [1985] Crim LR 727; *R v Bradshaw* (1986) 82 Cr App R 79; *R v Schafferius* [1977] Qd R 213 and *R v Tonkin and Montgomery* [1975] Qd R 1.

Refer also to the chapter titled 'Medical Evidence'.

[734] See *Ramsay v Watson* (1961) 108 CLR 642 at 649, [1961] HCA 65.

See also: *Mason* (1911) 7 Cr App R 67 and *R v Middleton* (2000) 114 A Crim R 258, [2000] WASCA 213.

Refer also to:
- the section titled 'Documentary Medical Evidence' in the chapter titled 'Documentary Evidence'; and
- the section titled 'Common Law Exceptions' in the chapter titled 'Hearsay Evidence'.

However, the 'purpose' of such a conversation is:

- not to prove the truth of what the complainant said happened; but
- to indicate the reason why the medical practitioner, health extension officer or nurse examined particular parts of the complainant's body.

[3.2.4] TELEPHONE CONVERSATION[735]

A simplistic example would be if a deceased speaks to an accused person on a telephone. The deceased then tells another person at that time that he or she is going to a location as arranged by the accused person. That witness who was with the deceased can give evidence that the deceased spoke to the accused person on the telephone immediately prior to leaving for a location as arranged by the accused person.

The 'purpose' of that evidence would be to prove:

> That the deceased spoke to the accused person and that the deceased left to see the accused person.[736]

The intention of the deceased was relevant at that time because it might be inferred that the deceased acted in accordance with that intention.[737]

---

[735] See also: *Ratten v R* [1972] AC 378, [1971] 3 All ER 801, (1971) 56 Cr App R 18, [1972] ALR 294.

[736] See *Pollit v R* (1992) 174 CLR 572, [1992] HCA 35.

[737] See *Walton v R* (1989) 166 CLR 283, per Wilson, Dawson and Toohey JJ at 300, (1989) 84 ALR 59, (1989) 63 ALJR 226, (1989) 38 A Crim R 276.

[3.2.5] CO-CONSPIRATORS RULE[738]

The acts and/or declarations of a co-conspirator or a party to an offence[739] may be admitted for the 'purpose' of:

> Establishing the truth of an express or implied assertion contained in them against each and every co-conspirator or party to the offence.[740]

However, there are the following provisos:

- such acts and/or declarations were committed in the furtherance of:
  - the conspiracy[741]; or
  - the joint offence; and
- there is independent evidence that links the co-conspirator or party to the offence, to:
  - the conspiracy; or
  - joint offence.[742]

---

[738] See also: *R v Starr* [2000] 2 SCR 144, 190 DLR (4th) 591, [2000] 11 WWR 1, 147 CCC (3d) 449, 36 CR (5th) 1, 148 ManR (2d) 161; *R v Mapara* 2005 SCC 23; *R v Terrence Walters, R v George Tovey, R v David Albert Padfield, R v Colin John Padfield* [1979] 69 Cr App R 115 and *R v Governor of Pentonville Prison; ex parte Osman* [1990] 1 WLR 277 at 316.

As regards the law in relation to the offence of 'Conspiracy', refer to the chapter titled 'Parties To Offences' in the text titled 'Injia on Criminal Offences in Papua New Guinea and the Pacific'.

Refer also to the subsection titled 'Joint Trials' in the section titled 'Joinder Of Charges' in the chapter titled 'Charges' in the text titled 'Injia on Criminal Practice and Procedure in Papua New Guinea and the Pacific'.

[739] Refer also to the chapter titled 'Parties To Offences' in the text titled 'Injia on Criminal Offences in Papua New Guinea and the Pacific'.

[740] Referred to as the 'co-conspirator's rule', see *R v Alick Au* [1993] 2 HKC 219 at 225; *HKSAR v Booth* [1998] 1 HKLRD 890 and *HKSAR v Cheng Sui-wa* [2003] 4 HKC 571.

[741] See *R v Chang* (2003) 173 CCC (3d) 397.

[742] See *R v Humphries* [1982] 1 NZLR 353; *R v Buckton* [1985] 2 NZLR 257; *R v Uea* (1989) 4 CRNZ 703; *R v Crowe* [1996] 3 NZLR 415; *R v Tauhore* [1996] 2 NZLR 641 and *R v Harris* [1998] 1 NZLR 405.

Usually the question of admissibility will relate to:

- directions;
- instructions;
- arrangements; or
- utterances accompanying acts.[743]

In order for an act or declaration to be admissible to prove the participation of another the Court must be satisfied that the act or declaration:

- was made by a conspirator;
- that it was reasonably open to the interpretation that it was made in furtherance of the alleged agreement; and
- that there is some further evidence beyond the document or utterance itself to prove that the other was a party to the agreement.[744]

[743] See *Tripodi v R* (1961) 104 CLR 1 at 7; *R v John Gray, R v Willam James Liggins, R v Mark Riding, R v Catherine Mary Rolands* [1995] 2 Cr App R 100 and *R v Brian Jones, R v Roy Williams, R v Edward Barham* [1997] 2 Cr App R 119 at 127-128.

[744] See *R v Derrick Davenport, R v Vincenzo Pirano* [1996] 1 Cr App R 221; *R v Brian Jones, R v Roy Williams, R v Edward Barham* [1997] 2 Cr App R 119 at 127-128 and *R v Platten* [2006] EWCA Crim 140.

[3.2.6] RES GESTAE[745]

The phrase 'res gestae' (literally, 'things done[746]') refers to:

> The inclusionary exception by which either the prosecution or defence are allowed to admit evidence which consists of, among other things, everything that is:
>
> - said; and
> - done
>
> in the course of an incident or transaction that is the subject of a trial.[747]

The 'res gestae exception' was justified at common law on the basis that all of the circumstances surrounding a relevant event should be admissible to give a true picture of what occurred.[748]

However, such evidence must be so closely and inextricably mixed up with the history of the guilty act itself so:

- as to form part of one chain of relevant circumstances; and
- could not be excluded in the presentment of the case,

otherwise the evidence would thereby be rendered unintelligible.[749]

---

[745] See also: *The State v Uraru Heneha and Warupi Aihi* (1998) N1686; *Pollit v R* (1992) 174 CLR 572, [1992] HCA 35; *Mills and others v R* [1995] 3 All ER 865; *Harriman v R* (1989) 167 CLR 590, [1989] HCA 50; *R v A* [2000] QCA 520; *R v Benz and another* (1989) 168 CLR 111, (1989) 89 ALR 339, (1989) 64 ALJR 94, (1989) 44 A Crim R 1; *Brown v R* (1913) 17 CLR 570; *R v McIntosh* (1969) 63 QJPR 23; *Ratten v R* [1972] AC 378 at 388-391, [1971] 3 All ER 801, (1971) 56 Cr App R 18, [1972] ALR 294; *R v W* [2003] EWCA Crim 1286; *The People (Attorney General) v Crosbie and Meehan* [1966] IR 490 and *The People (DPP) v Lonergan* [2009] IECCA 52.

[746] See also: New Zealand Law Commission, 2013, 'The 2013 Review of the Evidence Act 2006', Report 127, page 85.

[747] See Law Reform Commission of Ireland, 2010, 'Hearsay in Civil and Criminal Cases', Chapter 3.

[748] See New Zealand Law Commission, 2013, 'The 2013 Review of the Evidence Act 2006', Report 127, page 85.

[749] See *R v Bond* [1906] 2 KB 389 at 400.

HEARSAY EVIDENCE

The 'purpose' for such evidence is:

To throw light on other evidence by reason of its proximity in:

- time;
- place; or
- circumstances.[750]

In order to determine whether to admit such evidence the following principles[751] should apply:

- there must be no possibility of:
    - concoction; or
    - distortion

  when considering the circumstances in which the particular statement was made[752];

- the statement made must be 'sufficiently spontaneous' whilst taking into consideration the time factor and the other circumstances, ie., it must be so closely associated with the event which has excited the statement, that it can be fairly stated that the mind of the declarant was still dominated by the event[753]; and

- the 'weight[754]' to be given to such evidence should be based on the accuracy of the recollection of the statement when taking into consideration the ordinary infallibility of human recollection.

---

[750] See *The State v Wanjil* [1997] PNGLR 64, [1997] PGNC 213.

[751] See *R v Andrews* [1987] AC 281, per Lord Ackner at 300-301, [1987] 1 All ER 513, (1987) 84 Cr App R 382, [1987] 2 WLR 413, [1987] Crim LR 487.

[752] See *The State v Willie Orki Briza* (1976) No. 69.

See also: *R v Accused* (1997) 14 CRNZ 565 at 567.

[753] See *The State v Willie Orki Briza* (1976) No. 69.

See also: *R v Accused* (1997) 14 CRNZ 565 at 567.

[754] Refer also to the chapter titled 'Weight'.

Memories of the witnesses will fade over time.[755]

Memories are not permanently stored as if recorded on tape, unaltered, to be played back some time later as an exact recording of the event.[756]

Common sense and psychological research tells us that memory declines over time.[757]

[3.2.7] EVIDENCE OF POTENTIAL CUSTOMERS[758]

In relation to charges of:

- conducting a common gaming house[759]; and
- selling drugs[760],

the 'purpose' of leading evidence of statements of intending customers is:

To show the existence of and the nature of business or activity carried on at the premises.[761]

---

755 See *South Pacific Marketing (NZ Limited) v Maile* [1987] SILR 81, per Ward CJ at 87.

Refer also to the section titled 'Introduction' in the chapter titled 'Examination Of Witnesses' in the text titled 'Injia on Criminal Practice and Procedure in Papua New Guinea and the Pacific'.

756 See New Zealand Law Commission, 1999, 'Evidence: Total Recall?: The Reliability of Witness Testimony', Miscellaneous Paper 13, page 5.

757 See New Zealand Law Commission, 1999, 'Evidence: Total Recall?: The Reliability of Witness Testimony', Miscellaneous Paper 13, page 17.

758 See also: *Woodhouse v Hall* (1981) 72 Cr App R 39.

759 Refer also to the chapter titled 'Gambling Offences' in the text titled 'Injia on Criminal Offences in Papua New Guinea and the Pacific'.

760 Refer also to the chapter titled 'Drug Offences' in the text titled 'Injia on Criminal Offences in Papua New Guinea and the Pacific'.

761 See *Davidson v Quirke* (1923) 42 NZLR 552; *Lenthall v Mitchell* [1933] SASR 231; *McGregor v Stokes* [1952] VLR 347; *Marshall v Watt, Struthers, and County* [1953] Tas SR 1; *Gorman v Newton; ex parte Newton* [1958] Qd R 169, *Police v Machirus* [1977] 1 NZLR 288 and *R v Firman* (1989) 52 SASR 391.

[3.2.8] OPINION EVIDENCE

A witness called to give the 'opinion evidence' of an expert is entitled to express an opinion based on information that is:

- published; or
- unpublished

and usually in written form, received from other experts. Medical textbooks constitute a prime example. The relevant information must be of a type generally and reasonably relied upon and falling for evaluation within the relevant field of expertise.[762]

[3.2.9] DECLARATIONS IN THE COURSE OF DUTY

Where an oral or written statement was made by a person who was under a duty to do so because of his or her:

- occupation;
- trade;
- business; or
- profession,

the statement is admissible for its truth when the person subsequently dies.[763]

However, such a statement is inadmissible unless:

- the duty is specific; and
- it is a duty to:
  - do a particular act; and

---

[762] See *R v Wan Pui-hay* [1994] 2 HKCLR 47 at 48-49 and *Reid v Kerr* (1974) 9 SASR 367 at 390.

Refer also to the chapter titled 'Opinion Evidence'.

[763] See Cross on Evidence, 5th edition, 1979, Butterworths, page 560.

- record or report it when done.[764]

[3.2.10] DECLARATIONS AGAINST PECUNIARY OR PROPRIETY INTEREST

A statement made by a person of a fact which he or she knew to be against his or her:

- pecuniary interest; or
- proprietary interest

would, upon that person's death, be admissible in criminal proceedings as evidence of that fact.[765]

[3.3] STATUTORY EXCEPTIONS

[3.3.1] DYING DECLARATION[766]

STATUTORY PROVISION

Section 20 of the *Evidence Act* (Ch. 48) ['Dying Declarations'] states:

> 'A statement made orally by a person before his death relating to the circumstances resulting in his death is admissible in any legal proceedings if –
>
> (a) at the time when the person made the statement he believed, or may be reasonably supposed by the court to have believed, that his death was imminent, whether or not –
>
> (i) he entertained at that time any hope of recovery; or
>
> (ii) he thought that legal proceedings might eventuate; and

---

[764] See *R v O'Meally* [1952] VLR 499.

[765] See *R v Rogers* [1994] 158 JP 909.

[766] See also: *The State v Alex Kango* (2006) N3083, [2006] PGNC 115 and *R v Madobi-Modogai* [1963] PNGLR 252.

As regards the law in relation to 'Homicidal Offences', refer to the chapter titled 'Offences Against The Person' in the text titled 'Injia on Criminal Offences in Papua New Guinea and the Pacific'.

(b) at the time when the person made the statement he would have been a competent witness in the legal proceedings[767]; and

(c) the person making the statement could, if he had not died, have given direct oral evidence in the proceedings of the matter in the statement'.

GENERAL PRINCIPLES

The rationale for this exception is that a person aware of his or her imminent death would be most unlikely to fabricate any last words.[768]

The evidence of a deceased person is admitted to prove who committed the offence. Considering that a deceased person obviously cannot be cross-examined as to the truth of his or her 'dying declaration', ie., whether the accused person actually committed the offence and as a consequence killed him or her, such a declaration can be told to a Court by another person who heard it.

The purpose of such a declaration is:

> To prove what the deceased person said was the truth.[769]

It is therefore an exception to the 'hearsay rule'.[770]

For a statement of a declarant/deceased to be a dying declaration, it must meet the criteria set out in section 20 of the *Evidence Act* (Ch. 48) ['Dying Declarations'] as follows:

- at the time when the person made the statement he or she believed, or may be reasonably supposed by the court to have believed, that his or her death was imminent.

---

[767] Refer also to the section titled 'Competency And Compellability' in the chapter titled 'Witnesses' in the text titled 'Injia on Criminal Practice and Procedure in Papua New Guinea and the Pacific'.

[768] See *R v Woodcock* (1789) 1 Leach 500, 168 ER 352, per Eyre EB at 353.

[769] See *Subramanian v Public Prosecutor* [1956] 1 WLR 965.

See also: *Nembhard v R* (1982) 74 Cr App R 144, [1981] 1 WLR 1515, [1982] 1 All ER 183, [1982] Crim LR 41; *R v Howse* (2003) 20 CRNZ 826; *R v Andrews* [1987] AC 281, [1987] 1 All ER 513, (1987) 84 Cr App R 382 and *R v Baker* [1989] 1 NZLR 738.

[770] See *Subramanian v Public Prosecutor* [1956] 1 WLR 965.

See also: *Nembhard v R* (1982) 74 Cr App R 144, [1981] 1 WLR 1515, [1982] 1 All ER 183, [1982] Crim LR 41; *R v Howse* (2003) 20 CRNZ 826 and *R v Baker* [1989] 1 NZLR 738.

It is irrelevant the declarant/deceased entertained at that time:

    - any hope of recovery; or
    - thought that legal proceedings might eventuate;

- at the time when the declarant/deceased made the statement he or she would have been a competent witness in the legal proceedings[771]; and
- the declarant/deceased could, if he or she had not died, have given direct oral evidence in the proceedings of the matter in the statement.[772]

The religious beliefs of the declarant/deceased are irrelevant.[773]

[3.3.2] DEPOSITIONS

A statement made by a witness who is:

- dead[774];
- insane[775];
- so ill as not to be able to travel;
- kept out of the way by means of the procurement of the accused person or on his or her behalf; or

771 Refer also to the section titled 'Competency And Compellability' in the chapter titled 'Witnesses' in the text titled 'Injia on Criminal Practice and Procedure in Papua New Guinea and the Pacific'

772 See *The State v Stanley Kuma Kuru* (2011) N4264, [2011] PGNC 43.

773 See *The State v Enny Bulen* [1990] PNGLR 43; *The State v Willie Orki Briza* [1976] PNGLR 517; *R v Angalio Kaimagali* (1972) No. 725; *R v Ambimp* [1971-72] PNGLR 258 and *R v Kipali-Ikarum* [1967-68] PNGLR 119.

774 As regards a deceased witness, see *R v Manase* [2001] 2 NZLR 197; *R v Gera* [1978] 2 NZLR 500; *R v L* [1994] 2 NZLR 54; *R v Brooks* (1994) 11 CRNZ 670 and *R v Howse* [2003] NZCA 187.

775 As regards the competency of a mentally-ill witness to give evidence, refer to the section titled 'Competency And Compellability' in the chapter titled 'Witnesses' in the text titled 'Injia on Criminal Practice and Procedure in Papua New Guinea and the Pacific'.

- a person registered under the *Medical Registration Act 1980*[776]

may be admitted as evidence in the National Court pursuant to section 102 of the *District Courts Act* (Ch. 40).[777]

[3.3.3] PUBLIC DOCUMENTS[778]

During the 19th century, the English courts recognised that most public documents should be held admissible as evidence of the truth of their contents, thus constituting another extremely important exception to the hearsay rule. This exception is clearly based on both reliability and convenience.[779]

A 'public document' is a document that is produced by a public official:

- who was under a duty to make inquiry; or
- had personal knowledge of the matters stated, recorded or reported in the document for the use of the members of the public.[780]

---

776 Refer also to the chapter titled 'Medical Evidence'.

777 Refer also to:
- the section titled 'Admission Of Evidence Without The Calling Of A Witness' in the chapter titled 'Court Procedure' in the text titled 'Injia on Criminal Practice and Procedure in Papua New Guinea and the Pacific'; and
- the section titled 'Private Document' in the chapter titled 'Documentary Evidence'.

778 See also: *Myers v DPP* (1964) 48 Cr App R 348, [1965] AC 1001, [1964] 2 All ER 881, [1964] 3 WLR 145.

Refer also to the chapter titled 'Documentary Evidence'.

779 See Law Reform Commission of Ireland, 2010, 'Hearsay in Civil and Criminal Cases', Chapter 3.

780 See *Sturla v Freccia* [1880] 5 App Cas 623 at 623 and *Lilley v Pettit* [1946] KB 401, [1946] 1 All ER 593.

It is admitted as proof of its contents and is therefore an exception to the 'hearsay rule'.[781]

Such a document may speak for itself without the need to call any witness to verify the truthfulness of its contents.[782]

The rationale for the exception was that the truthfulness of the statement can be presumed from:

- the nature of the document; and
- the manner in which it was made.

It would be both impractical and unnecessary to require the statement maker to be a witness since that person could not generally be expected to recollect all of the matters described in the document.

[3.3.4] AFFIDAVIT

Pursuant to Division 2 of Part III of the *Evidence Act* (Ch. 48) ['Evidence by Affidavit'] an affidavit may be admissible as to the proof of its contents without the need to call evidence from a witness.[783]

---

[781] See *Lilley v Pettit* [1946] KB 401, [1946] 1 All ER 593.

See also:
- section 5 ['Acts of Parliament, etc.'];
- section 6 ['Regulations, etc']; and
- sections 38 to 51 ['Proof and Evidence in Certain Cases']

of the *Evidence Act* (Ch. 48).

[782] See *R v Patel* (1981) 73 Cr App R 117, [1981] 3 All ER 94, [1981] Crim LR 250.

[783] Refer also to:
- the chapter titled 'Documentary Evidence'; and
- the section titled 'Admission Of Evidence Without The Calling Of A Witness' in the chapter titled 'Court Procedure' in the text titled 'Injia on Criminal Practice and Procedure in Papua New Guinea and the Pacific'.

[3.3.5] COMPUTER RECORD

Pursuant to Division 5 of Part IV of the *Evidence Act* (Ch. 48) ['Computerised Information'] a computer record may be admissible as to the proof of its contents without the need to call evidence from a witness.[784]

[3.3.6] BANKER'S BOOK

Pursuant to Part V of the *Evidence Act* (Ch. 48) ['Special Provisions Relation to Banker's Books'] a banker's record may be admissible as to the proof of its contents without the need to call evidence from a witness.[785]

[3.3.7] BUSINESS RECORD

Pursuant to section 61 of the *Evidence Act* (Ch. 48) ['Business Records'] a business record may be admissible as to the proof of its contents without the need to call evidence from a witness.[786]

---

[784] Refer also to the chapter titled 'Documentary Evidence'.

[785] Refer also to the chapter titled 'Documentary Evidence'.

[786] Refer also to the chapter titled 'Documentary Evidence'.

IDENTIFICATION EVIDENCE

[1.0] INTRODUCTION[787]

The identity of the person who has committed an offence is often disputed in a criminal trial. When this happens, the admissibility of eyewitness evidence becomes crucial. The problem is that although such evidence may be compelling, it is not necessarily reliable.[788]

The public interest in:

- bringing wrongdoers to justice; and
- protecting the innocent from wrongful conviction

both require that:

- only reliable identification evidence be admitted; and
- unreliable identification evidence be excluded.[789]

Identification of an accused person should always be fairly conducted. In the absence of other credible evidence, it is unsafe to convict on identification evidence obtained through:

- unfair means; or
- means prejudicial to an accused person.[790]

Irrespective, there is no need for evidence of 'corroboration' before any 'weight[791]' or 'probative force' can be attached to identification evidence.[792]

---

[787] As regards ballistic evidence specifically, see *The State v Melchior Ibor* (2005) N2896.

Refer also to the chapter titled 'Forensic Evidence'.

[788] See New Zealand Law Commission, 1999, 'Evidence. Volume 1: Reform of the Law and Evidence. Volume 2: Evidence Code and Commentary', Report 55, page 53.

[789] See New Zealand Law Commission, 1999, 'Evidence. Volume 1: Reform of the Law and Evidence. Volume 2: Evidence Code and Commentary', Report 55, page 53.

[790] See *Taiya Balua v The State* (2006) SC878, [2006] PGSC 31.

[791] Refer also to the chapter titled 'Weight'.

[792] See *Kevin Mariano v The* State (2001) SCRA No. 71 of 2000.

IDENTIFICATION EVIDENCE

[2.0] EYEWITNESS IDENTIFICATION

[2.1] INTRODUCTION

Eyewitness identification is an act of the mind.[793]

The process of identification, in which a witness compares a remembered image with:

- a person; or
- an image of a person physically before them,

is complex and its accuracy can be influenced by a number of factors.[794]

Perception and memory are decision-making processes affected by:

- the totality of a person's abilities, motives and beliefs;
- the environment; and
- the way the recollection of the witness is eventually tested.[795]

There are dangers inherent in eye-witness identification evidence.[796]

Those dangers will become readily apparent if an eyewitness is shown a single photograph of a person who is said to be the suspect before giving evidence.[797] This phenomenon is known as the 'displacement effect'.[798]

---

[793] See *Alexander v R* (1981) 145 CLR 395 at 403, (1981) 34 ALR 289, [1981] HCA 17 and *R v EJ Smith* [1984] 1 NSWLR 462 at 464, (1984) 12 A Crim R 439.

Refer also to the section titled 'Introduction' in the chapter titled 'Examination Of Witnesses' in the text titled 'Injia on Criminal Practice and Procedure in Papua New Guinea and the Pacific'.

[794] See New Zealand Law Commission, 1999, 'Evidence. Volume 1: Reform of the Law and Evidence. Volume 2: Evidence Code and Commentary', Report 55, page 54.

[795] See New Zealand Law Commission, 1999, 'Evidence. Volume 1: Reform of the Law and Evidence. Volume 2: Evidence Code and Commentary', Report 55, page 54.

[796] See *Jimmy Ono v The State* (2002) SC698 and *The State v Marety Ame Gaidi* (2002) N2256.

[797] See *Alexander v R* (1981) 145 CLR 395, per Gibbs CJ at 400, (1981) 34 ALR 289, [1981] HCA 17; *R v Russell* [1977] 2 NZLR 20 at 27 and *R v Blick* (2000) 111 A Crim R 326 at 335, [2000] NSWCCA 61.

[798] See *Alexander v R* (1981) 145 CLR 395, per Stephen J at 409, (1981) 34 ALR 289, [1981] HCA 17.

Having been shown a photograph, the eyewitness's memory of it may be more clearly retained than the memory of the original sighting of the offender and may, accordingly, displace the original memory. Any subsequent identification, in court or in an identification parade, may on the identifying witness's part, in truth involve a matching of the person so identified with the remembered photograph, which has been displaced in the memory of the eyewitness his or her recollection of the original sighting.[799]

Such evidence has been described as being 'worthless'.[800]

The correctness of identification evidence is established by:

> Closely examining the circumstances in which the identification by each witness came to be made.[801]

However, there is a distinction between:

- 'eyewitness' evidence; and
- 'recognition' evidence.[802]

---

[799] See *Alexander v R* (1981) 145 CLR 395, per Stephen J at 409, (1981) 34 ALR 289, [1981] HCA 17.

[800] See *Alexander v R* (1981) 145 CLR 395, per Stephen J at 414 and Mason J at 426, (1981) 34 ALR 289, [1981] HCA 17; *Davies and Cody v R* (1937) 57 CLR 170 at 178, [1937] HCA 27; *R v Carusi* (1997) 92 A Crim R 52 at 55; *R v Agkul* [2002] 5 VR 537, [2002] VSCA 222 and *Aslett v R* [2009] NSWCCA 188.

[801] See *John Beng v The State* [1977] PNGLR 115, (1977) SC112; *Luingi Yandasingi v The State* [1995] PNGLR 268 and *Taiya Balua v The State* (2006) SC878, [2006] PGSC 31.

See also: *R v Breslin* (1985) 80 Cr App R 226.

As regards eye-witness identification based on non-facial features, see *Jimmy Ono v The State* (2002) SC698.

[802] See *Arthurs v Attorney-General for Northern Ireland* (1971) 55 Cr App R 161.

See also: *Davies v R* (1937) 57 CLR 170; *Kelly v R* (2002) 129 A Crim R 363 and *Al-Hashimi v R* (2004) 181 FLR 383, [2004] WASCA 61.

IDENTIFICATION EVIDENCE

In general, 'eyewitness evidence' describes:

> The evidence of an eyewitness who identifies an accused person as the offender in circumstances where the eyewitness first saw the accused person at or near the crime scene.[803]

Whereas, 'recognition evidence' describes:

> The evidence of a eyewitness who recognises an accused person as the offender in circumstances where:
>
> - the accused person was previously known to the eyewitness; or
> - the accused person had previously been seen by the eyewitness,
>
> other than at or near the crime scene.[804]

Although recognition may be more reliable than the identification of a stranger; even when an eyewitness is purporting to recognise someone whom he or she knows, mistakes in recognition of close relatives and friends are sometimes made.[805]

Whether the eyewitness who recognises an accused person knows his or her name is irrelevant.[806]

---

[803] See *Carr v R* (2000) 117 A Crim R 272, [2000] TASSC 183; *Kelly v R* (2002) 129 A Crim R 363, [2002] WASCA 134; *Al-Hashimi v R* (2004) 181 FLR 383, [2004] WASCA 61; *Peck v The State of Western Australia* [2005] WASCA 20; *R v Spero* (2006) 13 VR 225, [2006] VSCA 58 and *R v Defrutos* [2008] VSCA 55.

[804] See *Carr v R* (2000) 117 A Crim R 272, [2000] TASSC 183; *Kelly v R* (2002) 129 A Crim R 363, [2002] WASCA 134; *Al-Hashimi v R* (2004) 181 FLR 383, [2004] WASCA 61; *Peck v The State of Western Australia* [2005] WASCA 20; *R v Spero* (2006) 13 VR 225, [2006] VSCA 58 and *R v Defrutos* [2008] VSCA 55.

[805] See *Jimmy Ono v The State* (2002) SC698; *Piakali v The State* (2004) SC771, [2004] PGSC 20; *John Beng v The State* [1977] PNGLR 115; *The State v Natciai Tibone and Thomas Some* (1982) N361(M); *Patrick Towingo and two others v The State* (2008) SC983; *The State v Marety Ame Gaidi* (2002) N2256; *The State v Benny Damien* (2012) N4917, [2012] PGNC 253 and *The State v Samuel Kaka* (2013) N5082, [2013] PGNC 20.

[806] See *George Kalupai v The State* (1995) SC492; *The State v John Ate Alias Peter John Ate* (2001) N2055 and *The State v Yakoto Imbuni and others* (1997) N1558.

Irrespective, a witness giving identification evidence is telling the Court what he or she believes occurred.[807] A person recognises a person by comparing his or her current observation of that person with his or her recollection of that person.[808]

Where a case raises the issue of eyewitness identification, care must be exercised by the Court because there are dangers inherent in accepting or relying upon such identification.[809]

[2.2] ASSESSING VISUAL IDENTIFICATION EVIDENCE[810]

The fundamental principle of identification evidence based on the observations of an eyewitness is:

> The 'weight' or 'probative force' to be assigned to such evidence is determined by the circumstances under which the identification was made, ie., at the time of the commission of the offence or shortly thereafter or before, depending on the circumstances.[811]

A Court should:

- closely examine all of the circumstances in which the identification was made[812];and
- critically weigh up all of those circumstances

before relying on the identification evidence[813].

---

[807] See *Craig v R* (1933) 49 CLR 429 at 446, [1933] HCA 41.

[808] See *R v Benz* (1989) 168 CLR 110, [1989] HCA 64.

[809] See *Richard Liri v The State* (2007) SC883, [2007] PGSC 3.

[810] Refer also to the subsection titled 'Eliciting Evidence' in the section titled 'Examination-in-Chief' in the chapter titled 'Examination Of Witnesses' in the text titled 'Injia on Criminal Practice and Procedure in Papua New Guinea and the Pacific'.

[811] See *R v Breslin* (1985) 80 Cr App R 226.

[812] See *John Beng v The State* [1977] PNGLR 115, (1977) SC112; *Luingi Yandasingi v The State* [1995] PNGLR 268; *Taiya Balua v The State* (2006) SC878, [2006] PGSC 31 and *The State v Benny Damien* (2012) N4917, [2012] PGNC 253.

See also: *R v Breslin* (1985) 80 Cr App R 226.

[813] See *The State v Lasi Mauwe and Maki Onopika* (1999) N1885 and *The State v Kamo* (2006) N2991, [2006] PGNC 36.

However, what matters is the quality of the identification evidence, rather than its volume.[814]

The factors that should be considered, include:

- an honest and convincing witness may be mistaken[815], and therefore, a number of witnesses may all be mistaken[816].

  A perfectly honest witness could believe, and become increasingly convinced that he or she was right in so believing, that he or she had identified the right person when subsequently it could be shown in other ways that the witness had in fact made a mistake and identified the wrong person.[817]

  Therefore, a Court must be satisfied that the witness is both:

  - honest; and

  - accurate[818];

---

[814] See *R v Breslin* (1985) 80 Cr App R 226.

[815] See *John Beng v The State* [1977] PNGLR 115, (1977) SC112; *Jimmy Ono v The State* (2002) SC698; *Patrick Towingo and two others v The State* (2008) SC983; *Piakali v The State* (2004) SC771, [2004] PGSC 20; *The State v Kobale Rau* (1997) N1509; *The State v David Panake* (2010) N3963; *The State v Michael Monowi* (2009) N3588, [2009] PGNC 12; *The State v Andrew Nane John* (2007) N3201, [2007] PGNC 89; *The State v Zebedee Sod* (2012) N4826, [2012] PGNC 118; *The State v Benny Damien* (2012) N4917, [2012] PGNC 253; *The State v Marety Ame Gaidi* (2002) N2256 and *The State v Samuel Kaka* (2013) N5082, [2013] PGNC 20.

See also: *Kelleher v R* (1974) 131 CLR 534, per Gibbs CJ at 550-551, [1974] HCA 48; *R v Turnbull and others* [1977] QB 224, (1976) 63 Cr App R 132, [1976] 3 WLR 445, [1976] 3 All ER 549, [1976] Crim LR 565; *Festa v R* (2001) 208 CLR 593, [2001] HCA 72; *Longman v R* (1989) 168 CLR 79, per McHugh J at 108, [1989] HCA 60 and *Trudgett v R* [2008] NSWCCA 62.

[816] See *John Beng v The State* [1977] PNGLR 115, (1977) SC112; *Jimmy Ono v The State* (2002) SC698; *Taiya Balua v The State* (2006) SC878; *Piakali v The State* (2004) SC771, [2004] PGSC 20; *Patrick Towingo and two others v The State* (2008) SC983; *The State v Marety Ame Gaidi* (2002) N2256; *The State v Benny Damien* (2012) N4917, [2012] PGNC 253 and *The State v Samuel Kaka* (2013) N5082, [2013] PGNC 20.

See also: *R v Grant* [1996] 2 Cr App R 272 at 281; *R v Bentley* [1991] Crim LR 620; *R v Slater* [1995] 1 Cr App R 584 and *R v Thornton* [1995] 1 Cr App R 578.

[817] See *R v Johnson* [2001] 1 Cr App R 408 at 412.

[818] See *The State v Francis Vau Kamo* (2006) N2991, [2006] PGNC 36; *The State v Noutim Mausen* (2005) N2870, [2005] PGNC 95; *The State v David Panake* (2010) N3963 and *The State v Zebedee Sod* (2012) N4826, [2012] PGNC 118.

- what were the circumstances in which the accused person was observed?[819]
  - did the eyewitness have sufficient time to be able to identify the face of the accused person[820], ie., how long was the period of observation?[821];
  - what was the length of time that the witness was observing the accused person because the quality of the evidence may be poor if there was a fleeting glance?[822];
  - what was the accused person doing at that time?; and
  - how far away was the eyewitness from the accused person?[823];

---

[819] See *R v Uno Tam and Marau U'u* (1973) No. 766; *The State v Otto* [2007] PGNC 128 and The State v Danken Tilon (2010) N3966.

[820] See *John Beng v The State* [1977] PNGLR 115, (1977) SC112; *Patrick Towingo and two others v The State* (2008) SC983; *Jimmy Ono v The State* (2002) SC698; *Piakali v The State* (2004) SC771, [2004] PGSC 20; *The State v David Panake* (2010) N3963 and *The State v Kuku Hayala* (2009) N3774, [2009] PGNC 139.

See also: *R v Turnbull and others* [1977] QB 224, (1976) 63 Cr App R 132, [1976] 3 WLR 445, [1976] 3 All ER 549, [1976] Crim LR 565 and *R v Finlay* [2007] QCA 400.

[821] See *The State v Kapil Ouba* (2010) N4130 and *The State v Zebedee Sod* (2012) N4826, [2012] PGNC 118.

See also: New Zealand Law Commission, 1999, 'Evidence: Total Recall?: The Reliability of Witness Testimony', Miscellaneous Paper 13, page 13.

[822] See *Jimmy Ono v The State* (2002) SC698; *Piakali v The State* (2004) SC771, [2004] PGSC 20; *Patrick Towingo and two others v The State* (2008) SC983; *The State v Francis Vau Kamo* (2006) N2991, [2006] PGNC 36; *The State v Noutim Mausen* (2005) N2870, [2005] PGNC 95 and *The State v Benny Damien* (2012) N4917, [2012] PGNC 253.

See also: *Mills v The State of Western Australia* [2008] WASCA 219, per Buss JA.

[823] See *John Beng v The State* [1977] PNGLR 115, (1977) SC112; *Luingi Yandasingi v The State* [1995] PNGLR 268; *The State v Kapil Ouba* (2010) N4130 and *The State v Kuku Hayala* (2009) N3774, [2009] PGNC 139.

See also:

- *R v Turnbull and others* [1977] QB 224, (1976) 63 Cr App R 132, [1976] 3 WLR 445, [1976] 3 All ER 549, [1976] Crim LR 565 and *R v Finlay* [2007] QCA 400; and
- New Zealand Law Commission, 1999, 'Evidence: Total Recall?: The Reliability of Witness Testimony', Miscellaneous Paper 13, page 13.

- what were the prevailing lighting conditions, including:
  - was the identification made in broad daylight?;
  - was the identification made at dusk?;
  - was the identification made at dawn?; and
  - what were the prevailing lighting conditions inside or outside of the location, such as street lights?[824];
- how was the line of sight?
  - did the eyewitness have a clear front-on view of the accused person?[825];
  - was the line of sight of the accused person interrupted?[826];
  - did the eyewitness just see the accused person from the side?[827]; and

---

[824] See *John Beng v The State* [1977] PNGLR 115, (1977) SC112; *Luingi Yandasingi v The State* [1995] PNGLR 268; *The State v Francis Vau Kamo* (2006) N2991, [2006] PGNC 36; *The State v Kapil Ouba* (2010) N4130; *The State v Noutim Mausen* (2005) N2870, [2005] PGNC 95; *The State v David Panake* (2010) N3963; *The State v Michael Monowi* (2009) N3588, [2009] PGNC 12; *The State v Kuku Hayala* (2009) N3774, [2009] PGNC 139; *The State v Zebedee Sod* (2012) N4826, [2012] PGNC 118 and *The State v Benny Damien* (2012) N4917, [2012] PGNC 253.

See also:

- *R v Turnbull and others* [1977] QB 224, (1976) 63 Cr App R 132, [1976] 3 WLR 445, [1976] 3 All ER 549, [1976] Crim LR 565; and
- New Zealand Law Commission, 1999, 'Evidence: Total Recall?: The Reliability of Witness Testimony', Miscellaneous Paper 13, page 13.

[825] See *The State v Francis Vau Kamo* (2006) N2991, [2006] PGNC 36; *The State v Noutim Mausen* (2005) N2870, [2005] PGNC 95; *The State v David Panake* (2010) N3963; *The State v Zebedee Sod* (2012) N4826, [2012] PGNC 118 and *The State v Benny Damien* (2012) N4917, [2012] PGNC 253.

[826] See *The State v Francis Vau Kamo* (2006) N2991, [2006] PGNC 36; *The State v Noutim Mausen* (2005) N2870, [2005] PGNC 95; *The State v David Panake* (2010) N3963; *The State v Zebedee Sod* (2012) N4826, [2012] PGNC 118 and *The State v Benny Damien* (2012) N4917, [2012] PGNC 253.

[827] See *The State v Francis Vau Kamo* (2006) N2991, [2006] PGNC 36; *The State v Noutim Mausen* (2005) N2870, [2005] PGNC 95; *The State v David Panake* (2010) N3963 and *The State v Zebedee Sod* (2012) N4826, [2012] PGNC 118 and *The State v Benny Damien* (2012) N4917, [2012] PGNC 253.

- was the line of sight impeded in any way, as for example by passing traffic or a number of people in close proximity?[828];

- was the eyewitness's sighting of the accused person at the crime scene in poor conditions?[829]; and

- the quality of the evidence may be poor if there is a longer observation made in poor conditions[830];

- was the identification based on recognition evidence?

  - was the eyewitness purporting to identify a person who was:

    - a stranger; or

    - someone he or she recognised?[831];

  - was that previous knowledge of the accused person tenuous?[832];

  - what was the basis for knowing the accused person?;

---

[828] See *John Beng v The State* [1977] PNGLR 115, (1977) SC112 and *Luingi Yandasingi v The State* [1995] PNGLR 268.

See also:
- *R v Turnbull and others* [1977] QB 224, (1976) 63 Cr App R 132, [1976] 3 WLR 445, [1976] 3 All ER 549, [1976] Crim LR 565 and *R v Finlay* [2007] QCA 400; and
- New Zealand Law Commission, 1999, 'Evidence: Total Recall?: The Reliability of Witness Testimony', Miscellaneous Paper 13, page 13.

[829] See *Jimmy Ono v The State* (2002) SC698; *Piakali v The State* (2004) SC771, [2004] PGSC 20 and *Patrick Towingo and two others v The State* (2008) SC983.

[830] See *Jimmy Ono v The State* (2002) SC698; *Piakali v The State* (2004) SC771, [2004] PGSC 20 and *Patrick Towingo and two others v The State* (2008) SC983.

[831] See *The State v Francis Vau Kamo* (2006) N2991, [2006] PGNC 36; *The State v Noutim Mausen* (2005) N2870, [2005] PGNC 95; *The State v David Panake* (2010) N3963 and *The State v Zebedee Sod* (2012) N4826, [2012] PGNC 118.

[832] See *Mills v The State of Western Australia* [2008] WASCA 219, per Buss JA.

- did the eyewitness know the accused person before the time of the identification?[833];
- if so, how often?[834];
- if so, in what circumstances?;
- if so, over what period of time were those encounters?; and
- if only occasionally, had the eyewitness any special reason for remembering the accused person?[835];

- was there anything about the accused person that would have impressed itself upon the witness?[836];
- what was the emotional state of the eyewitness at the time of the identification?[837];

---

[833] See *John Beng v The State* [1977] PNGLR 115, (1977) SC112 and *Luingi Yandasingi v The State* [1995] PNGLR 268.

See also: *R v Turnbull and others* [1977] QB 224, (1976) 63 Cr App R 132, [1976] 3 WLR 445, [1976] 3 All ER 549, [1976] Crim LR 565 and *R v Finlay* [2007] QCA 400.

[834] See *John Beng v The State* [1977] PNGLR 115, (1977) SC112.

See also:
- *R v Turnbull and others* [1977] QB 224, (1976) 63 Cr App R 132, [1976] 3 WLR 445, [1976] 3 All ER 549, [1976] Crim LR 565 and *R v Finlay* [2007] QCA 400; and
- New Zealand Law Commission, 1999, 'Evidence: Total Recall?: The Reliability of Witness Testimony', Miscellaneous Paper 13, page 13.

[835] See *John Beng v The State* [1977] PNGLR 115, (1977) SC112.

See also: *R v Turnbull and others* [1977] QB 224, (1976) 63 Cr App R 132, [1976] 3 WLR 445, [1976] 3 All ER 549, [1976] Crim LR 565 and *R v Finlay* [2007] QCA 400.

[836] See *The State v Kapil Ouba* (2010) N4130.

[837] See *The State v Francis Vau Kamo* (2006) N2991, [2006] PGNC 36; *The State v Noutim Mausen* (2005) N2870, [2005] PGNC 95; *The State v David Panake* (2010) N3963; *The State v Zebedee Sod* (2012) N4826, [2012] PGNC 118 and *The State v Benny Damien* (2012) N4917, [2012] PGNC 253.

- was there any motive for giving false evidence as to the identity of the accused person?[838];
- was there any reliable evidence of other witnesses either:
    - confirming; or
    - contradicting

  the evidence of the eyewitness?[839];
- was there any special reason for remembering the accused person?[840];
- was there the existence of other evidence either:
    - direct; or
    - circumstantial,

  of facts or circumstances independently proved?[841];
- eyewitness identification evidence given by a police officer can be just as unreliable and therefore should be treated like any other eyewitness[842];
- how long elapsed between:

---

[838] See *R v Uno Tam and Marau U'u* (1973) No. 766; *The State v Otto* [2007] PGNC 128 and *The State v Danken Tilon* (2010) N3966.

[839] See *R v Uno Tam and Marau U'u* (1973) No. 766 and *The State v Otto* [2007] PGNC 128.

[840] See *The State v Kapil Ouba* (2010) N4130 and *The State v Kuku Hayala* (2009) N3774, [2009] PGNC 139.

[841] See *R v Uno Tam and Marau U'u* (1973) No. 766; *The State v Otto* [2007] PGNC 128 and *The State v Danken Tilon* (2010) N3966.

[842] See *The State v John Ate Alias Peter John Ate* (2001) N2055.

See also: *Reid (Junior) v R* [1989] 3 WLR 771, [1990] AC 363, (1990) 90 Cr App R 121, [1990] Crim LR 113; *R v Ramsden* [1991] Crim LR 295; *R v Tyler and others* (1993) 96 Cr App R 332, [1993] Crim LR 60 and *Powell v DPP* [1992] RTR 270, [1992] COD 191.

  - the original observation, ie., when the eyewitness first saw the accused person; and
  - the subsequent identification to the police?[843];

- how long after the time of the act of identification was the eyewitness asked about his or her description of the accused person by the police?[844]
- what was the version given to the police by the eyewitness of the circumstances in which the identification of the accused person was made?;
- what were the circumstances in which the description was recorded?
  - when was that description recorded?;
  - how was that description recorded?; and
  - who recorded that description?;
- was there any material discrepancy between:
  - the description of the accused person given to the police by the eyewitness;
  - the description of the accused person given to the Court by the eyewitness; and
  - the actual appearance of the accused person?[845];

---

[843] See *John Beng v The State* [1977] PNGLR 115, (1977) SC112 and *The State v Kapil Ouba* (2010) N4130.

See also: *R v Turnbull and others* [1977] QB 224, (1976) 63 Cr App R 132, [1976] 3 WLR 445, [1976] 3 All ER 549, [1976] Crim LR 565 and *R v Finlay* [2007] QCA 400.

[844] See *The State v Kuku Hayala* (2009) N3774, [2009] PGNC 139 and *The State v Kapil Ouba* (2010) N4130.

[845] See *John Beng v The State* [1977] PNGLR 115, (1977) SC112 and *The State v Kuku Hayala* (2009) N3774, [2009] PGNC 139.

See also: *R v Turnbull and others* [1977] QB 224, (1976) 63 Cr App R 132, [1976] 3 WLR 445, [1976] 3 All ER 549, [1976] Crim LR 565; *R v Finlay* [2007] QCA 400; *Pearsall* (1990) 49 A Crim R 439, per Hunt J 443-444 and *R v Swanston* [1982] 2 WLR 546.

- when there is a material discrepancy in the eyewitness identification evidence then the Court should:
    - consider such discrepancy; and
    - assess whether it is explicable in terms, other than dishonesty or unreliability[846];
- was there anything about the accused person that would have impressed itself upon the eyewitness?[847];
- was there a real question as to the accuracy or reliability of the eyewitness's powers of observation, recognition or recall?[848]; and
- what was the overall impression of the eyewitness as to his or her reliability and accuracy?[849]

[2.3] WARNING

As Lord Bingham stated in *R v Forbes*[850] identification evidence based on the observations of an eyewitness even when wholly honest may lead to the conviction of the innocent.

Therefore, the appropriate warning needs to be considered by a Court.

---

[846] See *The State v Francis Vau Kamo* (2006) N2991, [2006] PGNC 36; *The State v Noutim Mausen* (2005) N2870, [2005] PGNC 95; *The State v David Panake* (2010) N3963 and *The State v Zebedee Sod* (2012) N4826, [2012] PGNC 118.

[847] See *The State v Kuku Hayala* (2009) N3774, [2009] PGNC 139.

[848] See *R v Spero* (2006) 13 VR 225, [2006] VSCA 58, per Redlich AJA and *R v Turnbull and others* [1977] QB 224, (1976) 63 Cr App R 132, [1976] 3 WLR 445, [1976] 3 All ER 549, [1976] Crim LR 565.

[849] See *R v Uno Tam and Marau U'u* (1973) No. 766; *The State v Otto* [2007] PGNC 128 and *The State v Danken Tilon* (2010) N3966.

[850] [2001] 2 WLR 1 at 5.

IDENTIFICATION EVIDENCE

When such evidence represents a substantial part of the proof of a charge a Court should warn itself of acting on it[851] where:

- its reliability is disputed; or
- the witness may be mistaken.[852]

However, the need for such a warning depends on the circumstances of the case[853], for example:

- once a decision has been made by a Court as to:
  - the credibility of witnesses; and
  - whose evidence is acceptable[854],

  further considerations as to the treatment of the evidence may be futile[855];

---

[851] See *Jimmy Ono v The State* (2002) SC698; *Piakali v The State* (2004) SC771, [2004] PGSC 20; *Patrick Towingo and two others v The State* (2008) SC983; *The State v Kobale Rau* (1997) N1509; *The State v Francis Vau Kamo* (2006) N2991, [2006] PGNC 36 and *The State v Noutim Mausen* (2005) N2870, [2005] PGNC 95.

[852] See *John Beng v The State* [1977] PNGLR 115, (1977) SC112.

See also: *R v Turnbull and others* (1976) 63 Cr App R 132, [1976] 3 WLR 445, [1976] 3 All ER 549, [1976] Crim LR 565, [1977] QB 224, at 228; *Domican v R* (1992) 173 CLR 555 at 561, (1992) 66 ALJR 285, [1992] HCA 13; *R v Aziz* [1982] 2 NSWLR 322 at 328; *Kelleher v R* (1974) 131 CLR 534 at 551; *R v Burchielli* [1981] VR 611 at 616-619; *R v Bartels* (1986) 44 SASR 260 at 270-271 and *Jason Cape and others v R* [1996] 1 Cr App R 191.

[853] See *David Kandakason v The State* (1998) SC558.

See also: *R v Preston* [1961] VLR 761; *Raspor v R* (1958) 99 CLR 346, *R v Fox* [2000] 2 Qd R 430; *R v Spero* (2006) 164 A Crim R 583, [2006] NSWCCA 295, *DRE v R* (2006) 164 A Crim R 400, [2006] NSWCCA 280 and *Sepulveda v R* (2006) 167 A Crim R 108, [2006] NSWCCA 379.

[854] Refer also to the section titled 'Court Decision' in the chapter titled 'Court Procedure' in the text titled 'Injia on Criminal Practice and Procedure in Papua New Guinea and the Pacific'.

[855] See *David Kandakason v The State* (1998) SC558 and *Jimmy Ono v The State* (2002) SC698.

See however: *Gibson Gunure Ohizave v The State* (1998) SC595.

- when the accused person was already well known to the witness[856];
- when only a resemblance is claimed[857]; or
- when the defence is that the identification was a frame-up[858].

Both the prosecution and defence should outline to the Court the:

- strengths; and
- weaknesses

of the identification evidence.[859]

A Court should specifically warn itself that:

- a convincing witness may be mistaken; and
- a number of such witnesses could all be mistaken.[860]

Provided such a warning is given, no particular form of words need to be used.[861]

---

[856] See *Festa v R* (2001) 208 CLR 593, [2001] HCA 72.

[857] See *Festa v R* (2001) 208 CLR 593, [2001] HCA 72.

[858] See *R v Cape, Jackson and Gardner* [1996] 1 Cr App R 191, per Roch LJ at 198-199 and *Courtnell* [1990] Crim LR 115 at 116.

[859] See *R v Turnbull and others* (1976) 63 Cr App R 132, [1976] 3 WLR 445, [1976] 3 All ER 549, [1976] Crim LR 565, [1977] QB 224; *R v Fergus (Ivan)* (1994) 98 Cr App R 313; *R v Pattinson and Exley* [1996] 1 Cr App R 51; *R v Akaidere* [1990] Crim LR 808; *Smith v R* (1990) 64 ALJR 588 at 588 and *Keleher v R* (1974) 131 CLR 534 at 551.

[860] See *John Beng v The State* [1977] PNGLR 115, (1977) SC112; *Taiya Balua v The State* (2006) SC878; *Jimmy Ono v The State* (2002) SC698; *Piakali v The State* (2004) SC771, [2004] PGSC 20; *Patrick Towingo and two others v The State* (2008) SC983 and *The State v Benny Damien* (2012) N4917, [2012] PGNC 253.

[861] See *Jimmy Ono v The State* (2002) SC698; *The State v Marety Ame Gaidi* (2002) N2256 and *The State v Benny Damien* (2012) N4917, [2012] PGNC 253.

IDENTIFICATION EVIDENCE

Whilst there is no rule of law that the evidence of one witness as to the identification of an accused person is insufficient in proving a charge 'beyond reasonable doubt[862]', a Court should warn itself on relying on such evidence alone.[863]

If the quality of the eyewitness evidence is good, the identification may be reliable. If however, the quality of evidence is bad, the identification will be bad and there should be an acquittal in those circumstances[864], if there is no other evidence implicating the accused person 'beyond reasonable doubt[865]'.

[3.0] DISCLOSURE[866]

If in any case that the prosecution has reason to believe that there is a material discrepancy between:

- the description of an accused person given to the investigating officer by an eyewitness; and

- the actual appearance of the accused person

---

862 Refer also to the chapter titled 'Proof Of Issues' in the text titled 'Injia on Criminal Practice and Procedure in Papua New Guinea and the Pacific'.

863 See *John Beng v The State* [1977] PNGLR 115, (1977) SC112; *The State v Jason Baleng* (2006) N3395, [2006] PGNC 173; *The State v Francis Vau Kamo* (2006) N2991, [2006] PGNC 36 and *The State v Noutim Mausen* (2005) N2870, [2005] PGNC 95.

864 See *John Beng v The State* [1977] PNGLR 115, (1977) SC112; *Jimmy Ono v The State* (2002) SC698; *Piakali v The State* (2004) SC771, [2004] PGSC 20; *Patrick Towingo and two others v The State* (2008) SC983; *The State v Francis Vau Kamo* (2006) N2991, [2006] PGNC 36; *The State v Marety Ame Gaidi* (2002) N2256; *The State v Noutim Mausen* (2005) N2870, [2005] PGNC 95 and *The State v David Panake* (2010) N3963.

See also: *R v Turnbull and others* [1977] QB 224, (1976) 63 Cr App R 132, [1976] 3 WLR 445, [1976] 3 All ER 549, [1976] Crim LR 565 and *Domican v R* (1992) 173 CLR 555, (1992) 66 ALJR 285, [1992] HCA 13.

865 Refer also to the chapter titled 'Proof Of Issues' in the text titled 'Injia on Criminal Practice and Procedure in Papua New Guinea and the Pacific'.

866 See also: *Murphy v R* [2002] UKPC 3.

As regards the law in relation to 'Disclosure Of Prosecution Evidence', refer to the section titled 'The Prosecution Case' in the chapter titled 'Court Procedure' in the text titled 'Injia on Criminal Practice and Procedure in Papua New Guinea and the Pacific'.

it should supply the accused person and/or his or her legal representative with the particulars of the description the police were first given.[867]

Irrespective, if an accused person and/or his or her legal representative requests to be given particulars of such a description, the prosecution should supply it.[868]

Such disclosure should include any photographs taken of an accused person.[869]

[4.0] CONFRONTATION[870]

It is unfair to produce a lone suspect for identification purposes.[871]

The Courts treat it as indisputable that an eyewitness, if shown the accused person singly and as the person whom the police have reason to suspect, will be much more likely, however fair and careful the eyewitness may be, to assent to the view that the person he or she is shown in such circumstances:

- corresponds to his or her recollection; and
- is the accused person.[872]

---

[867] See *R v Turnbull and others* [1977] QB 224, (1976) 63 Cr App R 132, [1976] 3 WLR 445, [1976] 3 All ER 549, [1976] Crim LR 565.

[868] See *R v Turnbull and others* [1977] QB 224, (1976) 63 Cr App R 132, [1976] 3 WLR 445, [1976] 3 All ER 549, [1976] Crim LR 565.

[869] See *R v Fergus (Ivan)* (1994) 98 Cr App R 313.

[870] See also: *The State v Jacob Francis Paran* (2007) N3194, [2007] PGNC 83; *The State v Angaun Kakas, Kakalia Tulu, Sukulin Passomb and Kalain Kulu* (1994) N1217, [1994] PGNC 80; *The State v Henry Osare Kales* (2001) N2115; *R v Smith and Evans* (1908) 1 Cr App R 203; *Alexander v R* (1981) 145 CLR 395, (1981) 34 ALR 289, [1981] HCA 17 and *Domican v R* (1992) 173 CLR 555, (1992) 66 ALJR 285, [1992] HCA 13.

[871] See *Taiya Balua v The State* (2006) SC878.

[872] See *Michael Mini v The State* [1987] PNGLR 224 at 226, [1987] PGSC 13 and *Paul Papalamanan v Samson Nuakona* (1973) No. 771.

See also: *Davies and Cody v R* (1937) 57 CLR 170, [1937] HCA 27.

However, a confrontation is not objectionable if it is arranged not for the purpose of identification evidence, but simply to reassure the investigating officer that the accused person was the 'right' person.[873]

[5.0] IDENTIFICATION PARADE[874]

It is recognised at common law that the conduct of an identification parade is the most reliable means available for the identification of a suspect by an eyewitness.[875]

An identification parade offers safeguards which are not available when the witness is asked to identify the accused person in the dock at his or her trial, including:

- an identification parade is usually held much nearer the time of the offence when the witness's recollection is fresher; and
- the accused person is placed among a number of other persons of generally similar appearance which provides a check on the accuracy of the witness's identification by reducing the risk that the witness is simply picking out someone who resembles the offender.[876]

---

[873] See *Brown and Isaac v The State* [2003] UKPC 10.

[874] Refer also to the subsection titled 'Eliciting Evidence' in the section titled 'Examination-in-Chief' in the chapter titled 'Examination Of Witnesses' in the text titled 'Injia on Criminal Practice and Procedure in Papua New Guinea and the Pacific'.

See also: *R v Creamer* (1985) 80 Cr App R 248; *McGlashan v R* (2000) 56 WIR 444 and *Aurelio Pop v R* (2003) 62 WIR 18, [2003] UKPC 40.

[875] See *Alexander v R* (1981) 145 CLR 395, (1981) 34 ALR 289, [1981] HCA 17.

See also: Australian Law Reform Commission, 2005, 'Uniform Evidence Law', Report 112, NSWLRC Report 102 and VLRC Final Report, paragraph 13.47.

[876] See *Holland v HM Advocate* 2005 SC (PC) 1 at 17, [2005] UKPC D1 and *Neilly v R (The Bahamas)* [2012] UKPC 12.

However, there is no requirement to conduct such a parade.[877]

But an identification parade should be conducted whenever it will serve a useful purpose.[878]

The purpose of an identification parade is:

> To ensure that the identification of a suspect by a witness takes place in circumstances where the recollection of the identifying witness is tested objectively under safeguards by placing the suspect in a line made up of like-looking 'suspects'.[879]

But it may be futile conducting an identification parade:

- when the eyewitness cannot identify the accused person;
- when the eyewitness can only identify the clothing worn, and not the face of the accused person; or
- if there is a case of recognition with an offender well known to the eyewitness[880].[881]

Should an investigating officer decide that it is necessary to conduct an identification parade then it must be carried out fairly.[882]

---

[877] See *Taiya Balua v The State* (2006) SC878; *The State v Sela Gipe* (2000) N2058; *The State v Francis Vau Kamo* (2006) N2991, [2006] PGNC 36; *The State v Paul Dotaona* [2006] PGNC 67; *The State v Noutim Mausen* (2005) N2870, [2005] PGNC 95 and *The State v William Nanua Kapris and others* (2011) N4232, [2011] PGNC 24.

See also: *Raspor v R* (1958) 99 CLR 346 and *R v Preston* [1961] VR 761 at 762.

[878] See *R v Popat* [1998] 2 Cr App R 208, per Hobhouse LJ at 215, [1998] EWCA Crim 1035; *Goldson and McGlashan v R* (2000) 56 WIR 444, [2000] UKPC 9; *Brown and another v The State (Trinidad and Tobago)* [2003] UKPC 10; *Aurelio Pop v R* [2003] UKPC 40; *Ebanks v R* [2006] UKPC 6; *Pipersburgh v The State (Belize)* [2008] UKPC 11; *Ronald John v The State of Trinidad and Tobago* [2009] UKPC 12 and *France and another v R (Jamaica)* [2012] UKPC 28.

[879] See *Aurelio Pop v R* [2003] UKPC 40; *Pipersburgh v The State (Belize)* [2008] UKPC 11 and *Neilly v R (The Bahamas)* [2012] UKPC 12.

[880] See *Goldson v R* [2000] UKPC 9.

[881] See *R v Forbes* [2001] 1 AC 473, per Lord Bingham at 486.

[882] See *The State v Sela Gipe* (2000) N2058 and *The State v Thomas Some* (1982) N366(M).

See also: *R v Dickman* (1910) 5 Cr App R 135 at 142.

IDENTIFICATION EVIDENCE

The following best practice should be complied with in order for identification by means of an identification parade to be conducted fairly:

- an accused person should be advised that he or she has an option whether to participate in an identification parade[883];

- the identification parade must comprise of at least 8 persons[884];

- each of the persons in the identification parade should be of a similar description as the suspect, ie., approximately the same age, height, build and skin complexion.[885]

  It is entirely a matter for the police to select the people who, in addition to the suspect, are to participate[886];

- all unauthorised persons must be excluded;

- the suspect must be allowed to select his or her own position in the identification parade;

- the particulars of all persons who participated must be recorded, including names, addresses and identifying particulars, ie., age, height, build and skin complexion. Those details should be signed by each of those persons as a means of acknowledging the correctness of those details;

---

[883] See *The State v Thomas Some* (1982) N366(M) and *The State v Paul Dotaona* [2006] PGNC 67.

Section 32(2)(c) of the *Constitution of the Independent State of Papua New Guinea* ['Right to Freedom'] states:

> 'Every person has the right to freedom based on law, and accordingly has a legal right to do anything that and no person is obliged to do anything that is not required by law'.

Section 52(1) of that Constitution ['Freedom of Movement'] states:

> 'Subject to Subsection (3), no citizen may be deprived of the right to move freely throughout the country, to reside in any part of the country and to enter and leave the country, except in consequence of a law that provides for deprivation of personal liberty in accordance with Section 42 (*liberty of the person*)'.

See however: *The State v Kusap Kei Kuya* [1983] PNGLR 263.

[884] According to the general instructions of the New Zealand Police Force there should be at least 8 persons in an identification parade, see *R v Hewett* [2003] NZCA 291.

[885] See *The State v Thomas Some* (1982) N366(M).

[886] See *R v Thorne* [1981] Crim LR 702.

- an identification parade must not be arranged in such a way as to suggest or hint to the eyewitness who the suspect is[887];

- the eyewitness is not to be:

    - told; or

    - indicated as to

  who is the suspect[888];

- the eyewitness should not be told that the suspect is in the identification parade[889];

- an independent person should be requested to attend and observe the conduct of the identification parade;

- the eyewitness must be asked to identify the suspect without assistance. The use of questions such as:

  'Is that the man?' is impermissible[890];

  An eyewitness should merely be asked if he or she recognises anyone[891];

- the eyewitness should not see the suspect in police custody prior to participating in the identification parade; and

---

[887] See *Police v Meli* [2000] WSSC 55.

[888] See *Police v Meli* [2000] WSSC 55.

[889] See *The State v Thomas Some* (1982) N366(M); *The State v Paul Dotaona* [2006] PGNC 67 and *The State v Henry Among* [2007] PGNC 11.

[890] See *R v Chapman* (1911) 7 Cr App R 53.

[891] See *The State v Thomas Some* (1982) N366(M) and *The State v Paul Dotaona* [2006] PGNC 67.

- the eyewitness should not be called upon to identify the suspect twice at an identification parade. Once a clear identification has been made there is no useful purpose in repeating the identification and to do so only gives rise to suspicion that the first identification was perhaps not done properly.[892]

An accused person's choice not to participate in an identification parade is of no 'probative value[893]' and should not be led into evidence by the prosecution.[894]

[6.0] VOICE IDENTIFICATION[895]

Like eye witness identification, voice identification testimony has been regarded as legitimate and competent to establish identity in a criminal trial.[896]

Evidence that the voice of a person involved in an alleged offence is the voice of an accused person is admissible to prove identification of the accused person where:

- the voice is:
    - known; and
    - recognised

  by the witness; or

[892] See *R v Rifasia* (Solomon Islands Criminal Case No. 45 of 1976).

[893] Refer also to the chapter titled 'Weight'.

[894] See *R v Kiro* [1999] NZCA 100.

[895] See also: *R v EJ Smith* (1986) 7 NSWLR 444; *R v Clarence Osbourne* [1992] JLR 452; *R v Mackay* [1985] VR 623; *R v Harris (No. 3)* [1990] VR 310 at 314; *R v Zullo* [1993] 1 Qd R 572 at 578; *R v Keating (a)* (1909) 2 Cr App R 61; *R v Smith* (1984) 1 NSWLR 462; *Corke* (1989) 41 A Crim R 292 and *R v Brotherton* (1992) 29 NSWLR 95, (1993) 65 A Crim R 301.

[896] See *The State v Kipma* [1997] PNGLR 178, [1997] PGNC 208 and *The State v Dickson Wape* (1994) N1281.

See also: *R v EJ Smith* [1984] NSWLR 462, (1984) 12 A Crim R 439.

- the voice is not previously known to the witness, but has such distinctive features that it leaves a clear mental impression in the mind of the witness enabling him or her to draw the conclusion on hearing it later that it was the same voice.[897]

The reliability of voice identification varies with such factors including:

- the length and volume of speech heard;
- the witness's familiarity with the voice of the accused person; and
- the time elapsing between:
    - the occasion when the witness heard the voice of the accused person; and
    - the identification to the Court.[898]

If voice identification is in issue, the Court should consider the relevant principles enunciated in *R v Turnbull and others*[899] as regards a warning.[900]

[7.0] FINGERPRINT EVIDENCE

[7.1] STATUTORY PROVISION

Section 21 of the *Arrest Act* (Ch. 339) ['Finger-prints, etc'] enables a police officer to take the fingerprints and palm prints of any person on a charge of committing an offence.

---

[897] See *The State v Daniel* [1988-89] PNGLR 580 and *The State v Jimmy Kipma* (1997) N1543.

[898] See *Bulejcik v R* (1996) 185 CLR 375; *Festa v R* (2001) 208 CLR 593, per McHugh J at 619 and *Neville v R* [2004] WASCA 62.

[899] [1977] QB 224, (1976) 63 Cr App R 132, [1976] 3 WLR 445, [1976] 3 All ER 549, [1976] Crim LR 565.

[900] See *R v Hersey* [1998] Crim LR 281.

[7.2] GENERAL PRINCIPLES

The evidence of fingerprints or palm prints alone is sufficient evidence of identity to support a conviction[901], subject to:

- their location; and
- the circumstances of the case.

The fact of the individuality of the corrugations of the skin on the fingers of the human hand is recognised as to require very little, if any, evidence of it. A fingerprint is therefore in reality an unforgeable signature.[902]

A Court may take 'judicial notice[903]' that no two people have identical fingerprints.[904]

A fingerprint has been described as an unforgeable signature.[905]

If there are fewer than eight similar ridge characteristics, it is highly unlikely that a Court will exercise its discretion to admit such evidence and, save in wholly exceptional circumstances, the prosecution should not seek to adduce such evidence. If there are eight or more similar ridge characteristics, a Court may exercise its discretion in favour of admitting the evidence. How the discretion is exercised will depend on all the circumstances of the case, including in particular:

- the experience and expertise of a fingerprint expert[906];
- the number of similar ridge characteristics;

---

[901] See *R v Koito-Gaocatal* [1967-68] PNGLR 217, [1967] PGSC 26; *The State v Jack Kumul Ure Kore* (1999) N1856 and *The State v Jupui Kapera* (1986) N567.

See also: *Blacker v R* (1910) 10 CLR 604; *R v Morris (No. 2)* [1914] St R Qd 274, [1914] QWN 43, (1914) 8 QJPR 163, (1914) 9 QJPR 28; *R v Castleton* (1910) 3 Cr App R 74 and *R v Court* (1960) 44 Cr App R 242.

[902] See *Parker v R* (1912) 14 CLR 681.

[903] Refer also to the section titled 'Judicial Notice' in the chapter titled 'Court Procedure' in the text titled 'Injia on Criminal Practice and Procedure in Papua New Guinea and the Pacific'.

[904] See *The State v Jupui Kapera* (1986) N567.

[905] See *Parker v R* (1912) 14 CLR 681.

[906] Refer also to the chapter titled 'Opinion Evidence'.

- whether there are dissimilar characteristics;
- the size of the print relied on, in that the same number of similar ridge characteristics may be more compelling in a fingerprint of print than in an entire print; and
- the quality and clarity of the print on the item relied on, which may involve, for example, consideration of possible injury to the person who left the print, as well as factors such as smearing or contamination.[907]

[7.3] EVIDENCE TO CALL

[7.3.1] SCENES-OF-CRIME OFFICER

The following questions should be asked of the Scenes of Crime officer who attended the crime scene:

- "What is your full name?";
- "What is your current rank?";
- "Where are you currently stationed?";
- "What are your current duties?";
- "What is your experience in the taking of fingerprints?";
- "What is your qualification as regards the taking of fingerprints?";
- "Do you recall at (specify time) on (specify the date) attending the address of (specify the name of the complainant)?";
- "Did you take fingerprints at that address?";
- "Where were those fingerprints located?"; and

---

[907] See *R v Buckley* (1999) 163 JP 561at 568.

See also: *R v Koito-Gaocatal* [1967-68] PNGLR 217, [1967] PGSC 26.

- "Can you please produce the fingerprint lift/s?"

The prosecutor should seek to tender the fingerprint lift/s as an exhibit.

[7.3.2] FINGERPRINT EXPERT

The following questions should be asked of a Fingerprint Expert:

- "What is your full name?";
- "What is your current rank?";
- "Where are you currently stationed?";
- "Are you recognised as a fingerprint expert within the Royal Papua New Guinea Constabulary?";
- "What are current duties?";
- "What is your experience in the comparison of fingerprints?";
- "What is your qualification as regards the comparison of fingerprints?";
- "Do you recall receiving (specify the number) of fingerprint lifts on (specify the date) in relation to (specify the name of the complainant)?";
- "Who did you receive those fingerprint lifts from?";
- "Are these the fingerprint lift/s that you referred to in your evidence?";
- "Did you compare those fingerprint lifts against the fingerprint forms with the name (specify the name of the accused person) dated (specify the date that fingerprints were taken) taken by (specify who took the fingerprints)?";
- "When was the comparison done?";
- "Can you look at these fingerprint forms?";

- "What are they?";
- "Please tell the Court how you conducted the comparison?";
- "What did your comparison prove in your opinion?";
- "What are those photographic enlargements of?"; and
- "How many ridge characteristics are the same when comparing the fingerprint lift/s and the photographic enlargements?"

The prosecutor should then seek to tender:

- the document with the fingerprint lifts; and
- the fingerprint forms

as exhibits.

[8.0] DOCK IDENTIFICATION[908]

Where there is an out-of-court identification of an accused person the subsequent identification of that person in court, referred to as 'dock identification', is usually carried out to confirm that the person previously identified is, in fact, the accused person.[909]

It is not dock identification, but a pure formality, if the witness already knows the accused person.[910]

---

[908] Refer also to the subsection titled 'Eliciting Evidence' in the section titled 'Examination-in-Chief' in the chapter titled 'Examination Of Witnesses' in the text titled 'Injia on Criminal Practice and Procedure in Papua New Guinea and the Pacific'.

See also: *Peter Kawa Maima v the State* (1998) SC574; *Barnes v Chief Constable of Durham* [1997] 2 Cr App R 505; *R v Cartwright* (1914) 10 Cr App R 219; *R v Howick* [1970] Crim LR 403; *R v John* [1973] Crim LR 113 and *Grbic v Pitkethly* (1992) 65 A Crim R 12, (1992) 38 FCR 95.

[909] See *Grbic v Pitkethly* (1992) 65 A Crim R 12, (1992) 38 FCR 95 at 104.

[910] See *Stewart v R* (2011) 79 WIR 409, [2011] UKPC 12; *Tido v R* [2012] 1 WLR 115 [2011] UKPC 16 and *Neilly v R (The Bahamas)* [2012] UKPC 12.

Such in-court or dock identification is generally regarded as the most problematic of all forms of eyewitness identification.[911]

Evidence given by a witness identifying an accused person as the offender whom he or she saw at the time of an offence or in circumstances connected with an offence will generally be of very little 'weight[912]' if the identifying witness:

- has not seen the offender since that time; and
- is asked to identify the accused person for the first time in the court.[913]

Particularly, if the witness has not, by reason of previous knowledge of association, become familiar with the appearance of the accused person. In theory the manner in which an accused person was identified out of court goes to the weight, rather than to the admissibility of the evidence.[914]

However, it can never be suggested that dock identification is inadmissible.[915]

A Court should however only rely on such evidence with great care when considering the inherent dangers associated with such identification.[916]

---

[911] See *Davies and Cody v R* [1937] 57 CLR 170, [1937] HCA 27; *Festa v R* (2001) 208 CLR 593, [2001] HCA 72 and *Alexander v R* (1981) 145 CLR 395, per Gibbs CJ at 399 and Mason J at 426-427, (1981) 34 ALR 289, [1981] HCA 17.

See also: Australian Law Reform Commission, 2005, 'Uniform Evidence Law', Report 112, NSWLRC Report 102 and VLRC Final Report, paragraph 13.93.

[912] Refer also to the chapter titled 'Weight'.

[913] See *Alexander v R* (1981) 145 CLR 395, per Gibbs CJ at 399, (1981) 34 ALR 289, [1981] HCA 17.

[914] See *Alexander v R* (1981) 145 CLR 395, per Gibbs CJ at 399, (1981) 34 ALR 289, [1981] HCA 17.

[915] See *Festa v R* (2001) 208 CLR 593, per Gleeson CJ at 599, [2001] HCA 72; *R v Hallam* (1985) 42 SASR 126, per King CJ at 129-130; *R v Britten* (1988) 51 SASR 567, per King CJ at 572; *R v Demeter* [1995] 2 Qd R 626; *Pipersburgh v The State (Belize)* (2008) 72 WIR 108, [2008] UKPC 11; *Aurelio Pop v R* [2003] UKPC 40, (2003) 147 SJLB 692; *Young v The State (Trinidad and Tobago)* [2008] UKPC 27; *Maxo Tido v R* [2012] 1 WLR 115, [2011] UKPC 16; *Holland v HM Advocate* [2005] UKPC D1, 2005 SLT 563 and *Edwards v R* (2006) 69 WIR 360, [2006] UKPC 23.

[916] See *Aurelio Pop v R* [2003] UKPC 40, (2003) 147 SJLB 692; *Young v The State (Trinidad and Tobago)* [2008] UKPC 27; *R v Graham* [1994] Crim LR 212; *Williams (Noel) v R* [1997] 1 WLR 548 and *Pipersburgh v The State (Belize)* (2008) 72 WIR 108, [2008] UKPC 11.

The 'weight' that a Court will give dock identification will obviously be dictated by factors including:

- the circumstances under which the eyewitness initially identified the accused person;
- the time period between:
    - the initial observation of the accused person; and
    - the subsequent identification in the Court;
- whether the accused person was identified in an identification parade or other means of identification out-of-court; and
- whether the eyewitness knew the accused person prior to the commission of the offence.

[9.0] PHOTOBOARD

At common law, the courts allow the police to use a photograph of a person in the detection process[917], even though it may be one that might suggests that the person was in police custody when the photograph was taken.[918]

However, the police must ensure that the identification by means of a collection of photographs is correctly carried out.[919]

---

[917] See *The State v Sela Gipe* (2000) N2058.

[918] See *R v Dwyer* [1925] 2 KB 799.

See also: *Alexander v R* (1981) 145 CLR 395, (1981) 34 ALR 289, [1981] HCA 17.

As provided for by section 21 of the *Arrest Act* (Ch. 339) ['Fingerprints, etc'] there is the power to take photographs and other identifying particulars of any person on a charge of committing an offence.

Refer also to the section titled 'Fingerprint Evidence' in this chapter.

[919] See *R v Dickman* (1910) 5 Cr App R 135 at 142.

The following best practice should be complied with in order for identification by means of a photoboard to be conducted fairly to an accused person:

- there should be 12 photographs on a single board;
- each person should be of a similar description, ie., skin colour, colour of hair, hair length, beard or moustache;
- each photograph should be of the head and shoulders of the person;
- each photograph should be evenly spaced;
- a number should be written below each photograph; and
- the eyewitness should be asked whether he or she can identify any person on the photoboard by reference to the number below the photograph of that person.

[10.0] CLOTHING

The recognition of the clothing worn by an offender can assist in proving the identification of the accused person.[920]

[11.0] HANDWRITING EVIDENCE

[11.1] STATUTORY PROVISION

Section 31 of the *Evidence Act* (Ch. 48) ['Comparision of Disputed Hand-writings'] states:

> 'A comparison of a disputed hand-writing with a sample of hand-writing proved, to the satisfaction of the court, to be genuine may be made by witnesses, and the hand-writings and the testimony of the witnesses respecting them may be submitted to the court as evidence of the genuineness or otherwise of the hand-writing in dispute'.

[920] See *R v Hickin and others* [1996] Crim LR 584.

[11.2] GENERAL PRINCIPLES[921]

The issue whether an accused person is the author of a particular document, and therefore its authentication, can be proved by:

- an admission by the accused person[922];
- a witness who observed the accused person write the document[923];
- the evidence of a witness who:
  - had regularly corresponded with the accused person; and
  - is able to recognise the handwriting of the accused person to the satisfaction of the Court[924]; or
- the opinion evidence of a handwriting expert[925].[926]

A Court must be satisfied 'beyond reasonable doubt' that the disputed writing is genuine.[927]

---

[921] See also: *R v Smith (Hereford) (a)* (1909) 3 Cr App R 87 at 90.

[922] Refer also to the section titled 'Formal Admission' in the chapter titled 'Court Procedure' in the text titled 'Injia on Criminal Practice and Procedure in Papua New Guinea and the Pacific'.

[923] See *R v O'Brien* (1912) 7 Cr App R 29 and *R v McCartney and Hansen* (1928) 20 Cr App R 179.

[924] See *R v O'Brien* (1912) 7 Cr App R 29.

[925] See *R v Rickard* (1918) 13 Cr App R 140; *R v Tilley and Tilley* (1961) 45 Cr App R 360 at 364 and *R v Smith* (1968) 52 Cr App R 648, [1968] Crim LR 674.

Refer also to the section titled 'Expert' in the chapter titled 'Opinion Evidence'.

[926] See also: New Zealand Law Commission, 1994, 'Evidence Law: Documentary Evidence and Judicial Notice – A Discussion Paper', Preliminary Paper 22.

Refer also to the section titled 'Documentary Medical Evidence' in the chapter titled 'Documentary Evidence'.

[927] See *R v Ewing* [1983] QB 1039, (1983) 77 Cr App R 47.

IDENTIFICATION EVIDENCE

Although expert evidence is not essential for a Court to come to a conclusion on a comparison of disputed handwriting, a Court must warn itself of the dangers involved in proceeding without expert testimony.[928]

A photocopy of a disputed writing may be used for the purpose of comparison, if there is evidence that the original has been lost.[929]

---

[928] See *The State v Baine* [1990] 1 PNGLR 1 and *R v Magalu* [1974] PNGLR 188, [1974] PGSC 21.

See also: *R v Derrick* (1910) 5 Cr App R 162.

See however: *R v O'Sullivan* (1969) 53 Cr App R 274 and *R v Tilley and Tilley* (1961) 45 Cr App R 360.

[929] See *Lockheed Arabia v Owen* [1993] 3 WLR 468, (1993) 3 All ER 641, [1993] QB 806.

Refer also to the section titled 'Missing Exhibit' in the chapter titled 'Exhibits'.

[1.0] MEDICAL PRACTITIONER

Section 102 of the *District Courts Act* (Ch. 40) ['Statements of Witnesses Dead, etc'] refers to a 'person registered under the *Medical Registration Act 1980'* and section 37 of the *Evidence Act* (Ch. 48) ['Evidence of Scientific Examination'] refers to the term 'medical practitioner'.

Whilst the term 'medical practitioner' is not defined in the *Evidence Act* (Ch. 48), it is defined in section 3 of the *Interpretation Act* (Ch. 2) as meaning:

> 'a person registered, provisionally registered or temporarily registered as a medical practitioner under the *Medical Registration Act 1980*'.

The term 'registered medical practitioner' is defined in section 1 of the *Medical Registration Act 1980* as meaning:

> 'a person whose name appears on a register kept under Section 11(1)(a)'.

Section 11(1) of the *Medical Registration Act 1980* ['Registers to be Kept'] states (in part):

> 'The Medical Registrar shall keep separate registers of persons approved by the Board for –
>
> (a) registration as medical practitioners under Section 22'.

Section 22 of the *Medical Registration Act 1980* ['Approval of Registration'] states:

> 'Where, by personal interview or by any other means, the Board is satisfied that an applicant for registration, or provisional registration, as a medical practitioner –
>
> (a) is of good character and a fit and proper person to be registered, or provisionally registered, as a medical practitioner; and
>
> (b) possesses the minimum qualifications for registration, or provisional registration, set out in Section 23 or 24,
>
> the Board may approve the registration, or provisional registration, of the applicant as a medical practitioner'.

In compliance with sections 23 ['Minimum Qualifications for Registration'] and 24 ['Minimum Qualifications for Provisional Registration'] of the *Medical Registration Act 1980* a medical practitioner must:

- be duly registered as a 'medical practitioner';
- have acquired and completed the necessary studies in medicine and surgery; and

- have undergone clinical training at places as approved by the Papua New Guinea Medical Board.

[2.0] HEALTH EXTENSION OFFICER

A health extension officer is an 'allied health worker'.[930]

Section 39 of the *Medical Registration Act* (Ch. 398) ['Allied Health Workers'] states:

> 'The Board may prescribe –
>
> (a) categories of allied health work[931]; and
>
> (b) the course of studies to be undertaken by a person preparatory to registration as an allied health worker in each of the prescribed categories of allied health work'.

However, a registered nurse is not an 'allied health worker' under the *Medical Registration Act* (Ch. 398).

[3.0] NURSE

[3.1] REGISTERED NURSE

A registered nurse must be duly registered under the provisions of the *Medical Registration Act* (Ch. 398).[932]

---

[930] See section 39 of the *Medical Registration Act* (Ch. 398) ['Allied Health Workers'].

[931] See:
- section 2(3) ['Categories of Medical, etc Specialities']; and
- Part 3 of Schedule 2 ['Allied Health Workers']

of the *Medical Registration By-laws* (Ch. 398A).

[932] See Division 3 of Part III of the *Medical Registration Act* (Ch. 398) ['Registration of Nurses'].

[3.2] ENROLLED NURSE

An enrolled nurse must be duly enrolled under the provisions of the *Medical Registration Act* (Ch. 398).[933]

[4.0] HOSPITAL PATIENT RECORD[934]

Pursuant to section 61 of the *Evidence Act* (Ch. 48) ['Business Records'] a 'business record' may be admissible as to the proof of its contents without the need to call evidence from a witness.

Whilst a hospital patient record is a 'business record' for the purposes of section 61 it is not admissible, unless there is proof as to:

- how the document was made in accordance with section 61(2)(a);
- the trustworthiness of the source of information; and
- the method of preparation.[935]

Subject to satisfying that criteria to the satisfaction of the Court this provision only permits the tendering of the hospital patient record.[936]

Pursuant to Division 5 of Part IV of the *Evidence Act* (Ch. 48) ['Computerised Information'] a computer record may be admissible as to the proof of its contents without the need to call evidence from a witness and therefore, if a medical record is computerised then a printout of the record would be admissible.[937]

---

933 See Division 4 of Part III of the *Medical Registration Act* (Ch. 398) ['Enrolment of Nurses'].

934 Refer also to the section titled 'Documentary Medical Evidence' in the chapter titled 'Documentary Evidence'.

935 See *Doa Kerua v The State* [1981] PNGLR 357.

936 Refer also to the section titled 'Business Records' in the chapters titled 'Documentary Evidence' and 'Hearsay Evidence'.

937 Refer also to the section titled 'Computer Records' in the chapters titled 'Documentary Evidence' and 'Hearsay Evidence'.

[5.0] STATEMENT OF MEDICAL PRACTITIONER

Section 102 of the *District Courts Act* (Ch. 40) ['Statements of Witnesses Dead, etc'] permits the tendering of a statement of a 'medical practitioner' duly registered under the *Medical Practitioners Act 1980* in the National Court with the consent of the Court.[938]

[6.0] AFFIDAVIT OF MEDICAL PRACTITIONER[939]

[6.1] STATUTORY PROVISION

Section 37 of the *Evidence Act* (Ch. 48) ['Evidence of Scientific Examination'] states:

> '(1) An affidavit made by a medical practitioner who has made a medical, pathological or other scientific examination of a thing setting out –
>
> (a) his qualifications; and
>
> (b) that he has made the examination; and
>
> (c) the facts that he has ascertained and the conclusions at which he has arrived as a result of the examination,
>
> is admissible in evidence in any legal proceedings in a court.
>
> (2) Without affecting the admissibility of an affidavit made under Subsection (1), that subsection does not prevent a court, where it is satisfied, on application, that the justice of the case warrants its doing so, from –
>
> (a) requiring the medical practitioner who made the affidavit to attend and give evidence before the court if he is in the country and can be brought before the court without depriving the community or any part of the community of any essential service; or
>
> (b) arranging for the taking of his evidence orally by way of commission or in any other manner.

---

[938] See *The State v Samson Wailo (No. 2)* [1991] PNGLR 150, (1991) N1010, [1991] PGNC 83.

[939] Refer also to the section titled 'Documentary Medical Evidence' in the chapter titled 'Documentary Evidence'.

(3) Where –

(a) a person is charged with an indictable offence; and

(b) evidence is given on affidavit under Subsection (1); and

(c) the deponent does not give evidence in person,

the court shall not dispose of the matter summarily except with the consent of the accused'.

[6.2] GENERAL PRINCIPLES

Section 37 of the *Evidence Act* (Ch. 48) ['Evidence of Scientific Examination'] enables the evidence of a medical practitioner to be given by the use of an affidavit, including a certified statement.[940]

The legal requirements of this section are as follows:

- the medical examination must have been conducted by a medical practitioner, ie., the medical practitioner's qualification and confirmation of registration;
- the medical practitioner's experience;
- that the medical practitioner had made the examination; and
- the facts that the medical practitioner has ascertained and the conclusions which he or she had arrived at as a result of the examination.

[940] See *The State v Paulin Taupin; The State v Jim Kandamain* (1995) N1323, [1995] PGNC 18.

[7.0] STATEMENT/AFFIDAVIT REQUIREMENTS[941]

[7.1] INTRODUCTION

There are a number of requirements to be covered in:

- a statement from either a medical practitioner, health extension officer or nurse; and
- an affidavit from a medical practitioner.

[7.2] QUALIFICATIONS

[7.2.1] MEDICAL PRACTITIONER

A medical practitioner should state:

- I am a duly [provisionally] registered medical practitioner in Papua New Guinea under the *Medical Registration Act 1980.*
- I have successfully completed a degree in medicine and surgery from the [specify the name of the university].
- I have undergone clinic training as required by the Papua New Guinea Medical Board.

[7.2.2] HEALTH EXTENSION OFFICER

A health extension officer should state:

- I am a duly [provisionally] registered allied health worker in Papua New Guinea under the *Medical Registration Act 1980* as a 'health extension officer'.
- I have successfully completed [specify the qualification] from the [specify the name of the university/college, etc].
- I have undergone clinic training as required by the Papua New Guinea Medical Board.

[941] Refer also to the section titled 'Documentary Medical Evidence' in the chapter titled 'Documentary Evidence'.

[7.2.3] REGISTERED NURSE

A registered nurse should state:

- I am a duly registered nurse in Papua New Guinea under the *Medical Registration Act 1980.*
- I have successfully completed a course of studies from the [specify the name of the university/college, etc] as required under section 85(b) of *Medical Registration Act 1980* in order to be a duly registered nurse.

[7.2.4] ENROLLED NURSE

An enrolled nurse should state:

- I am a duly enrolled nurse in Papua New Guinea under the *Medical Registration Act 1980.*
- I have successfully completed a course of studies from the [specify the name of the university/college, etc] as required under section 91(b) of *Medical Registration Act 1980* in order to be a duly enrolled nurse.

[7.3] EXPERIENCE

[7.3.1] MEDICAL PRACTITIONER

A medical practitioner should state:

Since being provisionally registered as a medical practitioner in [year of completion] I have [outline a summary of the Medical Practitioner's experience].

[7.3.2] HEALTH EXTENSION OFFICER

A health extension officer should state:

Since being provisionally registered as an Allied Health Worker in [year of completion] I have [outline a summary of the health extension officer's experience].

[7.3.3] NURSE

A duly registered nurse or enrolled nurse should state:

Since being registered/enrolled as a registered/enrolled nurse in [year of completion] I have [outline a summary of the nurse's experience].

[7.4] HOSPITAL PATIENT RECORD[942]

A medical practitioner, health extension officer or nurse should state:

- I recall examining a patient by the name of [specify the name of the patient] on [specify the date of the examination] at [location of the examination].

- I recorded the results of my examination on a hospital patient record at the time of my examination.

- For the purpose of accuracy and in order to refresh my memory I would now like to refer to that hospital patient record.

The prosecution may tender that hospital patient record as an exhibit under section 61 of the *Evidence Act* (Ch. 48) ['Business Records'].[943]

[7.5] VERSION OF COMPLAINANT

A medical practitioner, health extension officer or nurse should state:

The patient told me that [outline a summary of the allegations].

---

[942] Refer also to the section titled 'Documentary Medical Evidence' in the chapter titled 'Documentary Evidence'.

[943] Refer also to the section titled 'Business Record' in the chapter titled 'Documentary Evidence'.

A medical practitioner, health extension officer or nurse is able to give evidence of what a complainant said during the course of an examination. However, the purpose of such a conversation is not to prove the truth of what the complainant said happened, but to indicate the reason why the medical practitioner, health extension officer or nurse examined particular parts of the complainant's body.[944]

[7.6] MEDICAL EXAMINATION FINDINGS

A medical practitioner, health extension officer or nurse should state:

- I then conducted an examination of the body of the patient.
- My observations in relation to that examination are as follows: [outline the observations]

[7.7] MEDICAL OPINION[945]

A Court may accept the opinion evidence of a health extension officer, notwithstanding that such a person is not a medical practitioner.[946]

A medical practitioner or health extension officer may base his or her opinion as to the medical condition of a patient on a medical textbook or article.[947]

---

[944] See *Ramsay v Watson* (1961) 108 CLR 642 at 649, [1961] HCA 65.

See also: *R v Tonkin and Montgomery* [1975] Qd R 1; *R v Schafferius* [1977] Qd R 213; *R v Henry* [1977] Qd R 204; *R v Smith* (1979) 69 Cr App R 378 at 386 and *Gordon v R* (1982) 41 ALR 64.

Refer also to the section titled 'Common Law Exceptions' in the chapter titled 'Hearsay Evidence'.

[945] Refer also to the section titled 'Expert' in the chapter titled 'Opinion Evidence'.

[946] See *The State v Aiaka Karavea and another* (1983) N452(M), [1983] PGNC 12; *The State v Onjawe Tunamai* (2000) N1989, [2000] PGNC 29; *The State v David Yakuye Daniel* (2005) N2869, [2005] PGNC 89 and *The State v Samson Bino* (2009) N3769, [2009] PGNC 150.

[947] An expert witness is entitled to express an opinion based on information, published or unpublished and usually in written form, received from other experts. Medical textbooks constitute a prime example. The relevant information must be of a type generally and reasonably relied upon and falling for evaluation within the relevant field of expertise, see *R v Wan Pui-hay* [1994] 2 HKCLR 47 at 48-49 and *Reid v Kerr* (1974) 9 SASR 367 at 390.

MEDICAL EVIDENCE

A medical practitioner[948] or health extension officer is entitled to support his or her opinion by referring to a professional practice with which he or she is familiar.

A nurse may also give opinion evidence, subject to the discretion of the court.

The following opinions may be given:

Bodily Harm[949]

- I am aware that the term 'bodily harm' is defined in section 1(1) of the *Criminal Code* (Ch. 262) as meaning 'any bodily injury that interferes with health or comfort'.

- Based on the results of my medical examination I am of the opinion that the patient did suffer an injury consistent with the legal definition of the term 'bodily harm' for the following reasons: [specify the reason/s].

Wounding[950]

- I am aware that the legal definition of the term 'wound' means that the whole skin was severed.

- Based on the results of my medical examination I am of the opinion that the patient did suffer an injury consistent with the legal definition of the term 'wound' for the following reasons: [specify the reason/s].

Grievous Bodily Harm[951]

- I am aware that the term 'grievous bodily harm' is defined in section 1 of the *Criminal Code* (Ch. 262) as meaning 'any bodily injury of such a nature as to endanger or be likely to endanger life, or to cause or be likely to cause permanent injury to health'.

---

[948] See *R v JAJ Smith* [1973] 1 WLR 1510, [1974] 1 All ER 376, (1973) 58 Cr App R 106.

[949] Refer also to the chapter titled 'Offences Against The Person' in the text titled 'Injia on Criminal Offences in Papua New Guinea and the Pacific'.

[950] Refer also to the chapter titled 'Offences Against The Person' in the text titled 'Injia on Criminal Offences in Papua New Guinea and the Pacific'.

[951] Refer also to the chapter titled 'Offences Against The Person' in the text titled 'Injia on Criminal Offences in Papua New Guinea and the Pacific'.

- Based on the results of my medical examination I am of the opinion that the patient did suffer an injury consistent with the legal definition of the term 'grievous bodily harm' for the following reasons: [specify the reason/s].

Cause Death[952]

- Based on the results of my medical examination I am of the opinion that the deceased did die from [...] for the following reasons: [specify the reason/s].

[952] Refer also to the chapter titled 'Offences Against The Person' in the text titled 'Injia on Criminal Offences in Papua New Guinea and the Pacific'.

OPINION EVIDENCE

[1.0] INTRODUCTION

At common law the general rule is that witnesses may not offer their opinion as evidence.[953]

The opinion rule is based on the distinction between fact and opinion.[954]

The opinion rule is based on the premise that some testimony is obtained by direct observation and is therefore factual, while other testimony is obtained by inference from observation and is therefore opinion.[955]

A witness must only give evidence of facts and it is up to the fact-finder to draw inferences from those facts, subject to the following exceptions:

- a non-expert, such as a police officer, may be allowed to give opinion evidence if:
    - it is a concise way of describing facts that the witness personally perceived; and
    - the facts cannot conveniently be stated other than in the form of an opinion; and
- a properly qualified expert witness may be allowed to give opinion evidence on matters within their field of expertise.[956]

The difference between the opinion evidence of an expert witness and a lay person is:

> The opinion of a lay person is based on his or her observations of the facts in issue which is not necessarily the basis of the admissibility of opinion evidence given by an expert witness.[957]

Considering that in most circumstances an expert witness will not observe the commission of an offence the expert witness uses his or her expertise to determine what occurred.

---

[953] See New Zealand Law Commission, 1991, 'Evidence Law: Expert Evidence and Opinion Evidence – A Discussion Paper', Preliminary Paper 18, page 1 and New Zealand Law Commission, 1999, 'Evidence. Volume 1: Reform of the Law and Evidence. Volume 2: Evidence Code and Commentary', Report 55, page 22.

[954] See New Zealand Law Commission, 1991, 'Evidence Law: Expert Evidence and Opinion Evidence – A Discussion Paper', Preliminary Paper 18, page 3.

[955] See New Zealand Law Commission, 1991, 'Evidence Law: Expert Evidence and Opinion Evidence – A Discussion Paper', Preliminary Paper 18, page 3.

[956] See New Zealand Law Commission, 1999, 'Evidence. Volume 1: Reform of the Law and Evidence. Volume 2: Evidence Code and Commentary', Report 55, page 22.

[957] See *Folkes v Chadd* (1782) 3 Doug KB 157, 99 ER 58, per Lord Mansfield.

OPINION EVIDENCE

An opinion by both an expert and a lay person may be given to a Court based on an experiment conducted in relation to the facts of the particular case.[958]

[2.0] EXPERT

[2.1] INTRODUCTION[959]

The opinion evidence of an expert should be as simplistic as possible.[960]

The criteria for the admissibility of opinion evidence from an expert is as follows:

- an opinion should not generally be offered on an issue if it is an ultimate issue that the Court has to decide, referred to as the 'ultimate issue rule'[961];
- the Court must be satisfied that there is an issue of fact the determination of which requires the application of:
    - expertise;
    - knowledge;

---

[958] See *Birks v Western Australia* (2007) 168 A Crim R 350, [2007] WASCA 29; *R v Ireland (No. 2)* [1971] SASR 6 at 14-15; *Chamberlain v R (No. 2)* (1984) 153 CLR 514 at 548, (1984) 51 ALR 225, [1984] HCA 7; *Thompson v R* (1986) 13 FCR 165 and *R v Neilan* [1992] 1 VR 57 at 74-75.

As regards the distinction between an experiment and a reconstruction, see *R v Baker* [1989] 3 NZLR 635.

[959] As regards:

- the history of expert opinion evidence, see *Dasreef Pty Limited v Hawchar* [2011] HCA 21, per Heydon J;
- preparation of an expert to give evidence, see Speech by The Honorable Justice PLG Brereton RFD, 'Aspects of Advocacy: The Effective Presentation of Evidence', College of Law, Advanced Family Law Weekend, 2006; and
- ballistic evidence, see *The State v Melchior Ibor* (2005) N2896 and the chapter titled 'Forensic Evidence'.

[960] See *Lewis v R* (1987) 88 FLR 104, per Maurice J at 123-124 and *R v Lucas* [1992] 2 VR 108, per Hampel J at 116-117.

[961] See New Zealand Law Commission, 1999, 'Evidence. Volume 1: Reform of the Law and Evidence. Volume 2: Evidence Code and Commentary', Report 55, page 22.

  - learning; or
  - experience

  beyond that of ordinary persons;

- the Court must be satisfied that the expert witness possesses sufficient of that expertise, knowledge, learning or experience to enable him or her to express an opinion on the issue of value;

- the expert's opinion must be based on proven admissible evidence, referred to as the 'factual basis rule'[962];

- the Court must know:
  - the 'facts'; and
  - the 'assumptions'

  upon which it is based;

- the Court must be satisfied that the subject of the testimony is supported by a body of expertise, knowledge, learning or experience that is sufficiently:
  - organised; or
  - recognised

  to be accepted as reliable;

- the Court must be satisfied that there must be reasons for the conclusion of the expert based on:
  - the proven facts or assumptions; and
  - the application of his or her expertise, knowledge, learning and/or experience; and

[962] See New Zealand Law Commission, 1999, 'Evidence. Volume 1: Reform of the Law and Evidence. Volume 2: Evidence Code and Commentary', Report 55, page 22.

- the Court must be satisfied that the expert witness must be able to provide:
    - impartial; and
    - objective

  evidence on the matters within his or her field of expertise.

A Court is, however, not bound by the opinion of an expert witness.[963]

It is up to the Court:

- whether to accept the evidence of an expert witness; and, if so
- to attach such 'weight[964]' as it sees fit.[965]

A Court may accept the opinion evidence of a health extension officer, notwithstanding that such a person is not a medical practitioner.[966]

---

[963] See *The State v Taupin; The State v Kandamain* (1995) N1323, [1995] PGNC 18.

See also: *R v Stockwell* (1993) 97 Cr App R 260; *R v Bailey* (1978) 66 Cr App R 31; *R v Rivett* (1950) 34 Cr App R 87; *R v Lanfear* [1968] 1 All ER 683; *R v Nawell* [1948] 1 All ER 744; *Beim v Collins* (1954) 28 ALJR 331 and *Hollingworth v Hopkins* [1967] 1 Qd R 168.

[964] Refer also to the chapter titled 'Weight'.

[965] See *The State v Paulin Taupin and The State v Jim Kandamain* (1995) N1323, [1995] PGNC 18.

See also: *Davie v Edinburgh Magistrates* [1953] SC 34, per Lord President Cooper at 40.

[966] See *The State v Aiaka Karavea and another* (1983) N452(M), [1983] PGNC 12; *The State v Onjawe Tunamai* (2000) N1989, [2000] PGNC 29; *The State v David Yakuye Daniel* (2005) N2869, [2005] PGNC 89 and *The State v Samson Bino* (2009) N3769, [2009] PGNC 150.

Refer also to:
- the section titled 'Documentary Medical Evidence' in the chapter titled 'Documentary Evidence';
- the subsection titled 'Eliciting Evidence' in the section titled 'Examination-in-Chief' in the chapter titled 'Examination Of Witnesses' in the text titled 'Injia on Criminal Practice and Procedure in Papua New Guinea and the Pacific; and
- the chapter titled 'Medical Evidence' in the text titled 'Injia on Investigatory Practice in Papua New Guinea and the Pacific'.

OPINION EVIDENCE

The prosecution or defence should be able to call an expert for the sole purpose of bolstering the credibility of another witness (the 'credibility' or 'bolster' rule[967]).[968]

At common law a report under the hand of an expert witness is generally inadmissible if he or she is not called as a witness.[969]

If the evidence of an expert witness will be expensive or timely, the prosecution or defence should consider:

- trying to obtain a 'formal admission[970]'; or
- tendering the report by consent[971].

---

[967] Refer also to the subsection titled 'Bolster Or Credibility Rule' in the section titled 'Examination-in-Chief' in the chapter titled 'Examination Of Witnesses' in the text titled 'Injia on Criminal Practice and Procedure in Papua New Guinea and the Pacific'.

See also: Queensland Law Reform Commission, 2005, 'A Review of the Uniform Evidence Acts', Report 60, page 123.

[968] See *R v Chard* (1971) 56 Cr App R 268.

See also:
- *R v B (an accused)* [1987] 1 NZLR 362 at 367; and
- Queensland Law Reform Commission, 2005, 'A Review of the Uniform Evidence Acts', Report 60, page 123.

[969] See *R v Abadom* [1983] 1 All ER 364, (1983) 76 Cr App R 48, [1983] 1 WLR 126.

Refer however to the section titled 'Documentary Medical Evidence' in the chapter titled 'Documentary Evidence'.

Refer also to the chapter titled 'Medical Evidence'.

[970] Refer also to the section titled 'Formal Admission' in the chapter titled 'Court Procedure' in the text titled 'Injia on Criminal Practice and Procedure in Papua New Guinea and the Pacific'.

[971] Refer also to the section titled 'Admission Of Evidence Without The Calling Of A Witness' in the chapter titled 'Court Procedure' in the text titled 'Injia on Criminal Practice and Procedure in Papua New Guinea and the Pacific'.

Where expert evidence refers to photographs, plans, calculations, analyses, measurements, survey reports or other similar documents, a copy of these must be provided to the opposite party at the same time as the exchange of reports.[972]

The prosecution should ensure that all of the relevant information which the expert has discovered (whether it supports the prosecution or the defence) is revealed to the Court.[973]

[2.2] ULTIMATE ISSUE RULE

An opinion should not generally be offered on an issue if it is an ultimate issue that the fact-finder has to decide, referred to as the 'ultimate issue rule'.[974]

There is no absolute rule against evidence from an expert witness that goes to the ultimate issue[975], but it must be necessary for the proper administration of the issues before the Court.[976]

However, an expert witness should not be permitted to usurp the function of the Court as regards making determinations of fact.[977]

Nor should an expert give an opinion as to the credibility of witnesses.[978]

---

[972] See *National Justice Cia Naviera SA v Prudential Assurance Co Ltd (The Ikarian Reefer)* [1993] 2 Lloyd's Rep 68, per Cresswell J at 81-82; *Stanton v Callaghan* [2000] QB 75, per Otton LJ at 107-108; *Meadow v General Medical Council* [2007] 2 WLR 286, [2006] EWHC 429 and *R v Harris* [2006] 1 Cr App R 5, [2002] NICA B51.

[973] See *R v Tihi* [1990] 1 NZLR 540 at 548.

[974] See New Zealand Law Commission, 1999, 'Evidence. Volume 1: Reform of the Law and Evidence. Volume 2: Evidence Code and Commentary', Report 55, page 22 and New Zealand Law Commission, 1991, 'Evidence Law: Expert Evidence and Opinion Evidence – A Discussion Paper', Preliminary Paper 18, page 16.

[975] See *R v Eade* [2002] NZCA 110.

[976] See *R v Makoare* [2001] 1 NZLR 318 and *R v Parrott* (2001) 150 CCC (3d) 449.

[977] See *G v DPP* [1997] 2 Cr App R 78; *R v Edwards* (1986) 20 A Crim R 463; *R v Haidley and Alford* [1984] VR 229; *R v Ashcroft* [1965] Qd R 81; *R v Wallace* (1978) 7 A Crim R 317; *R v Edwards* (1986) 20 A Crim R 463 and *Smith v R* (1990) 64 ALJR 588.

[978] See *R v Turner* [1975] 2 WLR 56, [1975] QB 834, (1975) 60 Cr App R 80.

See also: *R v O'Callaghan* [1976] VR 441; *R v Marquard* [1993] 4 SCR 223 at 248; *R v R (D)* [1996] 2 SCR 291 and *Doheny and Adams v R* [1997] 1 Cr App R 369, per Phillips LJ at 374.

However, medical evidence tending to show that a witness suffered from a disease, defect or abnormality of the mind is admissible on the issue of reliability of a witness's evidence.[979]

When there is no issue of mental illness, medical evidence as to an accused person's state of mind is inadmissible.[980]

[2.3] COMMON KNOWLEDGE RULE

An expert cannot give evidence on a matter within the knowledge and experience of the fact-finder, known as the 'common knowledge rule'.[981]

---

[979] See *Toohey v Metropolitan Police Commissioner* [1965] AC 595.

See also: *Farrell v R* (1998) 114 CLR 286.

Refer also to the sections titled 'Suspect Witness' and 'Vulnerable And Intimidated Witness' in the chapter titled 'Witnesses' in the text titled 'Injia on Criminal Practice and Procedure in Papua New Guinea and the Pacific'.

[980] See *R v Chard* (1972) 56 Cr App R 268 and *R v Turner* [1975] 2 WLR 56, [1975] QB 834, (1975) 60 CrAppR 80.

As regards the evidence of psychiatrists and psychologists generally, see:

- *R v Turner* [1975] 2 WLR 56, [1975] QB 834, (1975) 60 Cr App R 80; *R v B* [1987] 1 NZLR 362; *R v Smith* [1981] VR 907; *R v Accused* [1989] 1 NZLR 714; *R v Kyselka* (1962) 133 CCC 103; *R v MacKenney* (1981) 72 Cr App R78; *R v Toohey* [1965] 1 AC 595; *R v O'Callaghan* [1976] VR 441; *R v Fong* [1981] Qd R 90; *R v Weightman* (1990) 92 Cr App R 291; *R v Nelson* [1982] Qd R 636; *R v MacKinney and Pinfold* (1981) 76 Cr App R 271; *R v Barry* [1984] 1 Qd R 76, (1984) 10 A Crim R 143; *R v Laurie* [1987] 2 Qd R 762, (1986) 23 A Crim R 219; *Lowery v R* [1974] 1 AC 85 and *DPP v A and B C Chewing Gum* [1968] 1 QB 159; and
- New Zealand Law Commission, 1991, 'Evidence Law: Expert Evidence and Opinion Evidence – A Discussion Paper', Preliminary Paper 18, page 18.

[981] See *R v B (an accused)* [1987] 1 NZLR 362.

See also: New Zealand Law Commission, 1999, 'Evidence. Volume 1: Reform of the Law and Evidence. Volume 2: Evidence Code and Commentary', Report 55, page 22 and New Zealand Law Commission, 1991, 'Evidence Law: Expert Evidence and Opinion Evidence – A Discussion Paper', Preliminary Paper 18, page 15.

The Court must be satisfied that there is an issue of fact the determination of which requires the application of expertise, knowledge, learning or experience beyond that of ordinary persons.[982]

[2.4] COMPETENCY OF AN EXPERT

The competency of a witness to give opinion evidence as an expert is primarily for the Court as a question of fact.[983]

The Court must be satisfied that the expert witness possesses sufficient of that expertise, knowledge, learning or experience to enable him or her to express an opinion on the issue of value.[984]

Opinion evidence of an expert may be given by persons not qualified by:

- being the holder of a university degree; or

- long experience in some area of science,

but rather who have been in a position to observe facts outside the experience of an ordinary lay person as a result of their experience.[985]

---

[982] See *Carter v Kilmartin* (1991) 12 QLR 133; *Farrell v R* (1998) 194 CLR 286; *Kelliher (Village of) v Smith* [1931] SCR 672 at 684; *R v Abbey* [1982] 2 SCR 24 at 42; *R v Lavallee* [1990] 1 SCR 852 at 870; *R v Mohan* [1994] 2 SCR 9 at 23; *Osland v R* (1998) 197 CLR 316, (1998) 159 ALR 170, at 184, [1998] HCA 75; *Mallard v R* (2003) 28 WAR 1, [2003] WASCA 296; *R v Smith* [1979] 3 All ER 605 at 611 and *Mohan* [1994] 2 SCR 9 at 10, 1994 SCC 80.

[983] See *R v Middleton* (2000) 114 A Crim R 258, [2000] WASCA 213.

[984] See *R v Turner* [1975] 2 WLR 56, [1975] QB 834, (1974) 60 Cr App R 80, per Laughton LJ at 841 and 83.

See also: *R v Bonython* (1984) 38 SASR 45, (1984) 15 A Crim R 364; *Carter v Kilmartin* (1991) 12 QLR 133; *Quick v Stoland* (1998) 87 FLR 371 at 382; *Clark v Ryan* (1960) 103 CLR 486, per Dixon CJ at 491-492; *Murphy and others v R* (1988-1989) 167 CLR 94 at 111 and 130; *Hurst* [1995] 1 Cr App R 82; *Farrell v R* (1998) 155 ALR 652 at 655; *Hoyer v United States of America* (1955) 223 F 2nd 134 at 138; *R v Scheel* (1979) 42 CCC (2nd) 31 at 34-36; *R v Stubbs* [2006] All ER(D) 133, [2006] EWCA Crim 2312 and *Leo Sawrij v North Cumbria Magistrates' Court* [2010] 1 Cr App R 22, [2009] EWHC Admin 2823.

[985] See *Weal v Bottom* (1966) 40 ALJR 436; *Ritz Hotel Ltd v Charles of the Ritz Ltd (No. 7)* (1987) 14 NSWLR 107, per McClelland J at 109; *Ritz Hotel Ltd v Charles of the Ritz Ltd (No. 20)* (1988) 14 NSWLR 124, per McClelland J at 127; *R v Clare and Peach* [1995] 2 Cr App R 333 at 337-338 and *R v Duncan* [1969] 2 NSWR 675 at 678.

OPINION EVIDENCE

An expert witness should make it clear when a particular question or issue falls outside his or her expertise[986] and should confine his or her opinion to matters within his or her reasonable expertise[987].

If an expert gives an opinion that is not based on his or her expertise then such evidence is inadmissible.[988]

An expert may give 'hearsay evidence[989]' in relation to matters which demonstrate his or her expertise.[990]

It is generally the expertise itself that determines whether this admissibility requirement is satisfied.[991]

---

[986] See *National Justice Cia Naviera SA v Prudential Assurance Co Ltd (The Ikarian Reefer)* [1993] 2 Lloyd's Rep 68, per Cresswell J at 81-82; *Stanton v Callaghan* [2000] QB 75, per Otton LJ at 107-108; *Meadow v General Medical Council* [2007] 2 WLR 286, [2006] EWHC 429 and *R v Harris* [2006] 1 Cr App R 5, [2002] NICA B51.

[987] See *R v Murphy* [1980] QB 434 at 437; *R v Oakley* [1979] RTR 417 at 421; *Makita (Aust) Pty Ltd v Sprowles* (2001) 52 NSWLR 705, [2001] NSWCA 305; *R v Bonython* (1984) 38 SASR 45 at 47; *Clark v Ryan* (1960) 103 CLR 486 at 491-492, [1960] HCA 42 and *R v Bjordal* (2005) 93 SASR 237, per Debelle J at 245.

[988] See *Dasreef Pty Ltd v Hawchar* (2011) 243 CLR 588, [2011] HCA 21; *HG v R* (1999) 197 CLR 414 and *Makita (Australia) Pty Ltd v Sprowles* (2001) 52 NSWLR 705, [2001] NSWCA 305.

[989] Refer also to the chapter titled 'Hearsay Evidence'.

[990] See *Dasreef Pty Ltd v Hawchar* (2011) 243 CLR 588, [2011] HCA 21, per Heydon J.

[991] See *R v Silverlock* [1894] 2 QB 766.

See also: *R (Doughty) v Ely Magistrates' Court* [2008] EWHC 522 (Admin); *R v Robb* (1991) 93 Cr App R 161 at 164; *Henderson and others* [2010] 2 Cr App R 24, [2010] EWCA Crim 1269 and *Weller* [2010] EWCA Crim 1085.

[2.5] FACTS AND ASSUMPTIONS

The facts upon which the expert's opinion are based must be proved by admissible evidence, known as the 'factual basis rule'.[992]

Furthermore, before a Court can assess the value of such an opinion it must know:

- the 'facts' upon which it is based[993]; and
- the 'assumptions' upon which it is based.[994]

---

[992] See *R v B (an accused)* [1987] 1 NZLR 362; *Paric v John Holland Construction Pty Ltd* (1985) 62 ALR 85, (1985) 59 ALJR 844, [1985] HCA 58; *Bevan v Blackhall and Struthers (No. 2)* [1978] 2 NZLR 97 at 123; *ASIC v Rich* (2005) 218 ALR 764, [2005] NSWCA 152 and *Ramsay v Watson* (1961) 108 CLR 642 at 648, [1961] HCA 65.

See also: New Zealand Law Commission, 1999, 'Evidence. Volume 1: Reform of the Law and Evidence. Volume 2: Evidence Code and Commentary', Report 55, page 22; New Zealand Law Commission, 1991, 'Evidence Law: Expert Evidence and Opinion Evidence – A Discussion Paper', Preliminary Paper 18, page 27 and Australian Law Reform Commission, 1985, 'Evidence', Interim Report Volume 2, paragraphs 107-108.

[993] See *R v Turner* [1975] 2 WLR 56, [1975] QB 834, per Lawton LJ at 840, (1974) 60 Cr App R 80; *Holtman v Sampson* [1985] 2 Qd R 472 at 474; *Trade Practices Commission v Arnotts Ltd (No. 5)* (1990) 21 FCR 324, per Beaumont J at 327; *Arnotts Ltd v Trade Practices Commission* (1990) 24 FCR 313 at 349 and *Pownall v Conlan Management Pty Ltd* (1995) 12 WAR 370, per Anderson J at 389-390.

[994] See *R v Turner* [1975] 2 WLR 56, [1975] QB 834, per Lawton LJ at 840, (1974) 60 Cr App R 80.

See also: *Ramsay v Watson* (1961) 108 CLR 642 at 649, [1961] HCA 65; *R v Abadom* [1983] 1 All ER 364, (1983) 76 Cr App R 48, [1983] 1 WLR 126; *Paric v John Holland (Constructions) Pty Ltd* (1985) 59 ALJR 844 at 846, (1985) 62 ALR 85, [1985] HCA 58; *Steffen v Ruban* (1966) 84 WN (No. 1) NSW 264; *Pownall v Conian Management Pty Ltd* (1995) 12 WAR 370; *R v JP* [1999] Crim LR 401; *R v Smith* [1989] 3 NZLR 405; *R v Schafferius* [1977] Qd R 213 at 217; *R v Anderson* [2000] 1 VR 1 at 25; *Trade Practices Commission v Arnotts Ltd (No. 5)* (1990) 21 FCR 324; *Perry* (1990) 49 A Crim R 243 at 249; *Lee* (1989) 42 A Crim R 393; *Gordon v R* (1982) 41 ALR 64; *R v Tonkin* [1975] Qd R 1 at 17; *State Rail Authority of New South Wales v Earthline Constructions Pty Ltd (In Liq)* (1999) 73 ALJR 306, [1999] HCA 3; *Fernandez v Tubemakers of Australia Ltd* [1975] 2 NSWLR 190; *Commissioner for Government Transport v Adamcik* (1961) 106 CLR 292, per Taylor J at 298; *National Justice Cia Naviera SA v Prudential Assurance Co Ltd (The Ikarian Reefer)* [1993] 2 Lloyd's Rep 68, per Cresswell J at 81-82; *Stanton v Callaghan* [2000] QB 75, per Otton LJ at 107; *Meadow v General Medical Council* [2007] 2 WLR 286, [2006] EWHC 429 and *R v Harris* [2006] 1 Cr App R 5, [2002] NICA B51.

If an expert has:

- been misinformed about the facts;
- taken irrelevant facts into consideration; or
- omitted to consider relevant facts,

the opinion is likely to be valueless.[995]

However, the 'assumed' facts need not be itemised in an artificial way, but can be stated more informally.[996]

If an opinion relies on facts that must be proved or assumptions that must be verified, it is to the Court that they must be proved and verified, not to the expert witness.[997]

Before the opinion evidence of an expert can be of any value:

- the facts upon which it is founded must be proved by admissible evidence; and
- the opinion must actually be founded upon those facts or facts that are sufficiently similar.[998]

A bare unproven assertion of an expert witness should carry little 'weight[999]' or 'probative value'.[1000]

[995] See *R v Turner* [1975] 2 WLR 56, [1975] QB 834, per Lawton LJ at 840, (1974) 60 Cr App R 80 and *Pownall v Conlan Management Pty Ltd* (1995) 12 WAR 370, per Anderson J at 389-390.

See also: New Zealand Law Commission, 1991, 'Evidence Law: Expert Evidence and Opinion Evidence – A Discussion Paper', Preliminary Paper 18, page 27.

[996] See *Ramsay v Watson* (1961) 108 CLR 642, [1961] HCA 65.

[997] See *R v Turner* [1975] 2 WLR 56, [1975] QB 834, per Lawton LJ at 840, (1974) 60 Cr App R 80; *Ramsay v Watson* (1961) 108 CLR 642, [1961] HCA 65 and *Steffen v Ruban* [1966] 2 NSWR 622.

[998] See *Dasreef Pty Ltd v Hawchar* (2011) 243 CLR 588, [2011] HCA 21; *Ramsay v Watson* (1961) 108 CLR 642 at 648, [1961] HCA 65; *Paric v John Holland (Constructions) Pty Ltd* (1985) 59 ALJR 844 at 846, (1985) 62 ALR 85, [1985] HCA 58; *R v Perry* (1990) 49 A Crim R 243 at 249; *R v Hilder* (1997) 97 A Crim R 70 at 79 and *Bollock v Wellington* (1996) 15 WAR 1, per Anderson J at 3.

[999] Refer also to the chapter titled 'Weight'.

[1000] See *Davie v Magistrates of Edinburgh* [1953] SC 34 at 39-40.

If however other admissible evidence establishes that the matters assumed are sufficiently like the matters established to render the opinion of the expert of any value, even though they may not correspond with complete precision to the actual facts, the opinion will be admissible and material.[1001]

An expert witness should not omit to consider the material facts which could detract from his or her concluded opinion.[1002]

[2.6] BODY OF EXPERTISE, KNOWLEDGE, LEARNING OR EXPERIENCE

The Court must be satisfied that the subject of the testimony is supported by a body of expertise, knowledge, learning or experience that is sufficiently:

- organised; or
- recognised

to be accepted as reliable.[1003]

An expert witness will invariably rely on information in their field that is regarded as reliable.[1004]

[1001] See *Paric v John Holland Constructions Pty Ltd* [1984] 2 NSWLR 505 at 509-510; *Paric v John Holland Constructions Pty Ltd* (1985) 59 ALJR 844 at 846, (1985) 62 ALR 85, [1985] HCA 58 and *Bugg v Day* (1949) 79 CLR 442, per Latham CJ at 456 and Dixon J at 462, [1949] HCA 59.

[1002] See *National Justice Cia Naviera SA v Prudential Assurance Co Ltd (The Ikarian Reefer)* [1993] 2 Lloyd's Rep 68, per Cresswell J at 81-82; *Stanton v Callaghan* [2000] QB 75, per Otton LJ at 107-108; *Meadow v General Medical Council* [2007] 2 WLR 286, [2006] EWHC 429 and *R v Harris* [2006] 1 Cr App R 5, [2002] NICA B51.

[1003] See *R v Bonython* (1984) 38 SASR 45, (1984) 15 A Crim R 364; *R v B (an accused)* [1987] 1 NZLR 362 at 367; *Farrell v R* (1998) 155 ALR 652, per Kirby J at 661-662; *Osland v R* (1998) 197 CLR 316, (1998) 159 ALR 170, at 184, [1998] HCA 75; *Lewis v R* (1987) 88 FLR 104, per Maurice J at 123-124; *R v Gilfoyle* [2001] 2 CrAppR 57; *R v Anderson* (2000) 1 VR 1 at 25; *Mallard v R* (2003) 28 WAR 1, [2003] WASCA 296; *Dallagher* [2003] 1 Cr App R 12, [2002] EWCA Crim 1903; *Luttrell* [2004] 2 Cr App R 31, [2004] EWCA Crim 1344; *Reed* [2010] 1 Cr App R 23, [2009] EWCA Crim 2698; *Broughton* [2010] EWCA Crim 549; *Weller* [2010] EWCA Crim 1085; *Henderson and others* [2010] 2 Cr App R 24, [2010] EWCA Crim 1269 and *T* [2010] EWCA Crim 2439.

[1004] See *Jeffrey* (1991) 60 A Crim R 384 and *Borowski v Quayle* [1966] VR 382.

Refer also to the chapter titled 'Hearsay Evidence'.

However, a Court should not admit in evidence the results of any scientific test relevant to an issue which it has to determine, unless:

- it is established that it is a scientifically accepted instrument for its avowed purpose; and
- that the particular instrument used was working accurately,

if it is not a well-known instrument.[1005]

There should be evidence that:

- the scientific test had been undertaken by a suitably qualified person;
- that the process produces accurate results; and
- that the process was properly conducted.[1006]

Any information referred to by an expert cannot be tendered as an exhibit, although an expert witness may be cross-examined as to its contents.[1007]

The opinion evidence of an expert witness may be based on the examination or test conducted by another person.[1008]

[1005] See *Philpott v Boon* [1968] Tas SR 97, per Burbury CJ.

See also: *Mehesz v Redman (No. 2)* (1980) 26 SASR 244 and *R v Ciantar* (2006) 16 VR 26, [2006] VSCA 263.

[1006] See *Bevan v The State of Western Australia* (2010) 202 A Crim R 27, [2010] WASCA 101.

[1007] See *R v Allaway* (1922) 77 Cr App R 15.

[1008] See *Rowley v London and North West Railway* (1873) LR 8 Ex 221 and *R v Mason* (1912) 7 Cr App R 67.

See also: *R v Abadom* [1983] 1 All ER 364, (1983) 76 Cr App R 48, [1983] 1 WLR 126.

[2.7] CONCLUSION/S MADE

The Court must be satisfied that there must be reasons for the conclusion/s of the expert based on:

- the proven facts or assumptions; and
- the application of his or her expertise, knowledge, learning and/or experience.[1009]

If in order to give an opinion in a particular case, an expert relies upon assumptions of fact as the basis of the opinion, it is necessary to prove, in admissible form, those facts or facts which are sufficiently similar, in order to render the opinion of value.[1010]

If an expert's opinion is not properly researched because he or she considers that insufficient data is available, then this must be stated with an indication that the opinion is no more than a provisional one.[1011]

If, after exchange of reports, an expert witness changes his or her view on a material matter:

- after having read the other side's expert reports; or
- for any other reason,

such change of view should be communicated (through legal representatives) to the other side without delay and when appropriate to the Court.[1012]

[1009] See *R v Hipson* [1969] Crim LR 85.

See also: *R v Abadom* [1983] 1 All ER 364, (1983) 76 Cr App R 48, [1983] 1 WLR 126.

[1010] See *Dasreef Pty Ltd v Hawchar* (2011) 243 CLR 588, [2011] HCA 21, per Heydon J; *Ramsay v Watson* (1961) 108 CLR 642 at 648-649, [1961] HCA 65; *Paric v John Holland (Constructions) Pty Ltd* (1985) 59 ALJR 844 at 846, (1985) 62 ALR 85, [1985] HCA 58; *R v Perry* (1990) 49 A Crim R 243 at 249 and *R v Hilder* (1997) 97 A Crim R 70 at 79.

[1011] See *National Justice Cia Naviera SA v Prudential Assurance Co Ltd (The Ikarian Reefer)* [1993] 2 Lloyd's Rep 68, per Cresswell J at 81-82; *Stanton v Callaghan* [2000] QB 75, per Otton LJ at 107-108; *Meadow v General Medical Council* [2007] 2 WLR 286, [2006] EWHC 429 and *R v Harris* [2006] 1 Cr App R 5, [2002] NICA B51.

[1012] See *National Justice Cia Naviera SA v Prudential Assurance Co Ltd (The Ikarian Reefer)* [1993] 2 Lloyd's Rep 68, per Cresswell J at 81-82; *Stanton v Callaghan* [2000] QB 75, per Otton LJ at 107-108; *Meadow v General Medical Council* [2007] 2 WLR 286, [2006] EWHC 429 and *R v Harris* [2006] 1 Cr App R 5, [2002] NICA B51.

[2.8] IMPARTIALITY AND OBJECTIVITY

The Court must be satisfied that the expert witness must be able to provide:

- impartial; and
- objective

evidence on the matters within his or her field of expertise.[1013]

Where a expert witness witness has a material or significant conflict of interest the Court is likely to decline to:

- act on his or her evidence; or
- give permission for his or her evidence to be adduced.[1014]

[3.0] LAY PERSON[1015]

There are the following pre-requisites for admissibility of opinion evidence of a lay person:

- the witness must be stating a conclusion drawn from something personally perceived; and
- the opinion must be the only adequate mode in which to communicate the information to the Court.[1016]

[1013] See *Field v Leeds City Council* [2000] 1 EGLR 54; *Toth v Jarman* [2006] 4 All ER 1276, [2006] EWCA Civ 1028; *Polivitte Ltd v Commercial Union Assurance Co. Plc.* (1987) 1 Lloyd's Rep 379 at 386; *Whitehouse v Jordan* (1981) 1 WLR 246, per Lord Wilberforce at 256, [1980] UKHL 12; *National Justice Cia Naviera SA v Prudential Assurance Co Ltd (The Ikarian Reefer)* [1993] 2 Lloyd's Rep 68, per Cresswell J at 81-82; *Stanton v Callaghan* [2000] QB 75, per Otton LJ at 107; *Meadow v General Medical Council* [2007] 2 WLR 286, [2006] EWHC 429 and *R v Harris* [2006] 1 Cr App R 5, [2002] NICA B51.

[1014] See *Toth v Jarman* [2006] 4 All ER 1276, [2006] EWCA Civ 1028.

[1015] See also: *Marchesano v R* (2000) 116 A Crim R 237, [2000] WASCA 225; *R v Oakley* [1979] RTR 417, (1980) 70 Cr App R 7, [1979] Crim LR 205; *Anderson* (1992) 64 A Crim R 312 and *R v Murphy* [1980] 2 WLR 743.

[1016] See New Zealand Law Commission, 1991, 'Evidence Law: Expert Evidence and Opinion Evidence – A Discussion Paper', Preliminary Paper 18, page 10.

OPINION EVIDENCE

A 'lay person' may express his or her opinion, such as whether a person looked old, sick or angry.[1017]

However, there must be a factual basis for the opinion if it is to be ruled admissible by a Court.

When eliciting evidence of a lay person questions should be asked so that the witness describes the person or circumstances, prior to asking the witness his or her opinion.

For example, a police officer should not give evidence that a witness or accused person appeared affected by liquor without first giving evidence of what was the basis of such an opinion, such as the smelling of liquor on the breath of the person, slurred speech, or being unable to stand up, etc.

[1017] See *Cornell v Green* (1823) WL 2195 (Pa), 10 Serg & Rawl 14, per Gibson J at 16.

See also: *R v Carter; ex parte Gray* [1991] Tas R 174 at 175-176; *R v Whitby* (1957) 74 WN (NSW) 441 and *R v Von Elnem* (1985) 38 SASR 207 at 210.

PHOTOGRAPHIC EVIDENCE

A photograph is admissible as real evidence and is able to be tendered by either:

- the witness who took the photograph;
- a witness who is capable of advising the Court as to what is depicted on the photograph; or
- the witness who set up the camera in terms of the 'silent witness' theory[1018], ie., a camera that operates automatically.

A photograph of an accused person taken during the course of the commission of an offence is admissible.[1019]

[1018] See *Owners of Motorship Sapparo Maree v Owners of Steam Tanker Statute of Liberty* [1968] 2 All ER 195.

[1019] See *R v Cook* [1987] QB 417, (1987) 84 Cr App R 369, [1987] 2 WLR 775, [1987] 1 All ER 1049 and *R v Dodson and Williams* [1984] 1 WLR 971, (1984) 79 Cr App R 220, [1984] Crim LR 489.

POST-OFFENCE CONDUCT EVIDENCE

[1.0] INTRODUCTION

Under certain circumstances, the conduct of an accused person after the commission of an offence may provide 'circumstantial evidence[1020]' of the accused person's culpability for that offence[1021], referred to as 'evidence of post-offence conduct'[1022].

Such evidence includes:

- an accused person fleeing from the scene of the crime;
- an accused person fleeing from the jurisdiction in which it was committed;
- an accused person lying to the investigating officers or other persons in relation to an offence[1023];
- an accused person's silence in response to an allegation which he or she might reasonably be expected to deny[1024];
- the destruction of evidence[1025]; and

[1020] Refer also to the chapter titled 'Circumstantial Evidence'.

[1021] See *R v White* [1998] 2 SCR 72, 39 OR (3d) 223, 161 DLR (4th) 590, 125 CCC (3d) 385, 16 CR (5th) 199, 112 OAC 1.

[1022] See *R v White* [1998] 2 SCR 72, 39 OR (3d) 223, 161 DLR (4th) 590, 125 CCC (3d) 385, 16 CR (5th) 199, 112 OAC 1; *Zoneff v R* (2000) 200 CLR 234, 112 A Crim R 114, [2000] HCA 28, per Kirby J and *Martinez v The State of Western Australia* [2007] WASCA 143.

[1023] See *Mark McKey v R* [2012] NSWCCA 1.

[1024] See *R v MMJ* [2006] VSCA 226) and *Mark McKey v R* [2012] NSWCCA 1.

Refer also to:

- the section titled 'Right To Silence' in the chapter titled 'Confessional Evidence'; and
- the section titled 'The Defence Case' in the chapter titled 'Court Procedure' in the text titled 'Injia on Criminal Practice and Procedure in Papua New Guinea and the Pacific'.

[1025] See *R v Nguyen* [2001] VSCA 1 and *Mark McKey v R* [2012] NSWCCA 1.

Refer also to the chapter titled 'Administration Of Justice Offences' in the text titled 'Injia on Criminal Offences in Papua New Guinea and the Pacific'.

- attempts to influence the evidence of witnesses[1026].

Evidence of such after-the-fact conduct is commonly admitted to show that an accused person has acted in a manner which, based on human experience and logic, is consistent with the conduct of a guilty person and inconsistent with the conduct of an innocent person.[1027]

Evidence of post-offence conduct is not fundamentally different from other kinds of circumstantial evidence.[1028] In some cases it may be highly incriminating, while in others it might play only a minor corroborative role. Like any piece of circumstantial evidence it may be subject to competing interpretations and must be 'weighed[1029]' by the Court, in light of all the evidence, to determine whether it is:

- consistent with guilt; and
- inconsistent with any other rational conclusion.[1030]

However, when evidence of post-offence conduct is introduced to support an inference of consciousness of guilt it may be highly ambiguous.[1031]

Evidence tending to show consciousness of guilt can properly be treated as supportive of other evidence of guilt and should not be excluded from consideration because, on its own, it may not satisfy the standard of proof 'beyond a reasonable doubt[1032]'.[1033]

[1026] See *R v Smit and others* [2004] NSWCCA 409 and *Mark McKey v R* [2012] NSWCCA 1.

Refer also to the chapter titled 'Administration Of Justice Offences' in the text titled 'Injia on Criminal Offences in Papua New Guinea and the Pacific'.

[1027] See *R v Peavoy* (1997) 117 CCC (3d) 226, per Weiler JA at 238.

[1028] Refer also to the chapter titled 'Circumstantial Evidence'.

[1029] Refer also to the chapter titled 'Weight'.

[1030] See *R v White* [1998] 2 SCR 72, 39 OR (3d) 223, 161 DLR (4th) 590, 125 CCC (3d) 385, 16 CR (5th) 199, 112 OAC 1.

[1031] See *R v White* [1998] 2 SCR 72, 39 OR (3d) 223, 161 DLR (4th) 590, 125 CCC (3d) 385, 16 CR (5th) 199, 112 OAC 1.

[1032] Refer also to the chapter titled 'Proof Of Issues' in the text titled 'Injia on Criminal Practice and Procedure in Papua Nw Guinea and the Pacific'.

[1033] See *R v Morin* [1988] 2 SCR 345 at 354, 44 CCC (3d) 193, 66 CR (3d) 1, 30 OAC 81.

Refer also to the chapter titled 'Circumstantial Evidence'.

POST-OFFENCE CONDUCT EVIDENCE

Not in every case where there is post-conduct evidence should a Court regard such evidence as necessarily showing a consciousness of guilt.[1034]

[2.0] EVIDENCE OF FLIGHT[1035]

The 'evidence of flight' refers to:

> the sudden departure of an accused person from where he or she normally resides for no apparent reason

and may be a basis for showing a consciousness of guilt on the part of the accused person.[1036]

Such behaviour may provide evidence of corroboration[1037] in order to prove the guilt of an accused person, provided that guilt was the only reasonable explanation for that departure or flight[1038].[1039]

1034 See *Nguyen* (2001) 118 A Crim R 479, [2001] VSCA 1; *R v Chang* (2003) 7 VR 236, (2003) 140 A Crim R 573, [2003] VSCA 149; *R v Cook* [2004] NSWCCA 52; *R v SBB* (2007) 175 A Crim R 449, [2007] QCA 173 and *R v MC* [2009] VSCA 122.

1035 See also: *The State v Angaun Kalas and others* [1994] PNGLR 20; *The State v Avaka* (2000) N2024, [2000] PGNC 56; *R v Burge and Pegg* [1996] 1 Cr App R 163; *Woon v R* (1964) 109 CLR 529, per Windeyer J at 541-542; *Davis v The State of Western Australia* [2007] WASCA 267; *R v Wehlow* (2001) 122 A Crim R 63, [2001] QCA 193; *R v Box and Martin* [2001] QCA 272; *R v Rice* [1996] 2 VR 406, [1996] VSC 13; *R v Harron* [1996] Crim LR 581; *R v Richens* (1994) 98 Cr App R 43, [1993] 4 All ER 877; *R v Sharp* (1994) 98 Cr App R 144, [1993] 3 All ER 225; *R v Keeton* [1995] 2 Cr App R 241; *R v Durbin* [1995] 2 Cr App R 84; *R v Ensor* [1989] 2 All ER 586, [1989] 1 WLR 497, [1989] Crim LR 563, (1989) 89 Cr App R 139; *R v Rahmoun* (1986) 82 Cr App R 217 at 222; *R v West* (1984) 79 Cr App R 45 at 47-48; *Credland v Knowles* (1951) 35 Cr App R 46 at 57; *Hytch* (2000) 114 A Crim R 573; *ST* (1997) 92 A Crim R 390; *Appleby* (1996) 88 A Crim R 456 at 485; *Power and Power* (1996) 87 A Crim R 407 at 412-413; *Mason v R* (1995) 15 WAR 165 at 174; *Hunt* (1994) 76 A Crim R 363; *Bey* (1994) 98 A Crim R 158; *H* (1990) 49 A Crim R 396; *R v Mitchell* [2007] QCA 267; *R v T* [1994] QCA 45; *R v M* [1994] QCA 7 and *R v Cook* [2004] NSWCCA 52.

Refer also to the section titled 'Right To Be Present In Court' in the chapter titled 'Rights Of An Accused Person' in the text titled 'Injia on Criminal Practice and Procedure in Papua New Guinea and the Pacific'.

1036 See *R v Melrose* [1989] 1 Qd R 572, (1987) 30 A Crim R 332; *R v Gay* [1976] VR 577; *R v Dickson* [1983] 1 VR 227 and *R v Power* (1996) 87 A Crim R 407.

1037 As regards the law in relation to 'Evidence Of Corroboration Generally', refer to the section titled 'Suspect Witness' in the chapter titled 'Witnesses' in the text titled 'Injia on Criminal Practice and Procedure in Papua New Guinea and the Pacific'.

1038 See *R v Bridgman* (1980) 24 SASR 278.

1039 See *R v Melrose* [1989] 1 Qd R 572, (1987) 30 A Crim R 332.

POST-OFFENCE CONDUCT EVIDENCE

A sudden departure by a person who ordinarily stays close to home may give rise to quite different inferences from those which could be drawn from a journey by one who commonly moves about the country. The nature of the reasons, if any, given for the journey may also bear upon the proper conclusion to be drawn. Flight can be an indication of guilt.[1040]

Flight during the course of a trial may afford an even firmer foundation for drawing an inference of a consciousness of guilt on the part of an accused person.[1041]

Evidence of flight can be relevant even where an accused person is being tried on more than one charge.[1042]

[3.0] EVIDENCE OF LIES

By default, the common law has been reformed so that in effect lies can only be relevant to credibility and never indicative of guilt. The fact that people who lie are not necessarily guilty does not mean that guilty people never lie.[1043]

An accused person should not be convicted merely because a Court believes that he or she has told a lie.[1044]

Not in every case where it is established that an accused person has told a lie relevant to the matters in issue the Court will regard the telling of that lie as showing a consciousness of guilt.[1045]

[1040] See *R v Ed Adl* [1993] 2 Qd R 195.

[1041] See *R v Festa* [2000] QCA 73.

[1042] See *R v Dickson* [1983] VR 227; *R v Melrose* [1989] 1 Qd R 572, (1987) 30 A Crim R 332; *R v Chiu Siu-tung* [1996] 2 HKCLR 67 and *R v White* [1998] 2 SCR 72, 39 OR (3d) 223, 161 DLR (4th) 590, 125 CCC (3d) 385, 16 CR (5th) 199, 112 OAC 1.

[1043] See New Zealand Law Commission, 1999, 'Evidence. Volume 1: Reform of the Law and Evidence. Volume 2: Evidence Code and Commentary', Report 55, page 126.

[1044] See *DPP v John Fufue and Nelson Fafeloa v R* [1989] SBCA 5 and *Broadhurst v R* [1964] AC 441, per Lord Devlin at 457.

[1045] See *Edwards v R* (1993) 178 CLR 193, (1993) 68 ALJR 40, [1993] HCA 63; *R v Brennan* [1999] 2 Qd R 529 at 530, [1999] QCA 522; *R v Chevathen* (2001) 122 A Crim R 441 at 446 and *Zoneff v R* (2000) 200 CLR 234 at 244-245, (2000) 112 A Crim R 114, [2000] HCA 28.

POST-OFFENCE CONDUCT EVIDENCE

For good reason, it has been said that people confronted with allegations of wrongdoing may have other reasons not to tell the truth, such as:

- being confused;
- panicking;
- being in fear; and
- other innocent reasons.[1046]

Whilst the evidence of a lie told by an accused person out-of-court can support a prosecution case, such evidence alone cannot prove a case 'beyond reasonable doubt[1047]'.[1048]

Whilst a false statement by an accused person whether:

- in court; or
- out-of-court

may amount to corroboration, such a statement cannot take the place of lack of affirmative and material evidence.[1049]

As a general proposition a lie in itself can never prove guilt.[1050]

[1046] See *Allan Oa Koroda and Mariano Wani Simon v The State* [1988-89] PNGLR 131, per Kapi DepCJ at 133.

See also: *Edwards v R* (1993) 178 CLR 193, (1993) 68 ALJR 40, [1993] HCA 63; *Cleland v R* (1982) 151 CLR 1 at 23, (1982) 43 ALR 619, [1982] HCA 67; *Broadhurst v R* [1964] AC 441 at 457; *R v Dehar* [1969] NZLR 763 at 765; *R v Collings* [1976] 2 NZLR 104 at 116; *R v Kerim* (1987) 28 A Crim R 439 at 449; *Green v R* [1999] HCA 13; *Osland v R* (1998) 197 CLR 316, (1998) 159 ALR 170, at 184, [1998] HCA 75; *R v Baldwin and Chapman* (1973) 57 Cr App R 511, per Roskill LJ at 520; *R v Heyde* (1990) 20 NSWLR 234 and *HKSAR v Mo Shiu Shing* [1999] 2 HKLRD 155 at 168.

[1047] Refer also to the chapter titled 'Proof Of Issues' in the text titled 'Injia on Criminal Practice and Procedure in Papua New Guinea and the Pacific'.

[1048] See *R v Strudwick and Merry* (1994) 99 Cr App R 326.

[1049] See *The State v Vargi* [1991] PNGLR 54.

[1050] See *Allan Oa Koroka and Mariano Wani Simon v The State* [1988-89] PNGLR 131 at 133.

See also: *Yuen Kwai Choi v HKSAR* [2003] HKCFA 20, [2003] 2 HKLRD 176.

POST-OFFENCE CONDUCT EVIDENCE

Lies usually affect credibility only. The telling of a lie may affect the credibility of an accused person by influencing the Court in deciding whether to:

- accept; or
- reject

the evidence given or statement made by the accused person.[1051]

An accused person's making of a false statement to increase his or her appearance of innocence is not necessarily a proof of his or her guilt; but it is always evidence which ought to be submitted to the consideration of the Court.[1052]

There are circumstances in which the prosecution may want to use a lie told by an accused person to:

- assist the prosecution's case; or
- strengthen an inference of guilt against the accused person.[1053]

[1051] See *R v Mitchell* [2007] QCA 267; *Aubertin v The State of Western Australia* [2006] WASCA 229; *R v Toia* [1982] 1 NZLR 555; *R v Heyde* (1990) 20 NSWLR 234; *R v Manapouri* [1995] 2 NZLR 407 at 413; *R v Atkinson* [2000] NZCA 284 and *R v Renzella* [1997] 2 VR 88 at 92.

[1052] See *Moriarty v London, Chatham and Dover Railway Co* (1870) LR 5 QB 314, per Cockburn CJ at 319.

See also: *R v Farquharson* (2009) 26 VR 410 at 454.

[1053] See *Yuen Kwai Choi v HKSAR* [2003] HKCFA 20, [2003] 2 HKLRD 176.

A lie may be used, for example:

- as circumstantial evidence amounting to an implied admission of guilt on the part of an accused person[1054];
- to support identification evidence[1055]; and
- to provide evidence of corroboration[1056].

[1054] See *Edwards v R* (1993) 178 CLR 193, (1993) 68 ALJR 40, [1993] HCA 63; *R v Brennan* [1999] 2 Qd R 529 at 530; *R v Walton and Harman* [2001] QCA 309; *Zoneff v R* (2000) 200 CLR 234, (2000) 112 A Crim R 114, [2000] HCA 28 and *R v Heyde* (1990) 20 NSWLR 234.

In New Zealand a lie may be used as evidence of guilt when the lie is more consistent with guilt than with innocence. This is a less exacting test than in Australia, see *R v Federici* [2005] NZCA 153.

See also: *R v Dehar* [1969] NZLR 763; *R v Bills* [1981] 1 NZLR 760; *Dora v R* [2005] NZCA 162 and *R v Atkinson* [2000] NZCA 284.

The Australian cases follow similar authorities in Canada, see *R v White* [1998] 2 SCR 72, 39 OR (3d) 223, 161 DLR (4th) 590, 125 CCC (3d) 385, 16 CR (5th) 199, 112 OAC 1.

Refer also to the chapter titled 'Circumstantial Evidence'.

[1055] See *R v Goodway* [1993] 4 All ER 894, (1994) 98 Cr App R 11.

Refer also to the chapter titled 'Identification Evidence'.

[1056] See *John Jaminan v The State (No. 2)* [1983] PNGLR 318, per Amet J (as he then was) at 336.

See also: *R v Lucas* [1981] 1 QB 720, [1981] 3 WLR 120, [1981] 2 All ER 1008, (1981) 73 Cr App R 159, [1981] Crim LR 624; *Eade v R* (1924) 34 CLR 154 at 158; *Credland v Knowler* (1951) 35 Cr App R 49, per Goddard LCJ at 55; *R v Knight* [1966] 1 All ER 647 and *R v Baldwin and Chapman* (1973) 57 Cr App R 511, per Roskill LJ at 520-521.

As regards the law in relation to 'Evidence Of Corroboration Generally', refer to the section titled 'Suspect Witness' in the chapter titled 'Witnesses' in the text titled 'Injia on Criminal Practice and Procedure in Papua New Guinea and the Pacific'.

However, the following criteria must also be satisfied before a lie can be relied upon by the prosecution:

- the lie must have been deliberate.[1057]

  There is a difference between:

  - the mere conjection of a person's account of events; and

  - a finding that a person has lied.[1058]

  A lie is a deliberate untruth. To conclude that a statement is a lie is to conclude that the truth lies elsewhere. In some circumstances, a finding that a person lied will necessarily involve acceptance of the contrary. However, the fact that a person has lied does not of itself establish a specific contrary proposition[1059];

- the lie must have related to a material issue.[1060]

  There must be a close nexus between:

  - the lie; and

  - the matter in issue upon the trial

  to such an extent that the lie can be considered as showing a consciousness of guilt.[1061]

  The lie must reveal knowledge of the offence or of some aspect of it[1062]; and

[1057] See *The State v Kwale Dire* (2001) N2178.

See also: *R v Lucas* [1981] 1 QB 720, [1981] 3 WLR 120, [1981] 2 All ER 1008, (1981) 73 Cr App R 159, [1981] Crim LR 624.

[1058] See *Edwards v R* (1993) 178 CLR 193, (1993) 68 ALJR 40, [1993] HCA 63.

[1059] See *Edwards v R* (1993) 178 CLR 193, (1993) 68 ALJR 40, [1993] HCA 63.

[1060] See *R v Lucas* [1981] 1 QB 720, [1981] 3 WLR 120, [1981] 2 All ER 1008, (1981) 73 Cr App R 159, [1981] Crim LR 624.

[1061] See *R v Heyde* (1990) 20 NSWLR 234.

[1062] See *Edwards v R* (1993) 178 CLR 193 at 210-211, (1993) 68 ALJR 40, [1993] HCA 63.

- The lie must have sprung from:
    - a realisation of guilt; and
    - a fear of the truth[1063].[1064]

  The accused person must have told the lie because he or she perceived that the truth was inconsistent with his or her innocence and it must be a lie that an innocent person would not have told.[1065]

  The Court must only use the lie as evidence of guilt if satisfied that the accused person knew that telling the truth would implicate him or her in the offence.[1066]

Additionally, if a lie is being relied upon as evidence of corroboration[1067] the statement must clearly be shown to have been a lie by evidence, other than the witness whose evidence is to be corroborated.[1068]

[1063] See *Allan Oa Koroka v The State* [1988-89] PNGLR 131; *The State v Marianno Wani Simon and Alan Da Koroka* (1987) N600 and *The State v Vargi* [1991] PNGLR 54.

See also: *R v Small* (1994) 33 NSWLR 575, per Hunt CJ at 595 and *R v Colling* [1976] 2 NZLR 104, per McCartley P at 116.

[1064] See *The State v Vargi* [1991] PNGLR 54.

See also: *R v Lucas* [1981] 1 QB 720, [1981] 3 WLR 120, [1981] 2 All ER 1008, (1981) 73 Cr App R 159, [1981] Crim LR 624 and *Edwards v R* (1993) 178 CLR 193, (1993) 68 ALJR 40, [1993] HCA 63.

[1065] See *Edwards v R* (1993) 178 CLR 193 at 209, (1993) 68 ALJR 40, [1993] HCA 63.

[1066] See *The State v Vargi* [1991] PNGLR 54.

See also: *R v Lucas* [1981] 1 QB 720, [1981] 3 WLR 120, [1981] 2 All ER 1008, (1981) 73 Cr App R 159, [1981] Crim LR 624 and *Edwards v R* (1993) 178 CLR 193, (1993) 68 ALJR 40, [1993] HCA 63.

[1067] As regards the law in relation to 'Evidence Of Corroboration Generally', refer to the section titled 'Suspect Witness' in the chapter titled 'Witnesses' in the text titled 'Injia on Criminal Practice and Procedure in Papua New Guinea and the Pacific'.

[1068] See *Edwards v R* (1993) 178 CLR 193 at 211, (1993) 68 ALJR 40 at 49.

POST-OFFENCE CONDUCT EVIDENCE

A statement by an accused person may be proven to be a lie by either:

- an admission by the accused person[1069];
- evidence from witnesses, other than the complainant[1070]; or
- reason of its inherent improbability[1071].

Where a lie is relied upon to prove guilt, the lie must be precisely identified by the prosecution as should the circumstances and events that are said to indicate that it constitutes an 'admission against interest'.[1072]

[1069] See *Edwards v R* (1993) 178 CLR 193, (1993) 68 ALJR 40, [1993] HCA 63 and *R v Lucas* [1981] 1 QB 720, [1981] 3 WLR 120, [1981] 2 All ER 1008, (1981) 73 Cr App R 159, [1981] Crim LR 624.

[1070] See *Edwards v R* (1993) 178 CLR 193, (1993) 68 ALJR 40, [1993] HCA 63 and *R v Lucas* [1981] 1 QB 720, [1981] 3 WLR 120, [1981] 2 All ER 1008, (1981) 73 Cr App R 159, [1981] Crim LR 624.

[1071] See *R v Collings* [1976] 2 NZLR 104.

[1072] See *Edwards v R* (1993) 178 CLR 193 at 211, (1993) 68 ALJR 40, [1993] HCA 63.

PROOF OF AGE

[1.0] STATUTORY PROVISIONS

Section 57 of the *Evidence Act* (Ch. 48) ['Certificates Relation to Births, Deaths and Marriages'] states:

> 'A certificate relating to the birth, marriage or death of any person in –
>
> (a) the country; or
>
> (b) a state or Territory of Australia; or
>
> (c) the United Kingdom; or
>
> (d) a member state of the Commonwealth of Nations,
>
> if it purports to be issued by the officer authorized by the law of the place concerned is evidence of the matters stated without proof of the seal or stamp or signature or of the official character of the person appearing to have signed it'.

Section 63 ['Age'] states:

> 'In any legal proceedings, if the court does not consider that there is evidence or sufficient evidence to determine the age of a person the court, having seen the person, may itself determine the question'.[1073]

[1073] See *Tau Jim Anis and others v The State* (2000) SC642 and *The State v Samson Bino* (2009) N3769, [2009] PGNC 150.

PROOF OF AGE

[2.0] GENERAL PRINCIPLES

The age of the child may need to be proven 'beyond reasonable doubt[1074,1075]. Such proof cannot be based on the evidence of the complainant alone as to his or her age.[1076]

If there is no official record, evidence may be given by the parents or persons who know the child.[1077]

A Court may take 'judicial notice[1078]' of the age of a witness in obvious cases.[1079]

If the prosecution is relying on a birth ceritifcate a Court will require some evidence identifying the person whose birth is in question with the person specified in the certificate.[1080]

1074 Refer also to the chapter titled 'Proof Of Issues' in the text titled 'Injia on Criminal Practice and Procedure in Papua New Guinea and the Pacific'.

1075 See for example sections 343 ['Common Assaults'] and 344 ['Aggravated Assaults'] of the *Criminal Code* (Ch. 262) which provides for the charge of 'Common Assault' with a circumstance of aggravation that the victim was a male child under the age of 14 years.

1076 See *The State v Thomas Narop and Morris Kramer* (2009) CR No. 355 of 2006 and *The State v Peter Eddie (No. 1)* (2009) N3782, [2009] PGNC 173.

See however: *Smith v Police* [1969] NZLR 856 and *Apera v Crown* [2001] CKCA 1.

Refer also to the chapter titled 'Hearsay Evidence'.

1077 See *The State v Hayden* [1976] PNGLR 509, [1976] PGSC 5.

1078 Refer also to the section titled 'Judicial Notice' in the chapter titled 'Court Procedure' in the text titled 'Injia on Criminal Practice and Procedure in Papua New Guinea and the Pacific'.

1079 See *Dwyer v Bridges; ex parte Bridge and Dwyer v Brough; ex parte Brough* [1951] St R Qd 90.

1080 See Cross on Evidence, 7th edition, 2004, page 1371 and Phipson on Evidence, 15th edition, 2003, page 2272.

SIMILAR FACT EVIDENCE

[1.0] INTRODUCTION

The general rule was that evidence of propensity to offend was not admissible on the basis that such evidence is unduly prejudicial, and therefore contrary to a fair trial. However, despite this basic principle of non-admissibility, exceptions developed. These recognised the inherent potential for prejudice but allowed propensity evidence to be admitted. The most significant of these exceptions was the so-called 'similar fact' exception.[1081]

Similar fact evidence is a notoriously difficult area of evidential law that has been colourfully described as a 'pitted battlefield[1082]'.[1083]

Broadly speaking, it means evidence as to disreputable aspects of a defendant's character, other than evidence of the commission of the offence being tried.[1084]

The term 'similar fact' evidence covers:

> evidence of misconduct by an accused person, other than the charges currently before the Court, ie., other than those covered in the information or indictment[1085], whether arising:
>
> - before; or
> - after
>
> the offence charged[1086]

[1081] See New Zealand Law Commission, 2013, 'The 2013 Review of the Evidence Act 2006', Report 127, page 99.

[1082] See *Boardman v DPP* [1975] AC 421 at 445, [1974] 3 WLR 673 at 752, [1974] 3 All ER 887, (1975) 60 Cr App R 165, [1975] Crim LR 36.

[1083] See New Zealand Law Commission, 2008, 'Disclosure to Court of Defendants' Previous Convictions, Similar Offending and Bad Character', Report 103, page 20.

[1084] See New Zealand Law Commission, 2013, 'The 2013 Review of the Evidence Act 2006', Report 127, page 99.

[1085] See *John Makin and Sarah Makin v Attorney-General for New South Wales* [1894] AC 57 at 65.

[1086] See *The State v Bill Vevo* [2007] PGNC 1.

See also: *R v Witham* [1962] Qd R 49; *R v Barrington* [1981] 1 All ER 1132; *R v Hurren* (1962) 46 Cr App R 323 at 326; *R v Rodley* [1911-13] All ER 688, [1913] 3 KB 468, (1914) 9 Cr App R 688 and *R v Smith* [1914-15] All ER 262, (1916) 11 Cr App R 229.

which is said to be evidence of his or her:

- propensity; or
- disposition

to misconduct himself or herself either in:

- general; or
- specific

ways.[1087]

Such conduct must have significant probative value.[1088]

Such evidence, while generally inadmissible, may exceptionally be admitted where the probative value of the evidence in relation to an issue in question is so high that it displaces the heavy prejudice which will inevitably inure to the accused person where evidence of prior immoral or illegal acts is presented to the Court.[1089]

The Court is required to:

- make an assessment of probative value for the issue involved;
- then make an assessment of the prejudice which would be occasioned; and
- then decide whether that probative value outweighed prejudice.[1090]

[1087] See *R v Ball* [1911] AC 47.

[1088] See New Zealand Law Commission, 2008, 'Disclosure to Court of Defendants' Previous Convictions, Similar Offending and Bad Character', Report 103, page 20.

[1089] See *R v B (CR)* [1990] 1 SCR 717, per McLachlin J at 732.

See also: *R v Handy* (2002) 164 CCC (3d) 448.

[1090] See New Zealand Law Commission, 2008, 'Disclosure to Court of Defendants' Previous Convictions, Similar Offending and Bad Character', Report 103, page 20.

SIMILAR FACT EVIDENCE

Evidence that is received although it discloses the commission of offences, other than those of which the accused person is charged, is also referred to as 'propensity evidence'.[1091]

Such evidence is generally excluded because it is likely to operate unfairly to an accused person.[1092]

The common law 'similar fact rule' was developed because of concern at the prejudice to the accused person that may result through the use of evidence of other behaviour.[1093] The depth of this concern is evident in Viscount Sankey's description in *Maxwell v Director of Public Prosecutions*[1094] of the rule as:

> 'One of the most deeply rooted and jealously guarded principles of our criminal law'.

As regards the possible prejudicial effect of such evidence the following factors apply:

- the erosion of the presumption of innocence[1095];
- the danger of propensity reasoning; and
- circularity of reasoning.[1096]

1091 See *Pfennig v R* (1995) 182 CLR 461 at 464-465, (1995) 69 ALJR 147, (1995) 127 ALR 99, (1995) 77 A Crim R 149, [1995] HCA 7.

1092 See Queensland Law Reform Commission, 2005, 'A Review of the Uniform Evidence Acts', Report 60, page 131.

1093 See New Zealand Law Commission, 1997, 'Evidence Law – Character and Credibility A Discussion Paper', Preliminary Paper 27, page 75.

1094 [1935] AC 309 at 317.

1095 See section 37(4(a) of the *Constitution of the Independent State of Papua New Guinea* ['Protection of the Law'].

1096 See *Perry v R* (1982–83) 150 CLR 580 at 593-595, (1983) 57 ALJR 110.

See also: New Zealand Law Commission, 1997, 'Evidence Law – Character and Credibility A Discussion Paper', Preliminary Paper 27, page 77.

SIMILAR FACT EVIDENCE

The prosecution may not adduce evidence of other misconduct on the part of an accused person, if that evidence shows that the accused person had a propensity to commit:

- an offence; or
- the offence in question,

unless the evidence is sufficiently highly probative of a fact in issue to outweigh the prejudice it may cause.[1097]

In order to be admissible:

- such evidence must be directed to an issue in the case[1098] and should not be adduced merely to strengthen the evidence of a fact which:
    - was not denied; and
    - could not be the subject of rational dispute[1099]; and
- there must be 'a sufficient nexus' between:
    - the primary evidence on a particular charge; and

[1097] See *Roach v R* [2011] HCA 12.

See also: Cross on Evidence, 8th edition, 2010, page 709.

Refer also to the chapter titled 'Weight'.

[1098] See *DPP v Broadman* [1974] 3 WLR 673, [1974] 3 All ER 887, (1975) 60 Cr App R 165, [1975] Crim LR 36 [1975] AC 421, per Lord Morris at 439.

See also: *R v Lunt* (1987) 85 Cr App R 241 at 245; *Markby v R* (1978) 140 CLR 108, per Gibbs ACJ at 117; *Phillips v R* (2006) 225 CLR 303, (2006) 80 ALJR 531, (2006) 224 ALR 216 at 294, [2006] HCA 4 and *Pfennig v R* (1995) 182 CLR 461 at 483, (1995) 69 ALJR 147, (1995) 127 ALR 99, (1995) 77 A Crim R 149, [1995] HCA 7.

[1099] See *Noor Mohamed v R* [1949] AC 182 at 191-192, [1949] 1 All ER 365, and *R v Thompson* [1918] AC 221 at 232.

See also: *Attorney-General of Hong Kong v Siu Yuk-Shing* [1989] 1 WLR 236 at 240.

- the similar fact evidence.[1100]

As a general rule the evidence must bear a striking similarity to conduct by a relevant person, an accused person or another person who may have perpetrated the act.[1101]

The striking similarity should be to unusual and not common place features of the facts in issue.[1102]

However, striking similarity, underlying unity and other like descriptions of similar facts are not essential to the admission of such evidence, though usually the evidence will lack the requisite 'probative force' if the evidence does not possess such characteristics.[1103]

As a general rule the evidence must:

- bear a striking similarity to conduct by the accused person who may have perpetrated the act; and
- be evidence of acts by that person.[1104]

[1100] See *DPP v Kilbourne* [1973] 2 WLR 254, [1973] AC 729, [1973] 1 All ER 440, (1973) 57 Cr App R 381, per Lord Hailsham at 749.

See also: *Hoch v R* (1988) 165 CLR 292, per Brennan and Dawson JJ at 301 and *Phillips v R* (2006) 225 CLR 303, (2006) 80 ALJR 531, (2006) 224 ALR 216 at 294, [2006] HCA 4.

[1101] See *Anos Naime Maraga, Gaigo Arua Hariki and Hariki Bad v The State* (2009) SC968.

[1102] See *The State v Paul Ipor Daniel* [1988-89] PNGLR 580 and *The State v Bill Vevo* [2007] PGNC 1.

[1103] See *Pfennig v R* (1995) 182 CLR 461, (1995) 69 ALJR 147, (1995) 127 ALR 99, (1995) 77 A Crim R 149, [1995] HCA 7 and *DPP v P* [1991] 2 AC 447, [1991] 3 WLR 161, [1991] 3 All ER 337, (1991) 93 Cr App R 267, [1992] Crim LR 4.

[1104] See *Anos Naime Maraga, Gaigo Arua Hariki and Hariki Bad v The State* (2009) SC968 and *The State v Daniel* [1988-89] PNGLR 580.

SIMILAR FACT EVIDENCE

Similar fact evidence is inadmissible if it shows only that an accused person:

- has a propensity to commit an offence[1105];
- has committed offences in the past[1106];
- has a criminal disposition[1107]; or
- was the sort of person likely to commit the offence charged[1108],

but such evidence is admissible if it is relevant[1109] and it may be so relevant if it can:

- prove identity where the only other evidence is that the accused person had the opportunity to commit the offence[1110];
- prove identity where the similarities are sufficient to show that:
    - the accused person; and
    - the guilty person

[1105] See *Makin v Attorney-General for New South Wales* [1894] AC 57 at 65 and *DPP v P* [1991] 2 AC 447, [1991] 3 WLR 161, [1991] 3 All ER 337, (1991) 93 Cr App R 267, [1992] Crim LR 41.

[1106] See *Pfennig v R* (1995) 182 CLR 461, (1995) 69 ALJR 147, (1995) 127 ALR 99, (1995) 77 A Crim R 149, [1995] HCA 7 and *DPP v P* [1991] 2 AC 447, [1991] 3 WLR 161, [1991] 3 All ER 337, (1991) 93 Cr App R 267, [1992] Crim LR 41.

[1107] See *Pfennig v R* (1995) 182 CLR 461, (1995) 69 ALJR 147, (1995) 127 ALR 99, (1995) 77 A Crim R 149, [1995] HCA 7 and *DPP v P* [1991] 2 AC 447, [1991] 3 WLR 161, [1991] 3 All ER 337, (1991) 93 Cr App R 267, [1992] Crim LR 41.

[1108] See *Makin v Attorney-General for New South Wales* [1894] AC 57 at 65 and *DPP v P* [1991] 2 AC 447, [1991] 3 WLR 161, [1991] 3 All ER 337, (1991) 93 Cr App R 267, [1992] Crim LR 41.

[1109] Refer also to the chapter titled 'Relevance'.

[1110] See *R v Grovannone* (1960) 44 Cr App R 3; *R v Straffen* [1952] 2 QB 911, [1952] 2 All ER 657, (1952) 36 CrAppR 132; *Perkins v Jeffrey* [1915] 2 KB 702, [1914-15] All ER 172 and *Thompson v DPP* [1918] AC 221, (1917) 13 Cr App R 61.

See also: *R v W (John)* [1998] 2 Cr App R 289, [1998] Crim LR 668 and *R v Williams* (1987) 84 Cr App R 299, [1987] Crim LR 198.

have common characteristics which are so unusual that it is likely that they are one and the same person[1111];

- prove identity if it is of association with a person who has been proven to have committed a similar offence[1112];

- prove identity if there is an odd coincidence that the accused person has not explained, e.g. a thief is seen running into a house, later the accused person is identified in a identification parade and the house proves to be his or her father's house[1113];

- prove a system or course of conduct[1114];

- prove the commission of disputed facts[1115];

[1111] See *The State v Casper Otto* [2007] PGNC 128.

See also: *R v Morris* (1970) 54 Cr App R 69.

[1112] See *The State v Casper Otto* [2007] PGNC 128.

See also: *R v Davies and Murphy* (1971) 56 Cr App R 49.

[1113] See *The State v Casper Otto* [2007] PGNC 128 and *John Beng v The State* [1977] PNGLR 115.

See also: *R v Turnbull and others* [1977] QB 224 at 230, (1976) 63 Cr App R 132, [1976] 3 WLR 445, [1976] 3 All ER 549, [1976] Crim LR 565.

[1114] See *The State v Stafford Hambo* (2010) N4036.

See also: *Holder v R* [1980] AC 115, (1978) 68 Cr App R 120; *DPP v Broadman* [1975] AC 421, [1974] 3 WLR 673, [1974] 3 All ER 887, (1975) 60 Cr App R 165, [1975] Crim LR 36; *R v H* [1995] 2 AC 596; *R v Sims* [1946] KB 531, (1946) 31 Cr App R 158; *R v Lewis (PA)* (1983) 76 Cr App R 33; *R v Le Vard* [1955] NZLR 266; *R v Gill* (1906) 8 WALR 96; *R v Finlayson* (1912) 14 CLR 675, (1912) 7 QJPR 26; *R v Hurren* (1962) 46 Cr App R 323; *Hardgrove v R* (1906) 4 CLR 232; *R v Rhodes* [1899] 1 QB 77, (1899) 19 Cox CC 182; *R v Ollis* [1900] 2 QB 758; *R v Boyle and Merchant* (1914) 10 Cr App R 180; *R v Seaman* (1978) 67 Cr App R 234; *R v Mansfield* [1978] 1 All ER 134; *R v Slender* (1938) 26 Cr App R 155; *R v Porter* (1935) 25 Cr App R 59 and *R v Fisher* [1910] 1 KB 149.

[1115] See *Boardman v DPP* [1975] AC 421 at 458, [1974] 3 WLR 673 at 752, [1974] 3 All ER 887, (1975) 60 Cr App R 165, [1975] Crim LR 36; *Sutton v R* (1983) 152 CLR 528, (1984) 51 ALR 435, [1984] HCA 5 and *Hoch v R* (1988) 165 CLR 292.

- prove motive for committing an offence[1116];
- prove sexual intent or guilty passion[1117];
- to rebut a defence which would otherwise be open to the accused person[1118], including the defence of:
    - accident[1119]; or
    - mistake of fact[1120];
- prove knowledge by an accused person of some fact[1121];

[1116] See *R v Griffin (No. 1)* (1868) 1 QSCR 176.

[1117] See *R v Hewitt* (1925) 19 Cr App R 64; *R v Shellaker* [1914] 1 KB 414, (1914) 9 Cr App R 240 and *R v Marsh* (1949) 33 Cr App R 185.

See also: *Hoch v R* (1988) 165 CLR 292; *R v B* [1989] 2 Qd R 343 and *R v Witham* [1962] Qd R 49.

[1118] See *Makin v Attorney-General for New South Wales* [1894] AC 57 at 65 and *DPP v P* [1991] 2 AC 447, [1991] 3 WLR 161, [1991] 3 All ER 337, (1991) 93 Cr App R 267, [1992] Crim LR 41.

Refer also to the chapter titled 'Criminal Responsibility' in the text titled 'Injia on Criminal Offences in Papua New Guinea and the Pacific'.

[1119] See *Makin v Attorney-General for New South Wales* [1894] AC 57 at 65; *DPP v P* [1991] 2 AC 447, [1991] 3 WLR 161, [1991] 3 All ER 337, (1991) 93 Cr App R 267, [1992] Crim LR 41; *Holder v R* [1980] AC 115, (1978) 68 Cr App R 120; *R v Finlayson* (1912) 14 CLR 675, (1912) 7 QJPR 26; *Hardgrove v R* (1906) 4 CLR 232 and *R v Seaman* (1978) 67 Cr App R 234.

[1120] See *Makin v Attorney-General for New South Wales* [1894] AC 57 at 65; *DPP v P* [1991] 2 AC 447, [1991] 3 WLR 161, [1991] 3 All ER 337, (1991) 93 Cr App R 267, [1992] Crim LR 41; *R v Fisher* [1910] 1 KB 149; *R v Mortimer* (1936) 25 Cr App R 150; *Holder v R* [1980] AC 115, (1978) 68 Cr App R 120; *R v Finlayson* (1912) 14 CLR 675, (1912) 7 QJPR 26; *Hardgrove v R* (1906) 4 CLR 232; *R v Seaman* (1978) 67 Cr App R 234 and *R v Smith* (1915) 11 Cr App R 229.

See also: *R v Lewis (PA)* (1983) 76 Cr App R 33; *R v Butler* (1987) 84 Cr App R 12 and *R v Chandler* (1956) 73 WN (NSW) 605.

[1121] See *R v Mason* (1914) 10 Cr App R 169.

- show a state of mind of an accused person in respect to fraud offences by evidence of previous dishonoured cheques that may indicate that the accused person could not expect later cheques to be met upon presentation[1122];

- show the real and full relationship that existed between:

  - a complainant; and

  - an accused person[1123]; or

- rebut a defence of innocent association[1124].

However, similar fact evidence may be introduced even though no specific defence has been raised.[1125]

Similar fact evidence is 'circumstantial evidence[1126]'.[1127]

[1122] See *R v Hurren* (1962) 46 Cr App R 323; *R v Rhodes* [1899] 1 QB 77; *R v Ollis* [1900] 2 QB 758; *R v Boyle and Merchant* (1914) 10 Cr App R 180 and *R v Potter* (1935) 25 Cr App R 59.

See also: *R v Le Vard* [1955] NZLR 266 and *R v Gill* (1906) 8 WALR 96.

[1123] See *Wilson v R* (1970) 123 CLR 334, [1970] HCA 17; *Harriman v R* (1989) 167 CLR 590, [1989] HCA 50; *R v B* (1992) 175 CLR 599, [1992] HCA 68; *R v W* [1997] QCA 415; *R v R* [2000] QCA 27; *R v Chevathen and Dorrick* (2001) 122 A Crim R 441 at 449; *R v Self* [2001] QCA 338 and *R v Walker* [2007] QCA 446.

[1124] See *The State v Tanedo* (1975) N10.

See also: *DPP v Kilbourne* [1973] 2 WLR 254, [1973] AC 729, [1973] 1 All ER 440, (1973) 57 Cr App R 381; *Broadman v DPP* [1975] AC 421, [1974] 3 WLR 673, [1974] 3 All ER 887, (1975) 60 Cr App R 165, [1975] Crim LR 36; *R v Lewis* (1983) 76 Cr App R 33; *R v Chandor* (1958) 43 Cr App R 74 and *R v Lunt* (1987) 85 Cr App R 241.

[1125] See *Harris v DPP* [1952] 1 All ER 1044, (1952) 36 Cr App R 235, [1952] AC 694.

See also: *R v Anderson (M.)* [1988] 2 All ER 549, [1988] QB 678, (1988) 87 Cr App R 349.

[1126] Refer also to the chapter titled 'Circumstantial Evidence'.

[1127] See *The State v Bill Vevo* [2007] PGNC 1.

See also: *Martin v Osborne* (1936) 55 CLR 367, [1936] HCA 23 and *Sutton v R* (1983) 152 CLR 528, (1984) 51 ALR 435, [1984] HCA 5.

SIMILAR FACT EVIDENCE

Such evidence should be called after the evidence given in direct proof of the facts to be proved.[1128]

To enable a Court to be satisfied 'beyond reasonable doubt[1129]' of the guilt of an accused person:

- it is necessary not only that his or her guilt should be a rational inference; but
- that it should be the only rational inference that the circumstances would enable the Court to draw.[1130]

[1128] See *Chin v R* [1980] WAR 10.

[1129] Refer also to the chapter titled 'Proof Of Issues' in the text titled 'Injia on Criminal Practice and Procedure in Papua New Guinea and the Pacific'.

[1130] See *The State v Tom Morris* [1981] PNGLR 493; *Paulus Pawa v The State* [1981] PNGLR 498; *Allan Oa Koroka and Mariano Wani Simon v The State* [1988-89] PNGLR 131 at 139; *Garitau Bonu and Rosanna Bonu v The State* (1997) SC528; *The State v Derrick Sakatea Niso (No. 1)* (2005) N2929, [2005] PGNC 25; *The State v Nelson Tuli* (1997) N1534; *The State v Jupui Kapera* (1986) N567; *The State v Iamge Waea* (1990) N915; *The State v Koivi Ipai* (2010) N3972; *The State v Paul Yepei (No. 1)* (2004) N2570; *The State v Nigel Ongapa* (2008) N3314 and *The State v Dakoa* (2009) N3587, [2009] PGNC 13.

Similar Fact Evidence specifically, see also: *Pfennig v R* (1995) 182 CLR 461, (1995) 69 ALJR 147, (1995) 127 ALR 99, (1995) 77 A Crim R 149, [1995] HCA 7 and *Phillips v R* (2006) 225 CLR 303, (2006) 80 ALJR 531, (2006) 224 ALR 216 at 294, [2006] HCA 4.

Generally, see also: *Hodge's Case* (1838) 2 Lewin 227, 168 ER 1136, (1838) 2 Law CC 227; *Chamberlain v R (No. 2)* (1984) 153 CLR 521, (1984) 51 ALR 225, [1984] HCA 7; *Abbott v The State of Western Australia* [2005] WASCA 42; *R v Ramage* [1985] 1 NZLR 392 at 393; *Police v Pio* [1999] WSSC 50; *Edwards v R* (1993) 178 CLR 193 at 203; *McGreevy v DPP* (1973) 57 Cr App R 424; *Knight v R* (1992) 175 CLR 495 at 509-510; *Plomp v R* (1963) 110 CLR 234, per Dixon CJ at 243; *Shepherd v R* (1990) 170 CLR 573, per Dawson J at 578; *R v Griffin* 2009 SCC 28, [2009] 2 SCR 42 and *R v Comba* [1938] SCR 396 at 397.

However, a Court should decide whether the prejudicial effect of such evidence:

- 'far[1131]'; or
- 'totally[1132]'

outweighs its 'probative value[1133]'.[1134]

Therefore, the admission of similar fact evidence:

- is exceptional to other circumstantial evidence; and
- requires a strong degree of probative force.[1135]

Depending on the facts of the case the 'probative value[1136]' of such evidence may lie in the improbability of witnesses giving accounts of events having the requisite degree of similarity, unless the events actually occurred.[1137]

1131 See *DPP v P* [1991] 2 AC 447, [1991] 3 WLR 161, [1991] 3 All ER 337, (1991) 93 Cr App R 267, [1992] Crim LR 41 and *R v Lewis (P.A.)* (1983) 76 Cr App R 33.

1132 See *R v H* [1995] 2 AC 596 and *R v Yalman* [1998] Crim LR 569.

1133 Refer also to the chapter titled 'Weight'.

1134 Refer also to the chapter titled 'Discretion To Exclude Relevant Evidence'.

1135 See *The State v Casper Otto* [2007] PGNC 128.

See also: *DPP (UK) v Boardman* [1974] 3 WLR 673, [1974] 3 All ER 887, (1975) 60 Cr App R 165, [1975] Crim LR 36, [1975] AC 421, per Lord Wilberforce at 444; *Hoch v R* (1988) 165 CLR 292 at 294-295; *Markby v R* (1978) 140 CLR 108, per Gibbs ACJ at 117; *Perry v R* (1982) 150 CLR 580 at 586, per Gibbs CJ at 589, (1983) 57 ALJR 110; *Sutton v R* (1984) 152 CLR 528, per Gibbs CJ at 533, (1984) 51 ALR 435, [1984] HCA 5; *Pfennig v R* (1995) 182 CLR 461 at 481, (1995) 69 ALJR 147, (1995) 127 ALR 99, (1995) 77 A Crim R 149 at 481, [1995] HCA 7 and *Phillips v R* (2006) 225 CLR 303, (2006) 80 ALJR 531, (2006) 224 ALR 216 at 294, [2006] HCA 4.

1136 Refer also to the chapter titled 'Weight'.

1137 See *Boardman v DPP* [1975] AC 421, [1974] 3 WLR 673, [1974] 3 All ER 887, (1975) 60 Cr App R 165, [1975] Crim LR 36.

See also: *Hoch v R* (1988) 165 CLR 292; *Sutton v R* (1984) 153 CLR 528, (1984) 51 ALR 435, [1984] HCA 5; *Perry v R* (1982) 150 CLR 580 at 586-587, (1983) 57 ALJR 110; *Thompson v R* (1989) 169 CLR 1; *Martin v Osborne* (1936) 55 CLR 367, [1936] HCA 23 and *R v M* [1999] 1 NZLR 315 also reported as *R v Accused* (1998) 15 CRNZ 674 at 322 and 682.

SIMILAR FACT EVIDENCE

Evidence showing a:

- disposition; or
- propensity

for a co-accused to act in a certain way may be tendered by another accused person to disprove his or her guilt.[1138]

Evidence relating to a previous charge, where there has been an acquittal, is permissible as a matter of discretion and depending on fairness, although obviously great care is required before admitting such evidence.[1139]

Where evidence that would tend to prove:

- an earlier charge; or
- some element of an earlier charge

is admitted in a subsequent charge, the Court must accept the fact of the earlier acquittal and not use the evidence to:

- question; or
- discount

the effect of the acquittal.[1140]

[1138] See *R v Randall* (2004) 1 Cr App R 26, [2003] UKHL 69; *Lowery v R* [1933] HCA 35; *Knight v Jones; ex parte Jones* [1981] Qd R 98 at 101-104; *Winning v R* [2002] WASCA 44 and *R v Roughan and Jones* [2007] QCA 443.

Refer also to the section titled 'Joinder Of Charges' in the chapter titled 'Charges' in the text titled 'Injia on Criminal Practice and Procedure in Papua New Guinea and the Pacific'.

[1139] See *Washer v The State of Western Australia* [2007] HCA 48 and *R v Storey* (1978) 140 CLR 364, [1978] HCA 39.

See also: *R v Z* [2000] 2 AC 483, [2001] Crim LR 222, [2000] 2 Cr App R 281, [2000] 3 All ER 385, (2000) 164 JP 533, [2000] 3 WLR 117, [2000] UKHL 68; *R v Arp* [1998] 3 SCR 339; *Grdic v R* [1985] 1 SCR 810; *R v Degnan* [2001] 1 NZLR 280 and *R v Wilson* [1997] 2 NZLR 161.

[1140] See *Washer v The State of Western Australia* [2007] HCA 48 and *R v Storey* (1978) 140 CLR 364, [1978] HCA 39.

SIMILAR FACT EVIDENCE

Whether charges should be severed on the basis of the leading of similar fact evidence the admissibility of such evidence is distinct from whether the charges should be severed.[1141]

If a Court concludes that the evidence is admissible, then severance of the charges should be unlikely.[1142]

[2.0] PROCEDURE

The prosecution should advise the Court during the opening address if it intends to call similar fact evidence.[1143]

Such intention should also be raised at a pre-trial review conducted in accordance with Order 2 of the *Criminal Practice Rules 1987*.[1144]

A prosecutor must state precisely:

- what evidence is sought to be adduced, ie., the similar fact evidence;
- what is the relationship between:
    - that evidence; and
    - the other evidence sought to be admitted; and

[1141] See *R v Scarrott* [1977] 3 WLR 629, [1978] 1 All ER 672, [1978] QB 1016, (1977) 65 Cr App R 125, [1977] Crim LR 745.

Refer also to the section titled 'Joinder Of Charges' in the chapter titled 'Charges' in the text titled 'Injia on Criminal Practice and Procedure in Papua New Guinea and the Pacific'.

[1142] See *R v Christou* [1996] 2 WLR 620, [1996] 2 All ER 927, [1997] AC 117.

See also: *R v Wilmot* (1989) 89 Cr App R 341.

[1143] See *Boardman v DPP* [1974] 3 WLR 673, [1974] 3 All ER 887, (1975) 60 Cr App R 165, [1975] Crim LR 36, [1975] AC 421, per Lord Cross at 459.

Refer also to the section titled 'Addresses' in the chapter titled 'Court Procedure' in the text titled 'Injia on Criminal Practice and Procedure in Papua New Guinea and the Pacific'.

[1144] Refer also to the section titled 'Pre-trial' in the chapter titled 'Court Procedure' in the text titled 'Injia on Criminal Practice and Procedure in Papua New Guinea and the Pacific'.

- how the law relating to such similar fact evidence should be applied.[1145]

[3.0] SIMPLISTIC EXAMPLE

Suppose Janet Siapu decides to destroy the front windscreen of motor vehicles with bricks. On 15 May 2001 she approaches a motor vehicle and she destroys the front windscreen by throwing a brick through it. At the time of the offence there are no witnesses, however, she leaves the brick inside the motor vehicle.

On 19 May 2001 she again approaches another motor vehicle and she is seen by a police officer to throw a brick at the front windscreen. As a consequence the windscreen is destroyed. When approached by the police officer, she stated that she intended to throw the brick over the motor vehicle and that the brick struck the motor vehicle accidentally. No admissions are made in respect to both offences.

In such a situation the prosecution should charge Siapu with both offences and the facts surrounding the first offence could be used to negative the defence of 'Accident' as provided for by section 24 of the *Criminal Code* (Ch. 262)[1146] that was raised by the accused person.

However, even if there was a witness to the first offence and Siapu was subsequently arrested and sentenced before the second offence, the prosecution could still rely on the circumstances surrounding the first offence to negative the defence of 'Accident'. If the first offence had not been dealt with the prosecution should seek the permission of the Court to have both offences joined[1147].

When a Court decides whether Siapu was guilty of either or both charges the Court must ask itself whether there is a rational view of the evidence that is inconsistent with any reasonable hypothesis, other than the guilt of the accused person.

[1145] See *R v Clarke (R.L.)* [1995] 2 Cr App R 425, per Steyn LJ at 435.

[1146] As regards the law in relation to 'Accident', refer to the chapter titled 'Criminal Responsibility' in the text titled 'Injia on Criminal Offences in Papua New Guinea and the Pacific'.

[1147] Refer also to the section titled 'Joinder Of Charges' in the chapter titled 'Charges' in the text titled 'Injia on Criminal Practice and Procedure in Papua New Guinea and the Pacific'.

TAPE EVIDENCE

[1.0] VIDEO TAPE

A video tape is admissible as real evidence, to prove what is recorded, just as photographs are.[1148]

However, a video tape should be properly authenticated, ie., verified on oath or solemn declaration or affirmation.

A video tape may be authenticated by:

- the video camera operator;
- a person present when the video tape was recorded;
- a person qualified to state that what is recorded on the video tape is accurate; or
- a witness who testifies as to the automatic operation of the equipment, eg., an automatic surveillance camera.[1149]

A re-enactment of an offence on a video tape is prima facie admissible.[1150]

A videotape of poor quality may still be admissible.[1151]

A videotape recording of an interview with a suspect is admissible.[1152]

[1148] As regards video evidence generally, see *R v Sitek* [1988] 2 Qd R 284; *R v Maqsud Ali* [1966] 1 QB 688; *Kajala v Noble* (1982) 75 Cr App R 149; *R v Beames* (1980) 1 A Crim R 239 at 240-241; *R v Fowden and White* [1982] Crim LR 588 and *R v Grimer* [1982] Crim LR 674.

[1149] See *Taylor v Chief Constable of Cheshire* (1987) 84 Cr App R 191, [1986] 1 WLR 1479, [1987] 1 All ER 225, [1987] Crim LR 119.

[1150] See *Li Shu-Ling v R* (1989) 88 Cr App R 82.

[1151] See *Smith v R* (2001) 206 CLR 650, per Kirby J at 656 and *Li v R* (2003) 139 A Crim R 281, per Ipp JA at 294-295.

[1152] See *R v Travers* [1958] SR (NSW) 85, (1958) 74 WN (NSW) 484 and *Li Shu Ling v R* [1989] AC 270, [1988] 3 All ER 138, (1988) 88 Cr App R 82;

However, a transcript of such a conversation is only an aid to understanding.

See also: *R v Gardiner* [1979] VR 57.

Refer also to the chapter titled 'Confessional Evidence'.

TAPE EVIDENCE

[2.0] AUDIO TAPE

A tape recording is admissible provided:

- the accuracy of the recording can be proved;
- the voices recorded are properly identified; and
- the evidence is relevant and otherwise admissible.[1153]

[1153] See *R v Ali and Hussain* [1965] 2 All ER 464, [1966] 1 QB 688, [1965] 3 WLR 229, (1965) 49 Cr App R 230, per Marshall J at 238.

TRACKER DOG EVIDENCE

The evidence of tracking by a dog is admissible provided that:

- a dog handler can establish that the dog has been properly trained; and
- over a period of time the dog's reactions indicate that the dog is a reliable pointer to the existence of a scent from a particular individual.[1154]

Detailed evidence establishing the reliability of the dog in question is an essential requirement.

[1154] See *R v Pieterson and Holloway* [1995] 2 Cr App R 11.

See also: *R v Sykes* [1997] Crim LR 752.

VILLAGE APPREHENSIONS

The Courts must and ought to give due weight and consideration to the practice of handing over of suspects by community leaders in order to encourage the involvement of the communities in the task of improving law and order, unless a person affected by such a practice demonstrates by appropriate evidence that, the village leaders acted without any evidence pointing to his or her involvement in the commission of the offence.[1155]

[1155] See *Masolyau Piakali v The State* (2004) SC771, [2004 PGSC 20; *Jimmy Ono v The State* (2002) SC698 and *The State v Anis Noki* [1993] PNGLR 426 at 427.

APPENDIX

DRUG ANALYST AFFIDAVIT

IN THE DISTRICT COURT **IN THE MATTER OF POLICE**

HELD AT ... **AGAINST [NAME OF ACCUSED PERSON]**

I, [Full Name], **duly sworn make oath and say as follows:**

1. I am a drug analyst currently employed by [name of employer] at [location of work].
2. I am the holder of the following qualifications for the identification of [specify the dangerous drug such as cannabis and its derivatives]: [specify the qualifications]
3. At [location] on [date] I received a parcel from [person who handed in the parcel] of what appeared to me at that stage to be [specify the name of the dangerous drug] for the purpose of determining whether it was a dangerous drug as defined in the *Dangerous Drugs Act* (Ch. 228).
4. The recognised method used for the identification of such a dangerous drug is by [outline the usual method or methods used].
5. I analysed the dangerous drug by [outline as to how the dangerous drug was analysed].
6. As a consequence of that analysis I came to the conclusion that the substance was in fact the dangerous drug [specify the name of the dangerous drug, as referred to in the *Dangerous Drugs Act* (Ch. 228)].
7. The quantity of dangerous drug was [outline the weight of the dangerous drug].

....

[Full Name]

This page signed and sworn

at ... on ...

Before Me

....

Clerk of the District Court

INDEX

INDEX

Page

C

INDEX

INDEX

Page

E

F

INDEX

INDEX

INDEX

INDEX

INDEX

INDEX

Page

www.ingramcontent.com/pod-product-compliance
Lightning Source LLC
LaVergne TN
LVHW081024110926
847533LV00025B/27
* 9 7 8 9 9 8 0 8 7 9 1 8 9 *